THESE *Fiery*
Frenchified DAMES

Early American Studies

DANIEL K. RICHTER
Director, McNeil Center for Early American Studies,
Series Editor

Exploring neglected aspects of our colonial, revolutionary, and early national history and culture, Early American Studies reinterprets familiar themes and events in fresh ways. Interdisciplinary in character, and with a special emphasis on the period from about 1600 to 1850, the series is published in partnership with the McNeil Center for Early American Studies.

A complete list of books in the series is available from the publisher.

THESE *Fiery Frenchified* DAMES

Women and Political Culture in

Early National Philadelphia

SUSAN BRANSON

University of Pennsylvania Press

Philadelphia

TO MY PARENTS
Jeanne and George Branson,
who taught me the value of knowledge and
the power of love

Published by
University of Pennsylvania Press
Philadelphia, Pennsylvania 19104-4011

Library of Congress Cataloging-in-Publication Data

Branson, Susan.
   These fiery frenchified dames : women and political culture in early national
Philadelphia / Susan Branson.
      p. cm.—(Early American studies)
   Includes bibliographical references and index.
   ISBN 0-8122-3609-2 (cloth : alk. paper); ISBN 0-8122-1777-2 (pbk : alk.
paper)
   1. Women in politics—Pennsylvania—Philadelphia—History—18th century.
2. Women in public life—Pennsylvania—Philadelphia—History—18th century.
3. Women—Pennsylvania—Philadelphia—Social conditions. 4. Philadelphia
(Pa.)—History—18th century. 5. Philadelphia (Pa.)—Social conditions.
6. France—History—1789–1793. I. Title. II. Series.

HQ1236.5.U6 B75 2001
305.42'09748'11—dc21
                                                              00–069949

Contents

Plan of the city and suburbs of Philadelphia, 1794. Courtesy of the Library Company of Philadelphia.

Introduction

IN NOVEMBER 1793 a report direct from Paris described for Philadelphia readers a "Grand Festival dedicated to Reason and Truth" held at Notre Dame in Paris. This public ceremony included a group of young women dressed in white, who surrounded an Altar of Reason upon which a figure of Liberty stood.[1] The following August, Philadelphians echoed their French peers by celebrating the French Revolution in a similar manner. At ten o'clock in the morning participants assembled at the intersection of Market and Broad Streets. From there they paraded, accompanied by music, to the French minister Fauchet's residence two blocks away on the corner of Twelfth and Market Streets. Here "Maidens dressed in white and tri-color costumes" surrounded an altar of liberty reminiscent of the one constructed by Jacques-Louis David for the Notre Dame ceremony.[2] In Philadelphia, these symbols of French political street theater assumed an American form in which young women expressed their opinions and asserted their rights as participants in public political culture.[3] This book will explain how and why these Philadelphia women were a focal point of a very public, and a very political, activity.

The idea for this project began with my belief that the social, political, and intellectual ideas regarding women in the post-Revolutionary era contributed to a more significant change in women's public lives than most historians have recognized. There was more at work in the political consciousness of men and women in the early republic than just a conservative ideology that paid lip service to women's civic roles but in effect reinforced the identity of women with the private sphere. My starting point was a reconsideration of two historical paradigms: the concept of republican womanhood—a term developed more than twenty years ago by historians who examined post-Revolutionary rhetoric, prescriptive literature, and promotion of female education, and saw a conscious design to give women a part in the creation of a good society by allotting them the role of moral compass and educator of the private family—and the concept of separate spheres, which assigned women to domestic employments, homosocial relationships, and limited activity outside the home. Both of these constructs have been considerably modified by historians since they were first used twenty years ago, but neither of them has been abandoned.[4]

I find these paradigms unsatisfying for three reasons. First, historians have not adequately dealt with the *consequences* of the rhetoric generated by republican ideology as it concerned women—in other words, how it was applied to women's lives and activities. Some historians had imposed this ideological construct, but how accurate was it in assessing women's roles, both private and public? Second, most historical investigations still adhere to the notion of separate spheres— that legally, politically, and economically, women's status in the late eighteenth century was no different than it had been one hundred years earlier, and that this status limited women's public identities. I agree with their assessment that property rights, custody laws, and suffrage status remained unchanged, but I disagree with the conclusion that this framework confined women to domestic duties and private identities. Nor do I agree that republican womanhood, identified by historians as a concept designed to encourage women's education and knowledge of political affairs in order that they be better companions to husbands and more competent rearers of the next generation of male citizens, constrained women's civic activities. Women's public lives did begin to change in significant ways during the 1780s and 1790s, and these transformations laid the foundation for the long-term evolution of women's political, economic, and domestic status. Finally, I do not believe that historians have yet developed a sufficient explanatory device to connect the nascent protofeminism of individuals such as Judith Sargent Murray and Mary Wollstonecraft in the

1780s and 1790s with the public political activities of women in the second quarter of the nineteenth century.

Fundamentally, the task I set for myself is to look at the extent to which eighteenth-century women did not conform to the identities that twentieth-century historians have created for them and to begin to build a bridge between eighteenth-century women's history and nineteenth-century women's history. The purpose of this book, then, is to examine women's changing public roles as they resulted from the social, cultural, and political forces at work in American society in the last two decades of the eighteenth century. The Philadelphia ceremony just described is an example of what became possible for women in the early republic. To understand any society during a specific period requires examining the ways in which it is constantly shaped by myriad constituencies. Elite and middle-class women in early national Philadelphia, the primary focus of this study, were one of these constituencies. At the same time that family position and wealth provided such women with connections to the centers of national political, social, and cultural power that were taking shape in the capital city, their sex made them outsiders. Yet the forces at work in this era propelled these outsiders toward the center, and they took full advantage of the opportunity.

Three developments in particular made it possible for these women to achieve a greater share in the culture and politics of the new republic: a communications revolution that rapidly expanded the availability of printed materials and increased readership, the revitalization of cultural institutions such as theater and salons, and the development of a national political culture that simultaneously evolved into a party system with competing visions of the country's political and economic development, and responded to international events such as the French Revolution. Women took advantage of these developments to participate in the politics and culture of the day, initiate a discussion of their place in American society, and develop a consciousness as an important constituency for the competing political parties.

The tug-of-war between Federalists and Democratic Republicans was in many ways a competition over which party would control the meaning of the nation's political symbols, ceremonies, and celebrations, and therefore define the nature of people's participation in American society. Whose national vision would win out? The Federalists, who believed in social privilege and constituted authority, or the Democratic Republicans, who accepted a broad spectrum of males as citizens but rejected women and blacks as entitled groups?

The struggle for possession and control over the meanings of popular political culture occurred within the public sphere. Thus any study that attempts to define late eighteenth-century society as composed of public and private spheres must tackle the complex meaning of these concepts.[5] The idea of two gendered arenas of activity—men in public, outside the home, and women in private, within the home—was not new in the late eighteenth century. But during the Revolutionary era it received more attention, as female and male roles became a prominent theme in magazine essays, novels, and newspapers. Gender roles was a subject that provoked increasing anxiety as Enlightenment social and political philosophy suggested the possibility of alternatives to naturalized gender differences. The ideas and activities generated in the Revolutionary era challenged the association of the terms domestic/private/dependent with women, and public/citizen/independent with the innate attributes of men.[6]

As this book will demonstrate, the rhetoric of gendered spheres of public and private activity belies what was occurring in early national Philadelphia. Side by side with the formal politics that were the province of white males existed politically engaged constituencies including women, which fashioned alternatives to such political behavior and rhetoric.[7] What historians have begun to identify, then, are a multiplicity of public arenas that existed simultaneously. Like Venn diagrams, these arenas often intersected, overlapped, and included one another. In other words, while the apparent ideology of late eighteenth-century America was a republicanism which assumed that citizenship meant giving precedence to the public good over individual desires, and which defined itself in counterdistinction to dependence, weakness, and effeminacy, in practice the public sphere at the close of the eighteenth century had quite a different character, one influenced not only by republican ideology, but also by a Lockean liberalism that privileged the rights and freedoms of the individual over those of the state, and a culture of sensibility that placed value and importance on emotion and feeling and lent a legitimacy to the public dimensions of women's lives.[8] In this context, women's opinions, issues, and needs were acknowledged, debated, and sometimes incorporated into the wider political rhetoric and public culture, thus becoming integral to America's developing sense of itself as a nation.

This book examines the avenues through which women's presence became important or even central to the competition for control of the nation's political culture: print culture, political ceremonies, theater, and salons. Its chapter organization thus reflects this topical examination of culture and politics. Chapter 1 discusses how the explosion of printed materials—books, magazines, and newspapers—in postwar America allowed authors to reach a national audience and guaranteed a forum for the discussion of women's roles. Moreover, this print culture, replete with arguments, ideas, and contradictions, provided a contextual framework for the activities of many of the women who participated in the public political culture of the era.

Some of Philadelphia's public spaces were heavily contested by the political partisans of the day. Chapter 2 introduces the events and ideas that preoccupied American society at the end of the century and investigates how the French Revolution affected American women and acted as a catalyst to their collective political behavior. Women were present at many of the public celebrations and ceremonies in support of the French Revolution between 1789 and 1794. Then, after 1795, as relations between France and the United States deteriorated, women contributed to the Federalist anti-French military ceremonies that dominated public political space. Women used all of these occasions, and the opportunities afforded by the competition over dominance of this public space, to express their political sentiments and increase their presence as political participants.

Chapter 3 examines the theater, another contested political space where women were increasingly welcomed as spectators, performers, and playwrights in the early republic. Women not only contributed to the development of American theater, but also to the national political culture that used theatrical space as a forum for partisanship.

Women became a more prominent part of public political culture as participants in the displays staged in Philadelphia's playhouses by the Democratic Republicans and the Federalists in the 1790s. As actresses and playwrights they developed professional careers in an era when this was all but impossible for women to do in any other area. With a growing demand for new plays, especially for those with distinctly "American" content, female playwrights were able to stage their work and to express themselves on issues related to politics and to women's rights.

Chapter 4 explores how the salon, a social gathering place for elite men and women hosted by women of education and culture, functioned as an important part of the public sphere within which gender and politics were linked. The chapter focuses on Anne Willing Bingham, the daughter of a wealthy and socially prominent Philadelphia family and the wife of Federalist senator William Bingham. By adapting French ideas about women's social and cultural roles to an American setting, Bingham and other prominent Federalist women created the political salon—a new public space that came into existence coincident with a geographical location for a national political elite. Unlike the streets and the theater, the Federalists held firm control over this political space during the presidencies of Washington and Adams by providing women such as Bingham with access to men in power and opportunities to entertain the Federalist elite.

My work is part of a new historical orientation toward the intersection of political and cultural formations in the late eighteenth century. Recent studies of political rituals and celebrations have deepened our understanding of how public culture took shape in the early republic by exploring the specific constituencies that were responsible for its character.[9] My book enhances existing studies by identifying and exploring the cultural and political sites where women were prominent. We must look beyond the formal legal and political institutions, which limited or subsumed women's activities, to understand how and when women achieved a presence in the public sphere.

This book also argues that American politics and culture in the early republic must be understood within an international framework. The development of American society, and the place of women in it, was heavily influenced by French examples and ideas. The French claimed that the American Revolution helped spark their own, but the French Revolution was an equally important catalyst to the development of American political culture and to women's integral place in it.

In making the argument for women's engagement in the politics and culture of the early republic, this study has an urban focus with a particular, although not exclusive, concentration on events that occurred in Philadelphia. At the end of the eighteenth century Philadelphia was the "metropolis of America": the country's largest city and a major commercial center.[10] As the nation's capital from 1791 until 1800, it was the political arena par excellence for experiencing the conflicts between Federalists and Democratic Republicans. Philadelphia's citizens witnessed firsthand the workings of government, the men involved with it, and the partisanship that drew upon the international events of the day. The city was a magnet for anyone interested in government and politics; American men and women of all political views, international representatives of the major combatants in Europe's conflicts, and a large group of European and Caribbean refugees all resided there in the two decades following the American Revolution. Hence, Philadelphia's women witnessed and participated in events at the center of national power, propelled into this public arena by a response to domestic and international events. The multiplicity of street parades, processions, dinners, and protests underscore the diversity of women's participation in the political life of the capital city. Philadelphia was also the largest urban center, with 44,000 inhabitants in 1790, growing to 55,000 four years later, and 91,000 by 1810. In contrast, the next largest city, New York, had a population of 33,000 in 1790, followed by 18,000 in Boston, 16,000 in Charleston, and 13,000 in Baltimore. Consequently, Philadelphia had all the necessary ingredients to be the focal point of the nation's interests: diversity, density, culture, and politics. To observers, it truly may have seemed as though all the world was in Philadelphia.[11]

Class plays a defining role in the practices and activities examined in this book. It is the ideas articulated by middle class and elite women that have survived in letters, diaries, essays, and novels. It is our knowledge of the activities of these same women that delineate the extent to which gender defined participation in public cultural and political practices. Hence both the nature of available sources and the particular aspects of culture and society this study examines dictate this class orientation.

Middle-class and elite women did not necessarily articulate the aspirations, values, or ideologies of the wives and daughters of mechanics and tradesmen, nor of women of the laboring class. The politics of these less affluent women, including the thousands who were servants in middle-class households, the scores of women in the almshouses, or unknown numbers in boardinghouse rooms, was not captured in diaries nor discussed in newspapers. These groups may not have been the intended audience for the political ideologies of the day, but many probably did read novels and magazines, attend the theater, and participate in political celebrations or protests. Identifying their contributions and hearing their voices is difficult. We catch glimpses of them from time to time, inadvertently recorded in the letters and diaries of their wealthier employers and neighbors. And we can infer their presence in some of the public demonstrations and festivals in the streets by the descriptions of events. But poorer women, for the most part, remain silent.

This study begins in the early 1780s and ends when the capital moved to Washington in 1800. The republican ideology fostered by the American Revolution provided a language with which the implications of citizenship were explored in the decades following the peace in 1783. Both Federalists and Democratic Republicans struggled to define the meaning of liberty, independence, and civic responsibility for individual members of the polity. Peacetime economic recovery and development, encouraged by the policies of the federal government after 1789, allowed for the revitalization of cultural institutions such as the theater and an expanding print culture, including periodicals, which aimed to capture a female readership. The postwar era also witnessed the beginnings of innovations in female education, such as the Young Ladies Academy of Philadelphia. This school and others like it around the country had its origins in the encouragement of a civic role for women as wives and mothers responsible for inculcating civic virtue in husbands and sons.[12]

The creation of a federal government in the late 1780s precipitated the development of a political culture surrounding the presidency which included women in the levees hosted by Martha Washington and the salons created by the wives of elite Federalist women. And transatlantic political events influenced a growing partisanship in American political society, producing, by the election of 1796, the Democratic Republicans as an identifiable opposition party to the Federalists. Perhaps the most defining event of the last two decades of the eighteenth century was the French Revolution. Between the fall of the Bastille in 1789 and Napoleon's rise to power ten years later, the politics of revolution preoccupied American society. Initially jubilant that another nation sought liberty from tyranny, many Americans were frightened and angered by the more radical aspects of the French Revolution which deepened divisions between political factions.

Such circumstances, and the ideologies that shaped responses to the events of the era, allowed women's presence in the public sphere to become one of the defining features of American culture and society in the early republic, and laid the groundwork for future public activism. By 1800 these cultural and political practices were well underway when the seat of national power moved from Philadelphia to Washington and the political balance of power shifted with the transition from a Federalist to a Democratic Republican administration. After the crisis of 1798 and the XYZ Affair with France, American preoccupation with the French diminished. This study is meant to show the beginnings of practices and beliefs fostered during the late eighteenth century but which persisted into the nineteenth century.

Printed material in the 1790s epitomized the breadth of the discussion over women's authority and responsibilities in marriage, social relations, and participation in public political life. Though opinions on this issue varied, there was a tendency to favor increased female autonomy. This undercurrent of support for greater female participation formed the background to political salons, feminist writings, and public political activities. Women's wartime activities and the republicanism that emerged from the Revolution formed the basis for potentially radical changes in women's roles in postwar society. The reevaluation of gender relations questioned authorities such as religious teachings and legal precedent. It denaturalized traditional conceptions of femininity and made change at least feasible by forcing a defense of long-held beliefs. In the two decades that followed the war, women explored cultural and political possibilities, and in the process claimed for themselves a greater presence in the public sphere and a closer connection to the course of the nation. They were able to do so in part because of a legacy of action from the years of war in the 1770s and 1780s.

It was through individual experiences and collective action that many women came to believe that the promises of a newly independent nation applied to them. What distinguished the Revolutionary conflict from those that preceded it was its distinct ideology. Resistance to Great Britain required large numbers of colonists, for the first time, to put themselves in opposition to the mother country. More important, resistance was fostered on the understanding that Britain deprived its own citizens of their liberty. This concept of liberty took on multiple meanings as the need for collective effort encouraged unification of colonists in their resistance to perceived tyranny. This rhetoric of liberty and collectivity affected women as well as men. Revolutionary rhetoric and the Enlightenment ideology behind it nurtured a new political consciousness in women and provided many of them with new public, political roles. The acceptance, and often active encouragement, of women's public activities paved the way for the expansion of their presence in postwar society. The women who were eager patriots, besieged loyalists, or reluctant nonpartisans turned domestic duties into political acts, enhanced their civic presence in the new nation, and developed a collective consciousness of women's talents, interests, and potential.

War activities not only gained women visibility as public actors, it also affected how they thought of themselves. Rachel Wells, in New Jersey, contributed to the war effort by purchasing war bonds. Afterward she petitioned the Continental Congress for payment. She reminded these "gentlemen" that she had "Don as much to Carrey on the Warr as maney that Sett Now at ye healm of government." According to her lights, she, too, had been a patriot. Now she wanted her due. Wells's articulation of political sentiments, and her not-so-gentle reminder of her role in the war effort, express her self-conception as an engaged political individual.[13] Other women expressed similar sentiments as well as a confidence in their ability to perform tasks and undertake responsibilities previously denied to them. In New Hampshire, Mary Bartlett, wife of Congressman Josiah Bartlett, was left in charge of the farm during her husband's absence. After three years of running home and business single-handed, she began referring in her letters to "our farming business" instead of "your farming business."[14] Lucy Fluckner Knox, wife of General Henry Knox, was another woman left on her own while her spouse attended to war business. She expressed the hope that upon his rejoining her he would "not consider yourself as commander in chief of your own house—but be convinced . . . that there is such a thing as equal command."[15]

Individual women like Rachel Wells, Mary Bartlett, and Lucy Knox began to renegotiate their relationship to husbands as well as to the state during the Revolution. Collectively, women's behavior foreshadowed a conscious effort to place themselves squarely within the framework of postwar republican ideology, thus claiming a place in the civic body for wives and mothers. Women of the Revolution politicized traditional female roles when they claimed the authority to enforce boycotts or punish price gougers in their family purchases. At the same time, they looked ahead to an enhanced, permanent presence in the public sphere.

Women had a host of opportunities during the Revolution to accomplish this goal. Their experiences in the twenty years between 1763 and 1783 as decisionmakers, boycotters, rioters, fighters, active patriots, and ardent loyalists shaped their social and political consciousness. Spinners from New England's Congregationalist churches placed religious tradition within a political context by linking their faith with political principles. Boycott signers gave housewives' daily activities political meaning. The Ladies' Association of Philadelphia, building on the tradition of aid and benevolence that women of means extended to those in want, developed a new organizational, autonomous framework for women's public activities. Resistence to the war also provided opportunities for women to effect change and collectively influence political affairs. These female sources of civic identity fostered women's awareness of their rights as well as their responsibilities, and initiated developments which accorded women a more significant role in postwar society.

Many aspects of women's lives after the Revolution remained bounded by legal, economic, and social frameworks. The law continued to confine women to peripheral activity in the marketplace, restricted their property rights, and set limits on their autonomy in the home. No significant legal changes regarding child custody or ownership of property occurred in the 1780s or 1790s.[16] The constraints of the legal principle of *feme covert*—which denied most married and single women the right to sign contracts, make wills, or sue in a court of law—still bound most women to fathers and husbands. Only women of *feme sole* status, usually widowed, could act for themselves in a legal capacity. Though there were many female shopkeepers, mantuamakers, and sellers of all kinds of goods in the nation's urban areas, few women, if married, had the legal power to control capital for ventures in their own right.[17] Women were put into the same category as children, idiots, Indians, and slaves: they were judged to be dependents, lacking a free will, and consequently disqualified from voting. Only in isolated cases did the law recognize female political or economic autonomy. With the exception of New Jersey, where single or widowed women taxpayers or property owners could vote from 1776 until 1807 (as could blacks with the same economic qualifications), they were not citizens in a legal sense.

When asked to decide whether a woman was, as an individual, entitled to her property, the courts remained inconsistent. The courts settled in favor of Philadelphian Grace Galloway's claim to have her property restored to her because she did not share her estranged husband's Toryism.[18] In contrast, in the *Martin v. Massachusetts* case, the judge sided with the plaintiff, William Martin, and insisted that laws of coverture were still valid—a married woman remained under the control of her husband, unable to act as anything other than "'his instrument.'"[19]

Ironically, the key concept that did facilitate change in women's civic lives arose out of the same ideology that curtailed any hopes for legal or economic change. Civic virtue, which tied personal responsibility to the good of society, encompassed both men and women. Concepts of virtue promoted a popular, rather than legal, notion of citizenship, and encouraged broader familial and social roles for women. Through civic virtue women made claims on the republic both as wives and as educators of the rising generation.[20] In this capacity, they provided a moral grounding and good counsel to spouses and children, thereby ensuring the welfare of the state as well as the family. Future Supreme Court justice James Wilson, a member of the Constitutional Convention and a law professor at the College of Philadelphia, articulated the limits of women's political participation in 1788 when he stated that it would be improper for women to manage public affairs. Yet he included women in what he described as civil society: "the reading of newspapers and conversation among friends."[21] Hence women moved into the periphery of public culture through traditional paths as well as through changes in beliefs about individual rights and more representational government in the following century.[22]

The political model of the American republic as a consensual union of equals was reflected at the personal level in new precepts for marriage that included a new egalitarianism: the words equal, mutual, and reciprocal, rather than submission and obedience, described idealized postwar marital relations.[23] The new marital precepts were articulated through one of the fast growing mediums in the post-Revolutionary era: periodicals. One writer, identified only as a "Matrimonial Republican," suggested to readers that the word "obey" ought to be removed from the marriage service. Obedience, the writer argued, if at all necessary, ought to be mutual: "for the sake of their interest, inasmuch as two free opinions conjoined, are much more likely to produce a wise decision, than one haughty and exclusive."[24] Even fictional representations of marriage were expected to illustrate these new ideals. One theater critic, who claimed to be a "friend to the [female] sex," said of a character in the play *Wives As They Were and Maids As They Are*, "If *Lady Priory* is offered as a model by which wives of the present day ought to be formed, we trust no friend to the sex will consider it by [any] means perfect. She does not *love* her husband; but obeys him through dread; he is the *master*, and she the *servant*."[25]

One way to ensure domestic reciprocity and a harmony that only the uniting of equal minds could produce was to encourage the education of women. Education would guarantee the creation of a generation of women who would become "fit companions for republican men, and, especially, reliable guarantors of masculine virtue." Moreover, such women would make excellent mothers capable of passing on correct principles to the next generation.[26] Virtuous citizenship for men became a justification for improving female education. As the wives and mothers of citizens, women had a duty to be rational and informed. Many who turned their attention to this subject, like Benjamin Rush, "linked women's private development to political imperatives."[27] As John Adams informed his daughter Abigail, "It is by the female world, that the greatest and best characters among men are formed." Adams believed that there could be "nothing in life more honourable for a woman, than to contribute by her virtues, her advice, her example, or her address, to the formation of a husband, a brother, or a son, to be useful to the world."[28] The necessity for educated female republicans arose through two separate channels. One was the acknowledgment of the significance of maternal influence. The other was a developing emphasis on greater equality in marriage: women were to be intellectual and emotional companions to their spouses. The culture of sensibility, in full flower at the end of the eighteenth century in essays and fiction, with its emphasis on the primacy of emotions, fostered the notion that companionship of husbands and wives was important.[29]

New schools and academies for middle-class young women appeared everywhere in the postwar period. Most curricula still emphasized recitation, drawing, and embroidery over history, mathematics, classics, and philosophy. Though Benjamin Rush advocated education for women, he did so within the restricted limits of the female contribution to the appropriate rearing of future (male) citizens of the republic, and of widows' ability to provide for themselves. Still, the curricula sometimes included bookkeeping and writing, in line with the needs of unmarried women and widows.[30]

Quaker education for women was somewhat more academically oriented. Quakers were the first group to make formal provision for women's leadership within their faith. But even at Quaker schools, like

Westtown Friends School near Philadelphia, the content of young women's studies reflected the roles society expected them to fill. A man might need mathematical skills to calculate a ship's tonnage. A woman would also need mathematics, but she would put her knowledge to a more domestic use: calculating cloth yardage or recipe ingredients.[31] There was not a unified curriculum for girls and boys. New England educator Caleb Bingham explicitly delineated the proper direction for female education in the following manner. While America's sons prepared themselves "for the arduous, important and manly employment which America offers to the industrious," daughters were to attain the type of knowledge which would "enable them to become amiable sisters, virtuous children, and in the event, to assume characters more interesting to the public, and more endearing to themselves."[32]

The growing number of advertisements for periodicals, novels, lending libraries, schools, and private instruction testify to the increasing readership among educated men and women of the early republic. With growing literacy in the cities came new publications, especially periodicals, to cater to this new female readership. Many of the magazines aimed to contribute to female improvement. Some even claimed that they offered female readers a proper education. The editor of the *Lady's Magazine* informed readers they would find within its pages "everything requisite to disseminate knowledge of real life, to portray virtue, inspire the Female mind with love of religion, patience, prudence, and fortitude—in short with whatever tends to form the accomplished Woman, the complete Economist, and the greatest of treasures—a Good Wife."[33]

Yet not everyone agreed on the definition of a "good wife." An anonymous author in the *Columbian Magazine* complained that husbands valued their wives for the wrong qualities:

You hear from every quarter—My wife cannot make verses, it is true; but she makes an excellent pudding—she can't correct the press; but she can correct her children, and scold her servants with admirable discretion—she can't unravel the intricacies of political economy and federal government; but she can knit charming stockings—and this they call praising a wife, and doing justice to her good character—with much nonsense of the like kind.[34]

"Nitidia," the author of this complaint, argued that female education in the arts and sciences did not go far enough—political consciousness and political education were also a woman's province. Another author expressed the same sentiments more explicitly:

> Think of the cruel chain,
> Endure no more the pain
> Of slavery;—
> Why should a tyrant bind
> A cultivated mind
> By Reason well refin'd
> Ordained Free.[35]

Women, according to the anonymously written song, could no more tolerate "slavery" within marriage than Americans could endure it under the domination of Great Britain; domestic tyranny was just as abhorrent as political tyranny. This song illustrates the lessons republican ideology offered: reason, freedom, and self development, in contrast to slavery and tyranny. The articulation of such ideas in a printed context challenged the prescriptive roles expressed by men like James Wilson, Benjamin Rush, John Adams, and the editor of the *Lady's Magazine.*

The complexity of these issues was apparent as the nation celebrated ratification of the Federal Constitution in 1788. Ceremonies took place throughout the country, from Boston to North Carolina.[36] One of the largest Grand Federal Processions occurred in Philadelphia on July Fourth. It was a pageant designed to represent American society from top to bottom. Militia troops, Supreme Court justices, foreign consuls, farmers, manufacturers, artisans, and professionals all paraded in their appointed turn. Spectators crowded the "foot-ways, the windows, and the roofs of the houses." The line between spectators and participants blurred as more and more people joined the parade along the route. What had begun as five thousand marchers neatly organized by profession, ended as seventeen thousand men and women gathered on the large lawn at Bush Hill, on the western edge of the city.[37]

Along the way, the parade passed through the heart of the city, beginning at South and Third Streets, traveling north along Third to the northern limits of the city, turning back south on Fourth Street and then west on Market Street to Bush Hill, belonging to William Hamilton, one of the city's wealthy elite. Third Street housed a broad spectrum of Philadelphia society. As the marchers walked its length from south to north, they passed the elegant mansions of the Binghams, the Powels, and the Willings—three interrelated families who possessed a great deal of political power and social prestige in Philadelphia. Further to the north, Third Street became more commercial and less affluent. The procession here passed the doors of shopkeepers, innkeepers, tailors, hucksters, and laborers.

Spectators cheered for their fellow tradesmen and mechanics as the procession passed them; the celebration was an occasion for expressions of craft consciousness as well as citizenship. Many of the trades marched beside teams of horses pulling large floats (some of them thirty feet long) on which artisans performed their tasks: butchers carved meat, and printers struck off copies of Francis Hopkinson's ode written for the occasion, distributing it to the crowd. Potters shaped cups and bowls on a wheel, coachmakers constructed a carriage. All celebrated the industry and initiative of American workers and the quality of American-made goods.

The Manufacturing Society carried spinning and carding machines on its float. Two men worked the carding machine (which bore a sign boasting the machine's ability to card fifty pounds of cotton per day). A female spinner worked the spinning jenny. She represented "industrious poor" women workers assembled by the Pennsylvania Society for the Encouragement of Manufacture and the Useful Arts. The machines came from a factory at Ninth and Market Streets where poor women learned to use the mechanized spinners.[38]

On the same float, behind the carders and the lone spinner, was the machinery of John Hewson, textile printer. With Hewson and his assistant Mr. Lang sat Mrs. Hewson and her four daughters, dressed in cottons "of their own manufacture." All five of the women worked at "penciling a piece of sprigged chintz of Mr. Hewson's printing." Hewson's portion of the float was a colorful advertisement of his wares: a calico printer's flag with the motto "May the union government protect the manufactures of America," elaborately decorated with thirty-seven patterns of Hewson's design. The presence of the Hewson women, and the unnamed female spinner (mentioned only as "a native of, and instructed in, the city") illustrated the integral role women played in the family economy. Hewson depended upon his wife and daughters for his business success. The family, in turn, depended upon the Constitution and the unity of the nation to protect and promote domestic manufacturing. Plainly demonstrated to all observers was the fact that the Constitution *did* include women.[39]

Their inclusion, however, was problematic. Organizers intended the parade to be a living illustration of membership in the American nation. But the female wheel spinners, part of the Manufacturing Society's network of unmechanized labor and the only group of women invited to participate, refused to march in the parade because they perceived that the demonstration of the spinning jenny was a harbinger of their coming unemployment. Members of other female trades were not invited to march at all: weavers, seamstresses, tailoresses, glove, lace, and mantua makers were not present. Arabella Stewart, a milliner who lived on Third Street near Market, had no example of her trade to observe. Nor did shopkeeper Sarah Middleton, or Mrs. Sage, a widow who kept a school in the 1780s, but by 1791 ran a boardinghouse near the docks. Middleton had her shop on Sixth Street in the 1780s, but was listed as a huckster in 1791. This was a considerable step down the economic scale. For these women and innumerable others, opportunity came in small packages, if it came at all.[40]

Though the parade included the students of the university and principal schools of the city carrying the flag of "The Rising Generation," nowhere in the procession were the mothers who would rear this generation acknowledged. Women were not among the militia companies, the city's elite voluntary associations, or the professions. Only six—Mrs. Hewson, her daughters, and the unnamed spinner—were included with the trades. This vision of the nation displayed by the Grand Procession was hierarchical, white, and overwhelmingly male. But this was not the only manifestation of the public nation visible during this time of celebration.

Coexistent with the officially sanctioned Constitutional processions were several alternative ceremonies in which women celebrated the Constitution *as women*. In Woodstock, Connecticut, on July 2, two days before the Philadelphia procession, sixty-five young women gathered at the home of the Congregational minister. They spent the day spinning flax, and then they presented the yarn to the minister's wife. Simultaneously, several young men of the town built an oxcart for the minister and subscribed to have the women's yarn spun into cloth. At the completion of these tasks, the women and men participated in an "elegant entertainment," where "the American spinning wheel was the toast of the day." The Worcester (Massachusetts) *Spy* remarked that this event was probably the first instance "of the Ladies stepping forth as principals in a rejoicing on account of the present pleasing aspect of our political affairs." The reason for this particular form of celebration, according to the *Spy*, "seemed to be, that the Clergy may receive as great advantages from the New Federal Government as Civilians."[41] Like the spinning bees of the 1760s, this event placed the domestic virtues of the nation's women within a political context. It was a glance backward at traditional behavior, but at the same time, it was also a step toward the conscious, if tenuous, inclusion of women in the new republic.

Another Constitution celebration heralded female political activities of the decade ahead. On August 13, gentlemen from Waterford, New York, and the surrounding area held a procession to celebrate the Constitution. The following day, the women of Waterford held their own celebration. As the Lansingburgh *Federal Herald* reported, sixty-four women marched two by two through the town, carrying a copy of the Constitution before them. The author reported that "the countenances of the numerous and respectable beholders revealed the transporting joy which reign'd triumphantly within their breast on viewing the amiable espousers of the federal cause." At the edge of town the women "permitted a large number of gentlemen" to take tea and dance. Afterward the women proceeded back along their route and retired, again to dance, at a resident's home. Interest in this demonstration of female political expression was widespread: the event was reported throughout the country, as far away as South Carolina. The account of the Waterford event was reprinted twenty-five times, placing it among the most frequently reprinted essays, broadsides, and pamphlets concerning ratification.[42]

The Waterford and Woodstock events are evidence of women's increasing participation in the creation of a national civic culture in the early republic. Women's wartime activities offered the foundation upon which to build their post-Revolutionary lives. Republican rhetoric provided women with opportunities to redefine their relationship to the state. And the tradition of collective action continued to be a part of women's politics in the postwar era, but women also began to live their lives in an increasing number of new public spaces amidst an expanding, diverse popular culture. Women's public celebration of the Constitution was an indication of things to come. As this book will demonstrate, women became more visible, more public, and often more controversial, in the last two decades of the eighteenth century as they occupied a greater share of the young nation's public life.

CHAPTER ONE

Women and the Development of American Print Culture

BEFORE WOMEN stepped into the streets to partake in political celebrations, to attend plays, or to converse in salons, they were exposed to a growing body of written material about their status in the early republic. By the late eighteenth century American women had developed a new and more engaged relationship to print—a medium that both reflected current ideas about women's roles and promoted new ones. As the world of publishers and readership expanded with technological and educational developments, subjects of particular concern to women—education, friendship, courtship, marriage, children—occupied an increasing number of pages in the magazines and books of the day, including Philadelphia's *Lady's Magazine, Columbian Magazine,* and *Weekly Magazine,* and novels such as Susanna Rowson's *Charlotte Temple* and *Fille de Chambre,* Hannah Foster's *The Coquette,* Fanny Burney's *Evelina* and *Camilla;* the essays of Judith Sargent Murray in *The Gleaner;* and Mary Wollstonecraft's didactic *Vindication of the Rights of Woman.* The more American publications and British imports contained female-centered content, the more women were drawn to read them and to realize that these publications were a venue for their opinions. Moreover, such a potential audience was well developed among women who had a tradition of reading and writing to each other. Noted Philadelphia-area writers such as Elizabeth Graeme Ferguson, Hannah Griffitts, and Elizabeth Boudinot, for example, shared their writings among friends and acquaintances, an activity that created both educational and intellectual opportunities for the other women in their circles.[1]

Ultimately, these overlapping phenomena, all centered around the world of print, produced a new woman-centered public forum in which Americans discussed and debated women's familial, social, economic, and political roles. This forum was influenced by European writers and events. And as Americans participated in a transatlantic world of thought and culture they adapted old-world ideas to their new republican culture. This chapter will explore how popular magazines, novels, and didactic essays shared this American public forum that was for, about, and often by women.

None of the developments described above would have been possible without a rapid increase in literacy during the last quarter of the eighteenth century. The growing number of advertisements for periodicals, novels, and lending libraries in the nation's newspapers between 1785 and 1800 testifies to this increasing readership in the early republic, as do the expanded educational opportunities for men and women alike.[2] American readers, especially elites and gentry in the northern states and seaboard cities, had ample opportunity to purchase the latest books on any subject, and they stayed current on issues of the day through the popular periodicals that appeared with increasing frequency. Indeed, opportunities for access to print in the nation's urban centers abounded. As the United States reached a total population of five million in 1800, 219 booksellers in Boston, New York, Philadelphia, Baltimore, and Charleston served its citizens (compared to only 63 in 1773).[3] In Philadelphia, eighteen "Booksellers and Stationers" were listed in the 1795 city directory, all located within the city center. Along Market Street alone, in a four-block radius, there were six. Located among grocers, dry goods shops, and central markets, these booksellers were convenient to most citizens.[4]

Circulating libraries were another source of reading material, extending reading opportunities to those who could not afford to purchase books or magazines on a frequent basis. The number of these institutions increased dramatically in the last two decades of the eighteenth century. By one estimate, 376 social libraries were created between 1731 and 1800, while 266 of these opened in the 1790s alone. Social libraries, often referred to as subscription libraries, charged an annual membership fee and required the purchase of shares. These costs often placed social libraries beyond the means of all but the wealthy. The New York Social Library, for example, charged a two-hundred-dollar membership fee, and a two-dollar yearly fee. By contrast, in the small town of Carlisle, Pennsylvania, the Library Company operated on a more modest scale. It charged members eight dollars to join and one dollar and twenty-five cents per year.[5] A commercial circulating library, in contrast, rented books to the general public at considerably lower rates. Circulating libraries reached a wider readership of moderate-income readers in towns and cities from Pawlet, Vermont, to Baltimore.[6] The small farming town of Harwinton, Connecticut, had one. The Mechanics Library of New Haven catered to the area's artisan families.[7] Even the frontier town of Belpre, Ohio (settled in 1788), had a library by 1796.[8] Hocquet Caritat's lending library in New York City, probably one of the larger urban libraries, had fifteen hundred novels on hand. Borrowing privileges cost six dollars a year, but this fee could be paid in installments. The Annapolis Circulating Library offered readers the option of joining for a year, six months, three months, one month, or simply borrowing one book at a time with a small deposit. Arrangements such as those at the Annapolis and Caritat libraries put reading the most popular and current books, magazines, and essays within reach of artisans with modest incomes and their families.[9]

It was magazines, more than any other medium, that helped to develop an American public discourse on gender roles and gender relations in the early republic. As Charles Brockden Brown noted, "the controversy about the relative merit of the sexes has been carried on, of late years, with a good deal of vivacity."[10] In the late eighteenth century, periodicals offered readers one of the most interesting arenas for this discussion. Although there was no consensus on the issues discussed, the magazines devoted much space to the subject of gender relations. And for the first time, the recognition of a female audience influenced the development of periodicals.

There are two significant characteristics of the late eighteenth-century American magazines. First, they established a conversation among readers, and encouraged a dialogue between readers and the printed page by printing letters and comments. Precedents in British

Woman in the Ebenezer Larkin bookshop, Boston.
Trade Card Collection. Courtesy of the American Antiquarian Society.

magazines existed, but until the 1780s, Americans had been passive readers of British texts. By the 1790s readers were given the opportunity to respond to the essays, fiction, and commentaries in the magazines. Second, the volume of contributions on the topic of gender roles in magazines increased significantly in the early 1790s.[11] Through these publications, women, for the first time, were able "to constitute themselves as a distinct public in American life and letters."[12] Magazines also linked private and public life in a new way. Because they created conversations and dialogues, magazines did for a wider audience what salons did for only a few groups of elites: create intimate, private spaces where critical discussions took place. Through print, women's characters, behaviors, and futures were now a matter for public discussion.

The first American magazines specifically directed at women

appeared during the 1790s. British imports of established women's magazines, such as the *Lady's Magazine, or Entertaining Companion for the Fair Sex* (London, 1770-1811), and Eliza Haywood's *Female Spectator* (1744-46), the first periodical for women written by a woman, had been available to readers for many years.[13] Colonial magazines occasionally discussed women, but only rarely did women themselves contribute to them.[14] In Boston the *Gentleman and Lady's Town and Country Magazine* (1784-85) was the first American magazine to appeal to a female readership. *The Lady's Magazine and Repository of Entertaining Knowledge* was established in Philadelphia seven years later, and New York's *Lady and Gentlemen's Pocket Magazine of Literary and Polite Amusement* began in 1796. Magazines often served more than one region. Periodicals from Boston and New York, for example, were shipped south to Philadelphia, creating a national venue for regional authors such as Judith Sargent Murray.[15] Though reading choices were plentiful, many of the magazines were short-lived. *The Lady's Magazine and Repository of Entertaining Knowledge* and *Lady and Gentlemen's Pocket Magazine of Literary and Polite Amusement*, for example, did not last more than a year. The *Gentleman and Lady's Town and Country Magazine* published for only nine months, resumed as the *Gentlemen and Ladies' Town and Country Magazine* four years later, but lasted only nineteen months.[16] Almost all the magazines, whether for a general audience, such as Boston's *Massachusetts Magazine* (1789-96), New York's *New York Magazine* (1790-97), Philadelphia's *Columbian Magazine* (1786-92), the *National Magazine*, of Richmond, Virginia (1799-1800), or those specifically directed at female readers, contributed a wide variety of opinions on the topic of gender roles in the early republic.

Magazines wished to attract female readers, but they also actively encouraged women's contributions. Boston's *Gentleman and Lady's Town and Country Magazine* requested that women bestow to its pages "the elegant polish of the Female Pencil where purity of sentiment and impassioned Fancy are happily blended together."[17] The successor to this magazine, the *Gentlemen and Ladies' Town and Country Magazine*, proclaimed that its ambition was "the instruction and amusement of the Fair." And it conveyed the wish that "every Son of Science and Daughter of Genius" contribute to its pages.[18] In New

York, Noah Webster, as editor of the *American Magazine*, announced that he "flatters himself that many of the Ladies, who are favorites of Minerva and the Muses, will be found in the number of his correspondents."[19] The *Massachusetts Magazine* was even more pointed in its target audience: "The fair sex merits our highest attention. If their taste has not hitherto been consulted, or the delicacy of their fancy gratified, we flatter ourselves that the succeeding numbers will make compensation for the former negligence, and convince the last, best gift of heaven, that we reverence woman, the daughter of the sky."[20] New York's *Lady and Gentlemen's Pocket Magazine of Literary and Polite Amusement* went further in its assertion that there was "nothing of higher importance to a nation than the education, the habits, the amusements of the fair Sex."[21] Magazines facilitated women's entry into this new public space by accommodating both anonymous and pseudonymous contributions. Female correspondents were safely at a distance from public ridicule or attack. This anonymity allowed greater freedom of expression and more candor of opinion. This was true for onetime contributors and for regular authors such as Judith Sargent Murray, who wrote as "Constantia" for the *Massachusetts Magazine* in the early 1790s.

The contents of the magazines included prescriptive lessons, fables, stories, novellas, dialogues, poems, and letters from contributors. Most selections were designed to appeal to the "delicacy" of women's "fancy." If this was true, then seduction, murder, insanity, and suicide must be included among female reader's favorite subjects. Though there was a constant refrain in newspapers, instructional essays, and magazines condemning novel reading, as Robert Winans notes, "By the 1780s and 1790s the amount of fiction printed in the magazines far outweighed the number of essays denouncing it."[22] Much of this short fiction mirrored contemporary novels such as *The Coquette* and *The Power of Sympathy*, in which bad choices lead women to bad ends, but not before presenting in detail the pressures and problems women experienced.

Eager as readers were to indulge vicariously in sentiment and seduction, the majority of selections in the magazines were nonfiction. A lively conversation about women's political, social, and economic rights appeared in the magazines, representing a wide range of opinions on women's place in society and the home.[23] Women's physical and intellectual capabilities were frequently discussed. Occasionally their fitness for citizenship and a role in the civic body was taken up as well. With the exception of the Philadelphia *Lady's Magazine*, no other periodical took an editorial position either in favor of expanding women's roles and opportunities or of consistently arguing the dangers of changing the status quo. Measured in quantity, the articles that suggested women retain their traditionally defined roles, both in the domestic sphere and in society as a whole, outweighed the pieces advocating equality in marriage, the development of women's intellectual potential, or legal protections.

There was considerable contrast among the essays, poems, and other types of selections that argued either for or against the expansion of women's roles in the new republic. There were advocates who favored female modesty and "delicacy" (a highly ambiguous term used by very different authors for diverse purposes). Some selections, called "character studies," were meant to serve as examples to female readers of what a gentleman desired in a woman. Many of these emphasized that women needed to be delicate, refined, and unassertive. Fables also conveyed prescriptions for feminine behavior. "Elmina, or The Flower That Never Fades," subtitled "A Tale for Young Ladies," is one example. A fairy gives Elmina a flower that never fades. Its multicolored petals represent female virtues: vermillion for modesty, white for virtue, yellow for beneficence, and blue for gentleness. As long as Elmina practices these virtues the flower remains healthy, but, as the fairy cautions her, "whenever Elmina loses her temper or is angry, this charming flower will droop." Lest readers think that virtue is its own and only reward, a prince appears and marries Elmina.[24] Here was allegory with an explicit lesson: inner virtue reaps external rewards, including (and perhaps most important) marriage to the right man.

Some contributors took a more critical stance toward traditional expectations for women's behavior. Philadelphia's *Columbian Magazine* published many articles about gender roles such as "On the Supposed Superiority of the Masculine Understanding." The author, who identified herself only as "a Lady," argued that it was men who kept women subordinate, and she challenged, "Let them withdraw their injuries, and we shall easily spare their protection." Even more assertive was another piece, printed under "Maxims for the Ladies": "A woman, whose ruling passion is not vanity, is superior to any man of equal faculties."

Whereas some periodicals such as the *Columbian Magazine* published a range of opinions on women's roles, the Philadelphia *Lady's Magazine* consistently favored more egalitarian arguments about women's private and public roles. Editor Charles Brockden Brown, himself a critic of contemporary gender roles, publicly discouraged contributors who did not agree with his opinions. For example, rather than conveying a rejection privately, Brown chose to print the following: "S.L.'s piece we have received, but must assure him that, while he employs his pen in no other manner than in degrading ideas of *female learning*, he will be viewed by us as an object of contempt."[25] Brown's attitude alerted readers that the *Lady's Magazine* promoted a change in gender roles for women. It also advocated changes in gender relations, especially marital equality. One issue of the *Lady's Magazine* carried an article entitled, "Matrimonial Republican." The anonymous author suggested, perhaps sarcastically, that the word "obey" should not be included in the marriage ceremony, claiming that "we know it is virtually left out by nine out of ten who enter into that holy state." And bound at the back of the second volume of the same magazine, along with an advertisement for Mary Wollstonecraft's *Vindication of the Rights of Woman*, William Gibbons offered for sale a work entitled *Advantages and Disadvantages of a Married State.*[26] These selections highlighted the attitudes of the men and women who desired that marriage be a relationship of partners, in which husband and wife would jointly make decisions and both could act with a certain degree of autonomy in line with the current abhorrence of tyranny, both public and private. Increasingly, this theme was developed in the magazines and elsewhere.

Unlike the *Lady's Magazine*, most magazines neither vigorously advocated equality nor lamented that women were in subjection to their husbands. Instead, they offered selections such as "Rules and Maxims for Promoting Matrimonial Happiness." This particular article cautioned wives against arguing with their husbands, and suggested that a wife should "read frequently, and with due attention, the Matrimonial Service; and take care, in doing so, not to overlook the word Obey." This selection contrasted sharply with the *Lady's Maga-zine*'s "Matrimonial Republican."

Some articles recognized that women did have a certain degree of power within their domestic relationships, and the strategies they offered to wives for getting what they wanted involved not a challenge to the traditional patriarchal role of husband as a wife's superior, but rather suggested that a wife might cajole her husband, in the most demure manner, to achieve her ends. Delicacy and domestic diploma-cy, rather than direct rebellion, were advocated as the methods of attaining a woman's goals. One such article praised women for their yielding, compromising qualities, and pointed out that by such talents, women had ruled in France as a power behind the throne for hundreds of years.[27]

Another example of wifely manipulation appeared in the *Lady's Magazine*. This article included a letter, supposedly written from a real wife to her husband, in which she asked him to be more devoted to her. She gently chided the husband for his neglect, and mentioned that her friends and family did not approve of his behavior. The author of the piece claimed that the letter had the desired effect: the husband and wife, "lived many years after in the most perfect conjugal felicity." The author went on to caution that had the wife "taken the means too prevalent in this age, to work his reformation—it would not have suc-ceeded." In other words, if the wife had suggested that she had a right to certain behavior and attention from her husband, that their mar-riage relied on more than the tacit assumption that the husband was in authority and control, the wife would not have been able to make her husband change. In one of the rare cases in which a reader left mar-ginalia, the following comment was appended to this article: "Read this all you that wish to be happiest in a marriage."[28] Clearly neither authors, nor readers, came to any agreement about marriage. Some articles did present arguments and examples which promoted the idea of more power for women within the home. Not everyone was con-vinced that such a change should be promoted, but the magazines played a part in introducing this subject into the public discussion of women's roles.

In addition to essays, allegories, and poetry supporting increased equality for women in their domestic relationships, the magazines also contained much distinctly antifeminist material. Cautionary tales of bad wives and stories of young women gone astray because they disobeyed their parents appeared with great frequency. "The Prostitute," for example, detailed the precipitous fall of a rebellious daughter. Like the many novels of its time, this poem warned young women against giving in to ungoverned passion and too much female autonomy. Purportedly "humorous" anecdotes and rhymes about female termagants also found an audience in the periodicals. Reprints of epitaphs composed by surviving husbands on their deceased wives were prevalent. "Epitaph on a Violent Scold," and "Epitaph on a Scolding Wife" convey the tone of such selections.[29] These epitaphs demonstrated the misogynistic qualities still dominant in late eighteenth-century society. Reprinting such epitaphs for public amusement was part of a long "battle of the sexes," as Carla Mulford terms it, carried on in newspapers, magazines, and essays in the colonies, Britain, and Europe, throughout the eighteenth century. These battles often strayed from one public medium to another. For example, in *Poor Richard's Almanack* in 1737, Benjamin Franklin reprinted a popular British jest:

Woman are books in which we often spy
Some blotted lines and sometimes lines awry
And tho perhaps some strait ones intervene
In all of them erata may be seen
If it be so I wish my wife were
An almanack—to change her every year.

New Jersey poet Annis Boudinot Stockton replied in a poem circulated among her friends, "A Sarcasm Against the Ladies in a Newspaper; An Impromptu Answer":

"Woman are books"—in this I do agree
But men there are that cant read A B C
And more who have not genius to discern
The beauties of those books they attempt to learn
But thank our stars, our Critics are not *these*
The men of sense and taste we always please

Who know to choose and then to prize their books
With them into a world of error thrown
And our eratas place against their own.[30]

Many magazines tried to play to opposite constituencies simultaneously. While indulging readers who found humor in the stereotype of
the nagging wife, magazines also attempted to make good on their
claim that there was "nothing of higher importance to a nation than
the education, the habits, the amusements of the fair sex," by printing
advertisements for schools and private instruction for young women
available in the 1780s and 1790s.[31] Some magazines made extravagant
claims to their female readers, promising "everything requisite to disseminate knowledge of real life, to portray virtue, inspire the Female
mind with love of religion, patience, prudence, and fortitude."[32] But
the magazines also printed criticism of improvements for women.

A revealing short story published in Philadelphia's *Weekly Magazine*, titled, "The Plague of the Learned Wife," illustrates one aspect
of this criticism of female improvement. The narrator, a tradesman,
complains that his wife reads too much, and bothers him with reading
aloud passages containing "hard words." Her "bookish" interests also
mean that she is of no help to him in his business. From the husband's
point of view, there seems little to be gained from studying books:
"According to my notion now, neither tradesmen, nor tradesmen's
wives, nor any body belonging to them, have any business to talk like
skolards." Worse still, his daughter takes after her mother, and has
spurned an industrious young storekeeper because he did not come up
to her intellectual standards. The father concludes with a warning: "I
hope all unmarried tradesmen, when they have read this letter (for
your Magazine will undoubtedly fall into the hands of many such people), will take special care how they venture upon a bookish woman."
Issues of class and economics come to the fore in this selection. Neither the preservation of female "delicacy" nor "virtue" was the pressing
concern here. Rather, the author raised only the disturbing possibility
that a laboring woman's intellectual improvement, her aping of the
manners of her female "betters," could interfere with her ability to
contribute to the family economy.[33]

The magazines were a potpourri of arguments for and against changes in gender relations and women's roles. Some articles did not advocate substantial improvements for women, either within marriage or in terms of educational opportunities. But even opponents to change were just that: they responded to the general discussion in late eighteenth-century American society about women's public and private roles. If any one thing persuaded readers that women were capable of meeting intellectual challenges, it would have been the volume of contributions to the magazines from female authors. Many of these individuals chose to be known only by their pen names, such as "Laura," "Amelia," or "Constantia." There were real women behind these pseudonyms, many of whom circulated their work among friends. Elizabeth Graeme Ferguson was one of these authors. In addition to her literary works, which were read widely among her Philadelphia-area friends and fellow writers, Ferguson published twenty-seven poems in Philadelphia magazines and newspapers between 1784 and 1800. Many readers, then, already acquainted with female authors through salons or sororal networks, would have taken for granted that a "Laura" (Ferguson's pen name) really was a woman.[34]

The most prominent female magazine writer of the day was Judith Sargent Murray. No American author, male or female, articulated a position on gender roles and gender relations more clearly than Judith Sargent Murray. She was the first American woman to write essays for a large public forum in which women's concerns were consistently addressed. By the time her articles were reprinted as *The Gleaner* in 1798, she had won a national audience and garnered both praise and condemnation for her views. She first contributed an essay to the *Gentleman and Lady's Town and Country Magazine* in 1784 and began writing monthly essays for the *Massachusetts Magazine* in 1792. Murray may have been the first American women to have her own periodical venue. Under her pseudonyms "Constantia," then the "Gleaner," Murray expressed opinions on a wide variety of subjects, including women's rights, political affairs, and religious issues.

Many of Murray's opinions were shaped by personal experiences. She was raised in a well-to-do household in Gloucester, Massachusetts. Though she received no formal education, Murray read widely in the popular, political, and philosophical writings of the eighteenth

century. Her experiences with marriage, religion, and property ownership contributed to the development of a protofeminist consciousness
which found expression in both her private and personal writings.
Murray chafed at the legal limitations imposed on women; she resent-
ed the fact that she could not sell her own property without her husband's signature. As she told her brother, "The law acknowledges no
separate act of a *married* woman."[35] Her public writings, particularly
the magazine contributions, reflect her desire to see societal changes.
Murray believed much of the remedy lay in better education for young
women, and society's acknowledgment that women and men shared
many capacities and virtues.

Murray's proposals, like those of other proponents of female education, were a response to those prescriptions offered in conduct books,
such as John Gregory's *Father's Legacy to His Daughters*, and education
tracts, such as Jean-Jacques Rousseau's *Emile* (1762). Murray's opinions were diametrically opposed to those of Gregory and Rousseau.[36]
Murray strongly attacked claims of natural female inferiority. Education, she asserted, not nature, made women seem inferior to men. Yet
the intellectual equality of men and women was rarely recognized.
Worse still, the prevalent belief in woman's inferiority was a vehicle
used to prevent women from improving themselves. Dr. Gregory cautioned women to hide their intellectual accomplishments: "keep it a
profound secret, especially from the men, who generally look with a
jealous and malignant eye on a woman of great parts, and a cultivated
understanding." Rousseau wished to deny women any education that
was not domestic because they were unfit for anything else: reason,
according to Rousseau, was "beyond a woman's grasp."[37] Murray's
response to such ideas was strident: "But imbecility is still confin'd
/And by the lordly sex to us consign'd; /They rob us of the power t'improve, /And then declare we only trifles love."[38]

Murray argued that women possessed the four necessary elements
of intellectual powers—imagination, reason, memory, and judgment.
She did not shy away from criticizing male obstinacy on this point:
"Strange how blind self love renders you men; were you not wholly
absorbed in a partial admiration of your own abilities, you would long
since have acknowledged the force of what I am now going to urge."[39]
To counter claims that women could not exercise courage, fortitude, or

other "manly" virtues, Murray offered historical examples of women who embodied characteristics which proved them "in every respect, equal to men," including "supporting, with honour, the toils of government."[40] Murray clearly believed that politics was not the exclusive province of men. When author Sally Wood criticized "female politicians" in her novel *Julia, and the Illuminated Baron* (1800), Murray wrote to Wood, suggesting she reconsider. Murray asked, "May not a female be so circumstanced, as to render a correct, and even profound knowledge of politicks, the pride and glory of her character?" Because women were patriots and citizens, a knowledge of politics, which Murray defined as "a capability of distinguishing that which will probably advance the real interest of the Community," was as necessary for them as for men. She asked Wood, "Are not women equally concerned with men in the public weal?"[41]

The answer, according to Murray, was yes. And in order to be fit as members of the polity, women needed education. In "Desultory Thoughts upon the Utility of Encouraging a Degree of Self-Complacency, especially in female Bosoms," published in the *Gentleman and Lady's Town and Country Magazine* in 1784, Murray addressed her young female audience with the following advice: "A pleasing form is undoubtedly advantageous but, it must be your part, my sweet girl, to render yourself worthy of respect from higher motives: you must learn to 'reverence yourself,' that is, your intellectual existence."[42] Murray was careful to link the cultivation of the female intellect with practical talents. She advocated education which could "lay an early foundation for independence" and make women economically self-sufficient: "The sex should be taught to depend on their own efforts, for the procurement of an establishment in life."[43] Such resources could help widows and unmarried women attain economic security and independence. Talents were also necessary for married women: "The united efforts of male and female might rescue many a family from destruction."[44] Murray had personal reasons for asserting this: her first husband, John Stevens, became so indebted that he fled to Saint Eustatius in a desperate attempt to regain financial security. Stevens died shortly afterwards, leaving his wife without a "competency" to survive on.[45] Thus, Murray's advocacy sprang from her own needs and frustrations. Many readers, especially females, shared her concerns.

Murray's proposals were not extreme by eighteenth-century standards. They articulated succinctly and clearly many of the thoughts already current in the transatlantic world. American readers were familiar with Rousseau's ideas, but they were equally aware of his critics in the 1770s and 1780s. Madame de Staël's *Lettres sur Rousseau*, Madame d'Epinay's novel *Histoire de Madame de Montbrillant*, and her instructional guide for girls, *Les Conversations d'Emilie*, all advocated the type of female education Murray proposed, and they all attacked Rousseau's assessment of women's abilities. His harshest critic, Mary Wollstonecraft, affirmed the opinions in Murray's early essays, and Murray in turn praised Wollstonecraft's *Vindication of the Rights of Woman* in her essay "Observations on Female Abilities."[46] Murray's life experiences fostered her awareness of the confines of normative gender roles in the late eighteenth century. Her recognition of the need for social change prompted her to give voice publicly, albeit under a pseudonym, to her opinions. She found a ready audience in magazine readers prepared to entertain the prospect of change.

Whereas Murray gently urged her readers to advance the position of women in American society, Mary Wollstonecraft 's take-no-prisoners approach to the discussion of women's participation in private and public life made her one of the most controversial writers in the late eighteenth-century Anglo-American world. *A Vindication of the Rights of Woman*, published in London in 1792, was immediately reprinted in Boston and Philadelphia. The reason why her work garnered so much attention in the United States as well as in Britain was Wollstonecraft's ability to collect all the various arguments for the social, familial, and political advancement of women and put them in one place. As Rosemarie Zagarri has said, "Newspapers and magazines picked up her terminology and popularized a new language— the language of rights—by which Americans could understand, refer to, and analyze women."[47] By tying feminism to political theory, Wollstonecraft gave these ideas a more political, and therefore controversial, cast. Wollstonecraft benefitted from her time and place: the French Revolution raised the possibility of creating a radically new social, as well as political, structure. And French women, such as Olympe de Gouges and Madame Roland, demanded that women seize the opportunity to gain new rights for themselves.[48] American women were aware of these events, and were able to read Wollstonecraft's work within a transatlantic context of gender issues common to women in France, Britain, and the United States.

The occasion for Wollstonecraft's remarks was the French Revolution. While the Rights of Man were promoted in France, Wollstonecraft brought to the world's attention the fact that the Rights of Woman were unjustly neglected. Wollstonecraft's aim was "to render my sex more respectable members of society."[49] To do so, she first explained why traditional beliefs about women, and the behavior women were encouraged to practice, were wrong. Not surprisingly, one of her primary targets was Rousseau, who had claimed that "a woman should never, for a moment, feel herself independent, that she should be governed by fear to exercise her *natural* cunning, and made a coquettish slave in order to render her a more alluring object of desire."[50] It was not true, she asserted, that women really "governed" through obeying, or that their weakness was a virtue, designed by nature to afford them protection by men, nor that women were naturally the intellectual inferiors of men.

In many ways echoing Murray's precepts, Wollstonecraft urged her readers to replace traditional behavior and beliefs with new ones: men should treat women as intellectual equals. And women should take legal and financial command over themselves. Only by "allowing them to participate in the inherent rights of mankind" could women "become wise and virtuous."[51] Women's most important duty was "to themselves as rational creatures, and the next, in point of importance, as citizens, is that, which includes so many, of a mother."[52] Wollstonecraft wished to reenforce domestic roles rather than diminish or abandon them. She saw the need for good families in order to have good government. Women were instrumental to this plan. Her advocacy of better education, more serious pastimes, and better physical health, all contributed to making women "the friend, and not the humble dependent of her husband."[53] Self-control, rationality, order, and discipline were all necessary to producing good women capable of raising families, being good companions, and contributing to the polity.

Wollstonecraft urged that legal protections were necessary in order for women to exercise their abilities. Without civil existence in the state, women could not be independent: "But, to render her really virtuous and useful, she must not, if she discharge her civil duties, want, individually, the protection of civil laws; she must not be dependant on her husband's bounty for her subsistence during his life, or support after his death—for how can a being be generous who has nothing of its own? Or virtuous, who is not free?"[54] She even went so far as to suggest that women obtain political rights, although she was aware that this suggestion was extreme. Wollstonecraft acknowledged that it was more likely to "excite laughter" than agreement.[55]

Wollstonecraft's message was couched in terms which held particular appeal for American readers. Her chief arguments supported the notion that women were equally capable of virtue generally, and were therefore equally responsible for civic virtue. Wollstonecraft repeatedly mentioned civic virtue, the fundamental basis of a good and just society, throughout her essay. Both women and men needed to exercise it if society was to advance. Employing the language of the era, she asserted that the time was ripe "to effect a revolution in female manners—time to restore them their lost dignity—and make them, as a part of the human species, labour by reforming themselves to reform the world." Furthermore, she likened the subjection of women to "tyrannic kings and venal ministers." She linked civic virtue with republicanism: "as sound politics diffuse liberty, mankind, including women, will become more wise and virtuous."[56]

Ultimately Wollstonecraft's appeal, though made on behalf of women, had to persuade men. She argued that marriage, family, children, civil and political society would all be better off if women were given their due:

I entreat them to assist to emancipate their companion, to make her a help meet for them! Would men but generously snap our chains, and be content with rational fellowship instead of slavish obedience, they would find us more observant daughters, more affectionate sisters, more faithful wives, more reasonable mothers—in a word, better citizens. We should then love them with true affection, because we should learn to respect ourselves.[57]

One woman commented, after reading *A Vindication of the Rights of Woman*, "What a mind! How exquisitely sensible! And how extensive in all its powers."⁵⁸ Senator Aaron Burr wrote to his wife from Philadelphia that he found *A Vindication of the Rights of Woman* "a work of genius." He was particularly struck by Wollstonecraft's answer to Rousseau's *Emile*: "her comment on that work, especially what relate to female education, contains more good sense than all the other criticisms upon him which I have seen put together. I promise myself much pleasure in reading it to you."⁵⁹ Mary Moody Emerson in Massachusetts recommended that her sister-in-law Ruth Emerson (mother of Ralph Waldo Emerson) read Wollstonecraft's works, "about which we were so warmly disputing the last time I saw you." Emerson did not agree with all Wollstonecraft's ideas, but did approve of her suggestions for young women's education, the adoption of which promised to eliminate that "softness in girls which lays a foundation for many future ills in their lives."⁶⁰ Elizabeth Drinker, who was conservative in most of her opinions, acknowledged that Wollstonecraft articulated some of her thoughts: "In very many of her sentiments she, as some of our friends say, *speaks my mind*, in some others I do not, altogether coincide with her—I am not for quite so much independence."⁶¹ Drinker's response to Wollstonecraft was indicative of the interest and awareness many women had about their roles in the Republic, and at the same time indicates the hesitancy on the part of many women like Drinker to push for too much change too quickly. In this she differed from some of her sister Quakers such as Hannah Griffitts, who valued her "liberty."⁶² Wollstonecraft was greatly influenced by her acquaintance Thomas Paine. His *Rights of Man* (1791), an argument for more democratic government, irritated many American Federalists. But gender issues could transcend party lines. Even Abigail Adams, a model of high Federalism, was described by her husband as a "Wollstonecraft disciple."⁶³

The initial reception of *A Vindication of the Rights of Woman* in the United States was positive. Wollstonecraft confirmed the views already articulated in America among the middle and upper classes. Philadelphia printer Mathew Carey's confidence that he could sell fifteen hundred copies of his own printing of Wollstonecraft's book (a very large number for any book at that time), even after both the London and Boston editions were available, reflected a popular interest in what Wollstonecraft had to say. There were many advertisements for new and used copies of the book in the newspapers.⁶⁴ Several advertisements were bound into the back of newly published novels, a genre that publishers already recognized as having a large female readership. Wollstonecraft and her ideas gained a broad audience in the 1790s. Even people who may not have read her work knew who she was. When Charles Wollstonecraft (who ran a textile factory in Wilmington, Delaware) visited Philadelphia in 1796, Elizabeth Meredith identified him to her son as the "Brother to the Lady of that name who wrote the rights of Woman."[65]

It is not surprising that both the Boston *Massachusetts Magazine* (where most of Judith Sargent Murray's essays appeared) and Philadelphia's *Lady's Magazine* chose to print excerpts for their readers. Charles Brockden Brown included nine pages of passages from *A Vindication of the Rights of Woman* in the premier issue of *Lady's Magazine*. Significantly, Brown chose for the frontispiece of his magazine the same emblematical picture that the British *Lady's Magazine* used, but with a difference. In the British magazine illustration, a woman, the "Genius of the Ladies Magazine," kneels to Liberty, and presents her with a laurel crown and a copy of the *Lady's Magazine*. In the American version, this same woman kneels to Liberty, but this time she presents her with a sheet of paper titled "Rights of Woman." Thus Brown set the tone for his magazine: its contents would emphasize enhanced marital, social, and possibly political roles for American women.

The *Lady's Magazine* gave its readers a good sense of Wollstonecraft's arguments. Brown admitted in his commentary that he did not "agree with our fair authoress in all the points she contends for, yet to show her we are much pleased with her work, we shall be pretty copious in our review of it."[66] Tellingly, in his choice of selections from *A Vindication of the Rights of Woman*, Brown did not quote from her section "on the causes of the degradations of women," because, he claimed, Wollstonecraft had not said anything his audience had not already read about elsewhere.[67] He did include portions that discussed love, marriage, and female education. He also chose to print Wollstonecraft's criticism of Talleyrand and his French revolutionary government for its failure to give women a voice, and for denying them all "civil and political rights."[68] Brown's choice of selections may have reflected his own particular interests, or he may have included what he believed were the most interesting and compelling points in her essay.

Bookseller William Gibbons's advertisement for *A Vindication of the Rights of Woman* on the back page of the *Lady's Magazine and Repository of Entertaining Knowledge*, 1792. Courtesy of the Library Company of Philadelphia.

Frontispiece to the first volume of Philadelphia's *Lady's Magazine and Repository of Entertaining Knowledge*, 1792. The description reads: "The genius of the Ladies Magazine, accompanied by the Genius of emulation, who carries in her hand a laurel crown, approaches Liberty, and kneeling, presents her with a copy of the Rights of Woman." Courtesy of the Library Company of Philadelphia.

Wollstonecraft's ideas stimulated many to comment. In Ann Harker's commencement address at the Young Ladies Academy of Philadelphia in 1794 (printed and sold in the city almost immediately afterward), she asserted that women, as well as men, had their champions: "In opposition to your immortal Paine, we will exalt our Wollstonecraft."[69] A year later the *Philadelphia Minerva* printed a reverential song inspired by Wollstonecraft. Entitled "Rights of Woman," it upheld the claim of equal rights for women, and urged women to overthrow the oppression by man, "your tyrant lord." It especially praised Wollstonecraft for defending the "injured" rights of women, and ended with this verse:

John Opie's portrait of Mary Wollstonecraft, done from life in 1797. Courtesy of the Tate Gallery, London.

A voice re-echoing round
with joyful accents sound, "woman is free."
Assert the noble claim,
all selfish arts disdain,
hark how the note proclaim, "woman is free."

The promulgation of women's rights in such an accessible format argues for the widespread discussion of Wollstonecraft's work, and the gender issues it addressed.[70]

Portrait of Mary Wollstonecraft in *Eccentric Biography; or Memoir of Remarkable Female Characters Ancient and Modern*. These included "actresses, adventurers, authoresses, fortunetellers, gipsies, dwarfs, swindlers and vagrants." Worcester, 1804. Courtesy of the Library Company of Philadelphia.

One woman stimulated by Wollstonecraft's ideas was Annis Boudinot Stockton, New Jersey poet and wife of Declaration of Independence signer Richard Stockton. She wrote her daughter Julia Rush a long letter critiquing Wollstonecraft's work. Stockton admitted that she had difficulty getting a copy of *A Vindication of the Rights of Woman*, and assumed that her daughter, who lived in Philadelphia, would not only have been more likely to have read it, but also would have written to her mother about it: "I suppose it is an old thing with you—I wonder you never sent me your critique."[71]

Stockton's opinions on Wollstonecraft's ideas illustrate the extent to which gender issues had already permeated American society by the time Wollstonecraft wrote. Stockton, widely read and deeply thoughtful, dismissed Wollstonecraft's use of Rousseau as a straw man: "I think we need go no further than his Confessions, to discover that he had some *defect* in his brain or that he was a refined idiot, rather than an enlightened philosopher." Stockton was prepared to admit that Wollstonecraft might be right about the condition of women in Britain, but she believed that American women were not the "slaves" Wollstonecraft described: "the Empire of reason is not monopolized by men, there is great pains taken to improve our sex, and store their minds with that knowledge best adapted to make them useful in the situation that their creator has placed them." Stockton believed that American men, rather than taking efforts to oppose women's advancement, were "disposed to assist them by every means in their power," because "men of sense generally prefer such women as companions thro life." Stockton was perhaps overly optimistic in her opinion that "the women have their equal right of everything Latin and Greek excepted." But her letter demonstrates the extent to which Wollstonecraft's work provoked some Americans to consider the condition of women in their own country. Stockton herself had long felt that women were limited only by their lack of education, not their intellectual capacities. In 1768 Stockton published a poem in the *Pennsylvania Chronicle* in which she argued that women's faults lay in "education, not our Sex."[72] Stockton concluded her critique of Wollstonecraft by assuring her daughter that "a great deal of instruction may be gathered from [*A Vindication of the Rights of Woman*]. And

I am sure that no one can read it but they may find something or other that will correct their conduct and enlarge their ideas."[73] In Stockton's case, Wollstonecraft's message reaffirmed Stockton's own long-held beliefs.

Wollstonecraft's opinions touched the conversations and behavior of younger American men and women as well. Philadelphian Elizabeth Hewson, a single woman in her mid-twenties, reported to her brother that Wollstonecraft was hotly debated among her circle of friends, both male and female:

Many arguments are held on the subject, you know Sally is very warm and her brother seems to dispute on purpose. There was a great argument yesterday on female excellence. Sally contended warmly for our sex, I was not in spirits and did not say much which will most likely surprise you, for you know I am a pretty good hand for disputing, however if I had been inclined it would have been difficult to have got a word in between them.

She lamented, however, that another female friend had not "profited much by the reading of Mrs. Wollstonecraft."[74] Hewson's friend was "frightened" to hear her and another woman discuss riding in the local stage without a male escort. Hewson remarked to her brother, "I thought the Rights of Woman would have cured her of such ridiculous notions. I think you will agree with me that they are ridiculous."[75] Hewson later reported to her brother that they had gone on the local stage unaccompanied, showing that "we have profited by reading Mrs. Wollstonecraft. I assure you we are considered equal to Amazons in courage. The idea would be sufficient to make some ladies faint, but thanks to our stars we are endowed with stronger minds."[76] This example does not express the most radical ideas promulgated in *A Vindication of the Rights of Woman*. But it does describe how some women considered changes in their behavior as a result of Wollstonecraft's ideas, or at least justified their activities in those terms.

Student Priscilla Mason took Wollstonecraft's more radical ideas for social change to heart. Mason went further than her classmate Ann Harker at the Young Ladies Academy commencement ceremonies. In the presence of the school's students, instructors, and board of trustees, Mason used her "Salutatory Oration" to publicly state her views on women's rights. Mason's words clearly echoed Wollstonecraft, but her tone was more even more acerbic:

Our high and mighty lords (thanks to their arbitrary constitutions) have denied us the means of knowledge, and then reproached us for the want of it. They doomed the sex to servile or frivolous employments, on purpose to degrade their minds, that they themselves might hold unrivaled, the power and pre-eminence they usurped. Happily, a more liberal way of thinking begins to prevail. But supposing now that we possessed all the talents of the orator, in the highest perfection; where shall we find a theater for the display of them? The Church, the Bar, and the Senate are shut against us. Who shut them? *Man*; despotic man, first made us incapable of the duty, and then forbid us the exercise. Let us by suitable education, qualify ourselves for those high departments—they will open before us.[77]

One wonders how her audience reacted as they heard her words. With the exception of Harker and Mason, the other speakers emphasized how well prepared the women graduates were to be wives and mothers in the new republic, and to carry out more traditional duties. Prescriptive literature supported this traditional attitude. Mason's audience contained parents and relations, and, according to one observer, Pennsylvania and federal congressmen.[78] We can only speculate on what the congressmen thought of Mason's proposal that education would open the doors to congressional offices for women. Her speech, like the magazine essays, confirmed that there was no agreement about the uses of new female education. Some women, like Mason, were prepared to call publicly for advancement far beyond the confines of republican motherhood.

Women were not the only advocates of change. Though perhaps he did not envision women competing for his job, Annis Boudinot Stockton's brother, New Jersey congressman Elias Boudinot delivered a July Fourth oration at Elizabethtown in which he applauded the fact that "The rights of women are no longer strange sounds to an American ear, and I devoutly hope the day is not far distant when we shall find them dignifying in a distinguishing code, the jurisprudence of several states of the Union."[79]

Americans could reinforce the messages that resounded from public podiums with other writers who took up the cause of women's rights, often directly citing Wollstonecraft as their predecessor and inspiration. Mary Hays, a personal friend of Wollstonecraft, wrote *An Appeal to the Men of Great Britain in Behalf of Women* in 1798, reiterating many of the arguments in *A Vindication of the Rights of Woman*. That same year, Priscilla Wakefield's *Reflections on the Present Condition of the Female Sex* addressed women's need for economic independence, extending Adam Smith's idea of productive labor to include women of all classes. And she called for the development of female colleges to give women the same level of education as men. Mary Ann Radcliffe's *Female Advocate; or, An Attempt to Recover the Rights of Women from Male Usurpation* (1799) renewed Daniel Defoe's argument in *Roxana* that men employed a double standard for male and female behavior. Some authors shifted their focus from fictional portrayals to the education of real young women. Novelist and playwright Susanna Rowson, for example, opened an academy in Boston, wrote instructional texts, and became editor of the *Boston Weekly Magazine* (1801-1805).[80]

In Philadelphia, Charles Brockden Brown printed an essay titled "Rights of Women," a condensed version of his book-length essay *Alcuin*, in the *Weekly Magazine of Original Essays, Fugitive Pieces, and Interesting Intelligence*. Brown drew heavily on the ideas of both Murray and Wollstonecraft in his criticism of women's inferior position in American society.[81]

"Rights of Women" describes a Mrs. Carter—an amiable hostess who conducts a "lyceum" or salon and who provides excellent tea to go with the superb talk of her visitors. The narrator, a foil for Mrs. Carter's enlightened views on women, is a young, impoverished schoolmaster. On an afternoon visit to the pleasant home of his hostess, the narrator and others engage in political conversation. He asks his hostess if she is a Federalist. With heavy sarcasm, she replies:

Surely you are in jest. What! Ask a woman, shallow and inexperienced, as all women are known to be, especially with regard to these topics, her opinion on any political question! What in the name of decency have we to do with politics? The daringness of female curiosity is well known; yet it is seldom so adventurous as to attempt to penetrate into the mysteries of government.[82]

Mrs. Carter goes on to attack the inferior position of women in her society from every aspect. She asserts that female inferiority in reasoning, argument, and ideas is the sole result of lack of instruction and want of experience. In agreement with her, the narrator says, "They cannot read who never saw an alphabet. They who know no tool but the needle, cannot be skillful at the pen."[83] Furthermore, as Mrs. Carter asserts, there is no reason why women cannot learn what men learn. No inherent qualities distinguish men from women: "mere sex is a circumstance so purely physical; has so little essential influence, beyond what had flowed from the caprice of evil institutions on the qualities of mind or person."[84] Because women have been excluded from training for many professions, such as the law and medicine, they have thereby been deprived of the talents that would have given them "the means of subsistence and independence."[85]

Mrs. Carter, who is a widow, reiterates the inferiority to which the law condemns a woman upon her marriage, when she "loses all right to separate property." Because she owes her husband "unlimited obedience," in order to get what she wants, a wife must manipulate her husband with "blandishments and tears; not by appeals to justice, and addresses to reason. She will be most applauded when she smiles with most perseverance on her oppressor."[86]

Mrs. Carter provides her audience with strong evidence of the negative results of such limitations for women in the new republic. Feeling that Mrs. Carter has digressed somewhat from his initial inquiry, the narrator brings her back again to his original question, "Are you a federalist?" She first gives him the same reply: "And let me repeat my answer. What have I, as a woman, to do with politics?" And then she concedes that she is federalist insofar as she would defend the Constitution, and would prefer "a scheme of union and confederacy, to war and dissension." But her support of the government ends there. Mrs. Carter makes it quite plain that the lawmakers of the nation comprehended women in "their code of liberty as if we were pigs or sheep." She says that as long as women are perceived to

exist for no purpose but the convenience of the more dignified sex, that I cannot be entrusted with the government of myself: that to foresee, to deliberate, and decide belongs to others, while all my duties resolve themselves, into this precept, "Listen and Obey;" it is not for me to smile at their tyranny, or receive as my Gospel, a code built upon such atrocious maxims. No, I am no federalist.[87]

But Mrs. Carter does not stop merely with a lament about the current state of things. She further argues that the law, which "annihilates the political existence of at least one half of the community," should be changed. Women should have the right "to elect and to be electible."[88] To her, excluding women from suffrage makes no more sense than excluding "from all political functions everyone whose stature did not exceed five feet six inches."[89]

Such sentiments on women written by the individual who gave his magazine's readers nine pages from Wollstonecraft's *Vindication of the Rights of Woman*, and who portrayed forceful, intelligent women in his novels, should come as no surprise. But by the time Brown wrote his essay in 1798, the public and private agreement with Wollstonecraft's ideas had diminished. In its place was a negative criticism that not only targeted her ideas, but also attacked her character. The catalyst for this reversal was the publication of William Godwin's memoir of her in which Godwin revealed that she had a child out of wedlock with American Gilbert Imlay, and that she had attempted suicide more than once prior to marriage to Godwin. Critics seemed eager to demonstrate that Wollstonecraft's personal circumstances were the obvious consequence of her views. Freedom and equality for women could only (and in Wollstonecraft's case did) lead to ungoverned passion, illicit sex, illegitimate children, and attempted suicide. Wollstonecraft proved that transgressing gender roles was not only unseemly, it was morally dangerous. Letters to the magazines lamented Wollstonecraft's lack of self-control. Many readers found it impossible to separate the woman from her message. Elizabeth Drinker was among those readers who could not divorce Wollstonecraft's personal circumstances from her ideas. Seven years after her initial positive response to *A Vindication of the Rights of Woman*, she changed her mind. When Drinker learned the facts about Wollstonecraft's life, she commented: "To say the truth, I think her a prodigious fine writer— and should be charmed by some of her pieces, if I had never heard her character."[90]

Other criticism of Wollstonecraft arose directly from her attack on the "feminine" attributes of women. Gender lines in the eighteenth century were distinctly drawn between the "masculine" characteristics (rationality, strength, independence), and the "feminine" ones (dependency, weakness, and irrationality). John Adams's description of Wollstonecraft as a "Lady of a masculine masterly understanding," in his copy of her work on the French Revolution, demonstrated the very problem which Wollstonecraft sought to overcome: women's intellectual accomplishments and public activities should not need to be deemed "masculine conduct" in order to be praised. Portraits of Wollstonecraft after 1797 depict her as a masculinized tough, complete with what appears to be a five-o'clock shadow and a rakishly tilted man's top hat.

Like the magazine selections of the time, Wollstonecraft's essay contributed to an ongoing discussion about women at the end of the eighteenth century. The magazines may have helped her achieve a large audience. As Wollstonecraft's proponents had praised her in the early 1790s, critics sang their own tune later in the decade. In Vauxhall Gardens, a public pleasure grounds in Philadelphia, a popular song claimed women had the right to "prattle, with our tongues make a rattle, prattle, rattle prattle rattle husza, husza, for the rights of all Women husza."[91] Accepted or not, Wollstonecraft's ideas reached a broad audience. Men and women knew who she was and what she represented. Her work and her life engendered a backlash, but Wollstonecraft did help promulgate arguments for improving women's social, economic, and political place in the early republic. Knowledge of Wollstonecraft's personal life limited public praise for her ideas by the end of the century, yet privately many continued to agree with her, lamenting not her ideas, but the fact that Wollstonecraft's behavior made it impossible to defend her. As Margaret Murphey Craig explained, "Had she but lived to discover her errors and find the true path of female rectitude her works would have been invaluable and her memory immortal, but her unfortunate deviations make one rather wish to bury all in oblivion." Craig admitted that although Wollstonecraft continued to be "adore[ed] in secret," publicly, she was the subject of "the coarsest jests and most disgusting allusions." Craig sadly acknowledged that "there are no true lovers of virtue who would not

Music and lyrics for "The Rights of Woman" performed at Vauxhall Gardens. This comic song played on the stereotypical attributes of women, including their ability to "prattle" incessantly. *American Ladies Pocketbook for 1802*. Courtesy of the Library Company of Philadelphia.

support her cause if it could be supported, but it is best to let it rest in silence."[92] For all her reasonable proposals and compelling arguments, Wollstonecraft was ridiculed and dismissed because she violated the norms for feminine behavior. Most women, at least outwardly, accepted the contradictions between rhetoric and reality. They were content to "rest in silence" on many of the issues raised in the 1780s and 1790s.

Pundits such as the Rev. Samuel Miller expressed relief that "Wollstonecraftism" was over and that women recognized they were not suited, despite Priscilla Mason's rallying cry, for "The Academic

Chair, the Senate, the Bench of Justice [or] the train of War." Nevertheless, Miller reminded his readers that motherhood made women the most powerful "citizens" of the nation.[93] Miller was right about the diminishing admiration of, and references to, Mary Wollstonecraft. But he mistook the symptom for the cause. The innovations begun in the post-Revolutionary era fostered a generation of young women with the intellectual tools to make good choices about husbands, to develop their talents in order to achieve the "independence" Judith Sargent Murray called for, and ultimately, to produce granddaughters who would assert their right to fuller citizenship. By creating a new public forum that addressed the needs, desires, and abilities of women, magazines became a conduit for innovative thinking. This forum not only remained available to women in the following decades but continually widened in scope. The early nineteenth century's explosion of periodicals included a significant number of magazines for women. Though radical ideas such as those expressed by Mason were infrequent, they were not unknown. The number of publications and the opportunities for women as readers and writers guaranteed a place for the expression of a wide range of sentiments. The *Philadelphia Repository and Weekly Register*, for example, regularly included contributions from students at James Neal's Young Ladies Academy. In November 1800 one young woman penned "Observations on Female Politicians." The following year an "Advocate to the Fair" contributed arguments for "Female Improvement." Another "Friend to the Fair Sex" offered a "Plan for Female Education." In New York, the *Lady's Magazine and Musical Repository* reviewed works of interest to women such as *Condition of Women Under Republican Government*, a book that advocated a larger civic role for women. The magazine also presented a "Plan for the Emancipation of the Fair Sex," in which the writer argued that a necessary step in reestablishing the rights of women was "to petition the legislature to sanction their emancipation by law." The frequent attention to women's roles, even when not forthrightly encouraging radical changes such as those suggested above, often raised questions about marriage, education, and economic independence.[94]

The printed word could have such power in the late eighteenth century because reading was an active exercise, one that engaged individual readers with a text and groups of readers with each other. Marginalia illustrates this phenomenon, as does correspondence such as that between Annis Stockton and her daughter, or Elizabeth Hewson and her brother. Individuals used their reading to promulgate their own thoughts, such as when author Sally Wood praised Judith Sargent Murray's collection of essays, *The Gleaner*, in Wood's novel *Julia*, and when Henry Shelburne praised "Constantia" in *The Oriental Philanthropist*.[95] Readers and writers shared a community of ideas which was sustained by the men and women around the nation who contributed their poems, anecdotes, epigrams, and essays to this burgeoning American medium and who provoked agreement, amusement, irritation or opposition. When Elizabeth Meredith wrote to her son about her acquaintance Charles Wollstonecraft, she described him as the "Brother to the Lady of that name who wrote the rights of Woman." When Elizabeth Hewson rode unaccompanied by a male escort in the local stage, when her friends argued the merits of "female excellence," when Priscilla Mason stood in front of the Board of Trustees of the Young Ladies Academy and called for the admission of women to public offices, women's lives became of public interest. Armed with new ideas, and validated by the magazines' attention to women's concerns, American women began to make their presence known in the streets, the theater, and the salon.

CHAPTER TWO

American Women and the French Revolution

ARMED WITH the sentiments expressed in magazines and other forms of print culture, women were prepared to assume an expanded role in public events of the early republic. The popular American political culture that developed in response to the French Revolution provided them with ample opportunities to do so. Indeed, as early as 1789, as Americans were inundated with information, entertainments, and refugees from the conflicts in Europe and the West Indies, the French Revolution became a defining event in American political culture as well as a catalyst for the expansion of women's public roles. American women used public celebrations of the French cause as an avenue to the political sphere, adopting new clothing and forms of address and engaging in a wider array of public activities. By the end of the 1790s, deteriorating relations with France provoked American military preparations that included public ceremonies at which women in the capital presented militia banners and participated in protests against the French. In this deeply contested public political sphere, dominated first by the Democratic Republicans and then by the Federalists, partisanship encouraged women to assert their allegiances and expand their participation in public political culture.

Americans rejoiced as word reached the United States in 1789 that the French had risen in revolt to secure a republican government. The fall of the Bastille and the creation of the National Assembly filled them with satisfaction that yet another country had taken up "the flame of liberty, kindled at the taper of the American Revolution."[1] The United States became alive with activities related to the French Revolution, and the publication of Thomas Paine's *Rights of Man* in 1791 fueled the fervor. Some observers believed that men and women had "put away their wits and gone mad with republicanism. Their dress, their speech, their daily conduct were all regulated on strict Republican principles."[2]

As early as 1791, July Fourth celebrations frequently included toasts and tributes to the French.[3] That same year in Philadelphia, President Washington left the capital to attend a July Fourth dinner in Lancaster, Pennsylvania, where glasses were raised to the "King and National Assembly," and wishes were expressed that "the oppressed of all nations [might] find an asylum in America."[4] While perceived Jacobin excesses, American foreign policy problems, and the commercial upheavals attendant on political disharmony precipitated a sharp change in public opinion about the Revolution in the latter 1790s, Americans' initial response was strongly supportive. And the more information Americans received from overseas, the more they celebrated the French cause.

Philadelphia's women learned of Revolutionary events in a variety of ways. Newspapers reported on events abroad. Refugees told their anguished tales of hardship and horror. Mariners and ship captains brought firsthand reports into the city's coffeehouses and taverns. Indeed, information about the Revolution was so abundant that Philadelphian Mary Meredith complained to her brother in France that she had precious little domestic news to give him. "Our city affords none but french news and that you I suppose hear enough of."[5] Those men engaged in commerce with Britain and France were especially knowledgeable about current events, particularly the dangers of capture on the Atlantic, while the coffeehouses that catered to these merchants regularly supplied Philadelphians with as many foreign and domestic publications as they desired.[6]

Even without personal connections to France or access to the foreign press, women in the capital city had daily encounters with the myriad refugees from France and the French Caribbean who made Philadelphia their temporary home during the Revolution. As

Philadelphia women went about their daily business, they would have passed refugees on the street and walked by boardinghouses and private homes where French men and women resided. Poor's Young Ladies Academy of Philadelphia was located at 9 Cherry Street, half a block off North Third Street. Many of Poor's one hundred and fifty girls would have known about John Vallee's "French" boardinghouse half a block away, on the corner of Cherry and Fourth Streets. Across the street from the Academy lived "two French Blacks," as they were listed in Hogan's city directory. And one block north, on Race between Third and Fourth Streets, John Anthony and John Baptist Massieua ran a French bathing house.

Elizabeth and Henry Drinker's substantial house on Front Street between Arch and Race Streets, in the Mulberry ward, was two doors down from Gabriel Buche, a French merchant. John Boulanger's French boardinghouse was a half block around the corner on Race Street between Front and Second Streets. The Drinkers' house backed onto another French boardinghouse on Second Street, from where the Drinkers, if not always in visual contact with their neighbors, heard singing and music emanating from the house nightly.[7]

For a number of reasons, Philadelphia attracted large numbers of refugees from the revolution in the French Caribbean. The French minister (first Ternant, followed by Genêt, Adet, and Fauchet) resided there, and provided an obvious source of aid for political exiles as well as the principal point of contact with the French government. Furthermore, as the first French refugees arrived in the city, their presence attracted other refugees who were assured of finding a francophone environment of mutual support. By the late 1790s there were as many as five thousand French people living and working in the capital.[8] As the Comte de Moré noted, "les refugées français marquants que Philadelphie renfermait, comme l'arche de Noé."[9] In other words, the city was a Noah's Ark for émigrés: a refuge for a variety of French and Caribbean aristocrats, commoners, servants, and slaves.

Many visitors and residents commented on the physical presence of the French in Philadelphia. Second Street was known for its concentration of immigrants. As one eyewitness recalled, the city seemed full of the French, "of all shades from the colonies, and those from Old

France." To some (echoing Moré's comment), it appeared that Philadelphia was "one great hotel, or place of shelter for strangers hastily collected together from a raging tempest."[10] While they clustered principally in the Mulberry ward (which went east-west from Front to Sixth Streets, and north-south from Vine to Arch), enough French were scattered throughout the area to suggest that Philadelphians encountered them in all parts of the city.[11]

In addition to conversation with refugees, Philadelphia women received direct information on the Revolution from the personal observation of correspondents living in France. Even prior to the momentous events of 1789, American eyewitnesses reported their surveillance of the French political scene. Thomas Jefferson, in France until 1789, was alarmed by the political activities of French women. In a letter to Philadelphian Anne Willing Bingham, he compared the "Amazona" French women to the American "Angels," who were wise enough to know that politics was beyond their designated sphere.[12] Elizabeth Meredith's son, who resided in France from 1793 to 1799, was a careful (if biased) observer of the Revolution, providing his mother with details of events, as well as his own political analysis. Marianne Williams, who had lived in France for a period of her life, received extensive correspondence from her sisters Bethia Alexander and Isabelle Alexander Hankey. The two sent Williams their eyewitness accounts of the French National Assembly and Jacobin clubs. Bethia Alexander told Williams, "you must know that I sometimes assist at their meetings, in a little private corner destined for the ladies."[13] Alexander and Hankey also gave their sister an emotional account of the capture of the French king and queen as they attempted to flee the country in 1793. When the royal couple were apprehended in Varennes by a local grocer, the Queen, according to Alexander, "threw herself on her knees, wept, wrung her hands, begged his pity for her, for her children—great offers were made—but all could not be, the inflexible grocer stood firm."[14] Here was compelling information for Williams to share with her Philadelphia social circle: the powerless were becoming political actors.

Much of the information published was conveyed by ships that sailed from Liverpool and other British ports, and therefore carried much of the news of France as it was filtered through the British press. Hence many of the reports were negative in tone, particularly after Britain and France went to war in 1792. Nevertheless, the Democratic Republican papers, such as Philip Freneau's *National Gazette* and Benjamin Franklin Bache's *Aurora* in Philadelphia, carried more sympathetic news items and commentaries.[15] Freneau, for example, published the text of the Declaration of the Rights of Man and Citizen, a translation of the Marseillaise, and the entire constitution of the Republic of France, each on the front page of his paper.[16] All the American papers reported the battles fought on the Continent, infor-

Club Patriotique des Femmes. This sketch depicts a meeting similar to the one Isabelle Hankey described to her Philadelphia relations in 1793. Musée Carnavalet (Photo: Art Resource).

mation about various generals, the debates in the Legislative Assembly, and notices of trials and executions.

Besides contact with French refugees and correspondence with eyewitnesses, Philadelphia women drew on the wide array of newspapers available in the city. In addition, several short-lived French language newspapers came and went between 1784 and 1798, including *L'Étoile Américaine*. While these papers provided important news to French refugees in the capital, they were also a valuable resource for those Philadelphians with limited knowledge of the French language. For example, *L'Étoile Américaine*, which printed news side by side in English and French, was begun because "the French Revolution is at present a subject which engrosses nearly the whole public attention in all parts of the globe."[17] Yet while some American women read these French papers, most relied on the local city papers for news about the Revolution.[18]

French women of all classes were heavily involved in the Revolution—as participants in protests, marches, riots, committees and organizations, and even on the battlefield. But while reports on the activities of French women appeared in American papers frequently, they rarely made the front page. Nor did such notices appear in every issue. This inconsistent coverage of women was as much a reflection of the lack of exposure they received in the European press as it was of American editors' lack of interest in female activities. Most space in the French papers was devoted to details of the proceedings in the National Assembly, a political arena where female emancipation and other rights were rarely discussed. The places where women's issues were debated, such as the Cercle Social, whose members included the women's rights activists Marquis de Condorcet and Etta Palm d'Aelders, were rarely mentioned.[19] Nevertheless, as Isabelle Hankey's letters attest, news reports coupled with the private correspondence that reached the United States gave American women an opportunity to learn of these revolutionary women's activities.[20]

American papers mentioned a variety of events in which French girls and women were prominent. The arrest and trial of Charlotte Corday, assassin of the Jacobin Robespierre's revolutionary compatriot Jean-Paul Marat, reached American readers, as did a description of the funeral procession for him through the streets of Paris on July 18, 1793. His body was borne aloft, uncovered, so the wounds were clearly visible to the crowd. Four women carried the bathtub in which he had been killed. An "Amazon," according to the report, held aloft Marat's shirt, "stained with blood," at the top of a pike.[21]

Another report described the arrest of female "counterrevolutionaries" led by Madame La Combe, charged with rallying male citizens who had been routed by gunfire August 10, 1792, and participating in street fighting. These Jacobin women also had formed their own political club, the Citoyennes Républicaines Révolutionnaires, and called for changes the political opposition, the Girondists, did not want.[22] The revolutionary government thus criticized the actions of these women for their political views, for refusing to abide by "the sacred principles of the constitution," rather than for overstepping the boundaries of women's accepted roles. Here, then, gender took a backseat to partisanship. Although French revolutionaries had ambivalent feelings about women's place in the polity, until the Jacobin government eliminated women's right of association in October 1793, on the grounds that they were inciting counterrevolutionary activity, such collective political organization was a model of women's new relationship to the state under a republican government, a model American women might consider. Indeed, as they read such reports, American women had a clear example of female political activism and of women's place in the political sphere.[23]

French women's political demonstrations were not just admired by American women, they were sometimes emulated. In the summer of 1792, for example, Pauline Léon and a delegation of women presented the French Legislative Assembly with three hundred signatures in petition of women's right to bear arms. As Léon argued, "We are *citoyennes* and we cannot be indifferent to the fate of the fatherland." Although the assembly tabled any discussion of the petition, tacit assent to women's desire to defend their nation allowed them to carry arms in the Paris processions a few months later.[24] These events inspired a similar martial spirit among a group of Philadelphia women. In the summer of 1798, at the height of a feared invasion of American shores, the *Philadelphia Gazette* reported that a group of women had formed a martial "Corps-de-Reserve" in the city. They proposed to "hold themselves in readiness to issue forth against the enemies of [their] beloved country."[25] While there were several accounts of individual American women contributing to the military success of the American forces during the struggle against Great Britain, nowhere did they instigate the collective action supposedly contemplated by these American women.[26]

By the mid-1790s, the Jacobins had shut down women's political clubs and reversed or ignored earlier initiatives which extended some political rights to women, and Americans began to see the darker side of revolution. Indeed, when the political wind changed, a woman's revolutionary politics could suddenly seem counterrevolutionary, and the guillotine disregarded sex as well as rank. Two prominent women, Madame Roland and Olympe de Gouges, paid the price for their principles. Roland, the wife of the minister of the interior, was guillotined for her role in her husband's political affairs as well as for her own writings.[27] News that she was brought before the Revolutionary Tribunal and her subsequent execution were announced in the American papers, which also reported what the British papers had to say about these actions. Their comment on Roland's death was that she "died like the heroine who had participated in her husband's counsels, and advised his measures."[28] In truth, Roland used her husband's position to achieve her own political ends. She not only wrote most of his speeches and correspondence, but was often consulted instead of her husband.[29] Actress and playwright Olympe de Gouges was also executed, notwithstanding her plea of pregnancy.[30] De Gouges had been condemned to death for her political writings, notably her call for women's rights to liberty, property, and the vote in *The Declaration of the Rights of Women* (1791).[31]

Charlotte Corday, killer of the Jacobin leader Marat, was perhaps the most prominent counterrevolutionary of whom American women had knowledge. Freneau's Democratic Republican *National Gazette* gave a detailed account of Marat's assassination and Corday's trial.[32] Corday was portrayed as a woman who took drastic action out of a sense of patriotism. She denied the influence or assistance of anyone; no man was the guiding hand behind her actions. What some Americans remembered about her, however, was her political heroism, not her counterrevolutionary treason. Fourteen years later, American playwright Sarah Podgson's *Female Enthusiast* was performed in Charleston, South Carolina. The drama portrayed Corday as an intelligent woman who acted "in the cause of virtue" to save her nation from corruption.[33]

Prominent individuals such as Roland and Corday were not the only female political activists whose executions were announced in the Philadelphia papers. *L'Étoile Américaine* noted numerous executions of "women of diverse classes," estimating that the lives of between two hundred and three hundred people every week ended at the guillotine. Marie Magdaleine Coutelet, a worker in hemp manufacturing, was one such unfortunate, executed for "hawking about some writings tending to the establishment of royalty."[34] The message was clear: French women of political convictions, regardless of class, risked the same fate as their male counterparts. As factionalism rose to fever pitch and as the revolutionary government contended with enemies at home and abroad, no political transgression was too small to be ignored by the tribunals.

No other execution of a French woman captured more attention in the United States than that of Queen Marie Antoinette. Many American papers reprinted British versions of the trial, the execution, and even letters to the editor, leaving little space for pro-Revolutionary celebration of the downfall of the monarchy.[35] Moreover, as Federalists gained a stronger voice in public opinion, more and more reprints from the British press made their way into the American newspapers. In the capital, the pro-French press, led by Benjamin Franklin Bache's *Aurora* and Philip Freneau's *National Gazette*, was increasingly challenged by John Fenno's *Gazette of the United States* and later William Cobbett's *Porcupine's Gazette*. They presented the queen as an "unhappy victim of democratic fury" who met her end with "natural dignity" and viewed her "murder" as an "instance of unrelenting cruelty, of systematic injustice, and diabolical atrocity."[36]

It was Marie Antoinette the "unfortunate and unprotected woman," rather than Marie Antoinette the queen, who was victimized by these "unmanly indignities."[37] Unlike the king, she was accused not only of political crimes—conspiracy against the nation—but of gross sexual misconduct as well. The most extreme of the allegations, all of which were detailed in American newspapers, was that she had sexual relations with her own son.[38] Whatever the results of these manipulations at the trial in France, Philadelphia women, propelled by their reading of the British version of events, felt disgust for her accusers and sympathy for the woman. The *Gazette of the United States* printed an elegy, "Moral reflections of the death of Maria Antonietta," written by "Philenia."[39]

News of her trial outraged American women, while the strongest reactions came from those who had always had the least amount of sympathy with the Revolution. Abigail Adams remarked that the revolutionaries, "not content with loading her with ignominy, whilst living, blacken her memory by ascribing to her the vilest crimes."[40] Quaker Mary Parker Norris was so affected by the news that she "could not get to Sleep the night I saw it in the papers." As to the charges leveled against the queen, Norris remarked that, "Wisdom has took its flight from France, or they would never have thought of exhibiting such a Charge against her, which nobody in their Senses can believe, but posterity will judge."[41] Elizabeth Drinker had much the same comment to make. Like Norris, she judged the trial and the sentence "beyond description cruel."[42] With such a conjunction of misogyny and revolution, it is not surprising that all three of these women became staunch Federalists. As the Democratic Republicans continued to support the French cause, and as Federalists increasingly linked their political opponents with the excesses of the French Jacobins, many women such as Norris and Drinker had one more reason to align themselves with a party that privileged order over liberty.

Others, however, were not so sensitive to the political abuse of a woman whom they believed to be guilty of crimes against the French nation. According to a story passed along by Philadelphia Federalists, one of the "democratic" taverns renamed itself the "guillotined Queen of France." Its signboard displayed "a decapitated female, the head lying by the side of the bleeding trunk."[43] Another report claimed to have heard "more than one young woman, under the age of twenty, declare that they would willingly have dipped their hands in the blood of the Queen of France."⁴⁴ Much of this rumor and hearsay was anti-French propaganda, designed to sever the ties of fraternity between the French and their American supporters. No small part of it may also have been misogynistic, as much about the inappropriateness of female political figures as of the institution of monarchy.

When women wanted more detailed information about events in France, they supplemented their knowledge gleaned from the newspapers and correspondence with books and other printed material. In addition to Edmund Burke's *Reflections on the French Revolution* and Wollstonecraft's *Vindication of the Rights of Man*, curious Philadelphians also purchased maps "of the present seat of war in France" and French calendars that explained how to decipher the new Republican calendar that was adopted in 1793.⁴⁵

Philadelphia's newspapers advertised this material and sold them at their offices. The *Aurora* sold what it termed "Political Novelties," which meant books and pamphlets with political content, including Rabaut's *History of the French Revolution*, Paine's *Age of Reason*, Priestley's *Letters on Religion*, Barlow's *Advice to Privileged Orders, Part III*, and Robespierre's *Report on Political Morality*. Most of the newspaper offices, regardless of their political leanings, sold copies of the French constitution in English. Benjamin Franklin Bache's *Aurora* office also offered it in French for immigrant customers.⁴⁶ And those Philadelphia women who kept a pocket diary could have a daily reminder of a Franco-American hero: William Birch advertised *The American Ladies Pocket Book for 1798*, which contained "an elegant frontispiece of the Marquis de la Fayette and his family in the castle of Olmutz, with an illustration, being an account of the principal events in the public life of the marquis, with a sketch of the sufferings of himself and his unfortunate family."⁴⁷

Another source of information on the Revolution was the many personal and public histories published (or republished) in the United States. Martha Washington was an avid reader of works about the French Revolution. She and the president received all the newspapers available in the capital. In addition to reports on events in France in the "foreign news" column of these papers, she purchased a six-volume history of the French Revolution in April 1793.⁴⁸ The following year she purchased another history of the Revolution, as well as English-woman Helen Maria William's pro-Revolutionary "Letters," written during a stay in France.[49] Elizabeth Drinker was particularly fond of reading about the victims of the French Revolution. After finishing the three octavo volumes of the *Private Memoirs Relative to the Last Year of the Reign of Lewis the Sixteenth, late King of France,* by A. F. R. Bertrand de Moleville, she remarked that it was "a very interesting and affecting account." Americans of anti-Gallic sentiments had plenty of fodder for their animosity in John Robison's *Proofs of a Conspiracy against all the Religions and Governments of Europe, carried in the Secret meetings of Free Masons, Illuminati, and Reading Societies* (London, 1798), in which the author recounted tales of sansculotte women who bit off the limbs of their victims. Drinker, decidedly anti-French, but perhaps not totally gullible, deemed this "a curious work."[50]

Reading these accounts allowed American women to compare the French Revolution with their own. Instances of female heroism or assertiveness vied for space with examples of extreme cruelty. Indeed, there was enough variety among the accounts for Americans to take away contradictory messages. After reading Madame Roland's memoirs, for example, Quaker Susanna Emlen remarked, "I have compared with wonder and I hope some little gratitude the security and peace that *we* personally enjoy with the terrible anarchy and confusion which then prevailed in her unhappy country."[51] Though French women were portrayed in the American press as heroines, patriots, and defenders of their nation, American women were just as divided over the revolution as men were. Religion and political sentiments often affected how women responded. For Quakers such as Drinker, Norris, and Emlen, all of whom had lived through their own nation's Revolution, perhaps no amount of female heroism could make up for the "terrible anarchy" brought on by political upheaval. For women such as Martha Washington or Abigail Adams, on the other hand, whose Anglican and Puritan creeds were not compromised by their staunch support of the War for Independence, they may have found affirmation of their belief that the French were sliding into dangerously "democratic" ways quite different from the tenor of the American experience. Clearly, as these women's opinions attest, there was not one, but many interpretations of the Revolution.

Women in Philadelphia did not have to rely on what they read in order to experience the French Revolution. The capital city held enough entertainments and diversions to satisfy the curiosity of those eager for news of anything connected with events in France. Moreau de St. Méry, an exile from Saint Domingue, displayed a stone from the Bastille at his bookstore on Front Street, a great curiosity that many passersby stopped to see.[52] Along with symbols of liberation there were also reminders of death. Having read of the scores of French men and women whose lives ended at the guillotine, spectators had the opportunity to watch one in action. In 1794 the *Aurora* advertised that Philadelphians could pay to see the demonstration of a operational guillotine including a victim, whose head, as the advertisement described, was severed from its body, and then dropped into a waiting basket.[53] The performance, as William Cobbett said, occurred "twenty or thirty times every day, during one whole winter, and part of the summer," for the diversion of citizens in the capital city.[54] For those too squeamish to view this reenactment, there was a detailed description of the device—how it worked and what it looked like—printed in the *National Gazette*. Not everyone found such entertainment diverting. Elizabeth Graeme Ferguson's satirical poem, "God Save the Guillotine," was meant to remind her readers that it was a machine of death as well as an agent of political change.[55]

A decidedly less sanguine entertainment was the exhibit of automatons, "Citizen Sans Culotte and Mr. L'Aristocrate." Advertised in the newspapers, this pair of life-size wind up mechanisms performed to such acclaim that their stay in the capital was extended. Martha Washington and her granddaughter went to see the show and later returned, bringing the president along with them.[56] For the delight of the audience these two opposing political figures "salute the company and seem to rival each other to please the spectators with their agility." They could even dance, although Mr. L'Aristocrate, it was noted, could not "be prevailed upon to dance to the Carmagnrol or Ça-ira."[57]

In addition to such popular spectacles, the songs of the Revolution often greeted the ears of Philadelphia's pedestrians. John Fanning Watson reported that "the Marseilles Hymn was learned and sung by the citizens everywhere, to which they added the American song of 'Hail Liberty Supreme Delight.'" Philadelphia's Democratic Republican newspapers, including the *Aurora* and the *National Gazette*, print-ed the lyrics to many of the French patriotic songs (with translations), including "Ça Ira." They also printed American pro-French songs "God Save the Rights of Man" and "Patriotic Stanzas on the Anniver-sary of the Storming of the Bastille."[58] American women did not have to rely on reports of the Revolution abroad to learn about its princi-ples, its supporters, or its foes. The Revolution was as close at hand as the music stand in their parlors.

Fireworks, parades, feasts, and festivals (much like those being per-formed in Paris) greeted the eyes and ears of American women from Boston to Charleston. These various entertainments, festivals, and celebrations offered women the opportunity both to observe and to participate in popular demonstrations of political culture, if they chose. In the 1780s, women celebrated the Constitution by adorning themselves with red, white, and blue sashes at balls and suppers. They could even wear a "Federal hat" complete with thirteen rings and a replica of the "federal ediface." In the 1790s, dress again became one way that women demonstrated their political support, this time for the French Revolution.[59] In France, dress and political affiliation were closely linked. The color of a hat cockade, even its fabric (silk smacked of aristocracy, wool was solidly republican) signaled to observers the wearer's political sentiments. The French government even enter-tained the idea of a national uniform, calling on artist Jacques-Louis David for a design.[60]

Wealthy, fashion-conscious Americans adopted the new French style of dress.[61] The newspaper advertisements, especially in the cap-ital city, for shopkeepers selling the latest French fabrics, accessories, gloves, fans, laces, and shoes, and French men and women offering their services as seamstresses and tailors, confirm that some Ameri-cans began to prefer French dress over British when it came to imported fashions.

After her return from Europe, Philadelphian Anne Bingham had Thomas Jefferson send her the latest "Modes de Paris"—the fashion journals. She informed Jefferson that the journals "have furnished our ladies with many hints, for the decoration of their persons." Jefferson, in turn, offered to send Bingham any items she requested, but she responded that "at present I am well stocked, having lately received a variety of articles from Paris." Bingham was also well stocked in French face cream, which she ordered in quantities of twenty-four at a time.[62]

Dresses such as those worn by Bingham were in the neoclassical style. Aided in part by Jacques-Louis David's elaborately planned civic rituals and costume designs, which deliberately evoked the Greek polis, Joséphine de Beauharnais (soon to be Madame Bonaparte) and other elite women helped popularize the free-flowing, less constricting dresses that exposed more of the breasts and outlined the figure.[63]

Head coverings also reflected French style. William Cobbett noticed many "bold, daredevil, turban-headed females" on the streets of the capital. These women emulated the headdress of middle-class female revolutionaries.[64] Another popular piece of headgear displayed by American women was the Phrygian cap. In 1793, the Républicaines Révolutionnaires adopted this ancient symbol of liberty.[65] American women had seen this cap as well as the republican style of dress in the circulated portraits of Madame Roland, whom they knew from the newspapers and Roland's published memoirs. The turban, much disliked by Cobbett, did not become fashionable until after Napoleon's Egyptian campaign in 1798. Also popular, according to the *Journal des Dames et des Modes*, was a turban-style kerchief, called a "fichu à la Marat" named for the headdress worn by the martyred Jacobin in Jacques-Louis David's painting of Jean-Paul Marat "quand il fut assassiné dans sa baignoire."[66] Ironically, the French concern to politicize their clothing by making it more "à la democrate," at the beginning of the Revolution, was adopted from America: a magazine of haute couture in Paris, the *Journal de la Mode et de Goût*, recommended a bonnet to its readers which it claimed was "à l'américaine."[67] Thus, a two-way transmission of Revolutionary apparel occurred, as the symbolic value of women's fashions was shared across the Atlantic.

These practices did not sit well with all American women, however. Echoing the political attitudes prevalent in the mid-1790s concerning the need for American neutrality, Miss Priscilla Mason of Philadelphia warned that women should not be "slaves" to foreign

Fashion plate from the *Journal des Dames et des Modes* (1798).
Turbans such as the one shown here were adopted by Philadelphians as well as Parisians, much to the dismay of William Cobbett. British Museum; photo: Courtauld Institute of Art, London.

fashion. Rather, she believed they should be encouraged to develop a truly American style of dress. This suggestion for a political boycott echoed women's consumption boycotts of the American Revolution.[68] Philadelphia's popular magazine the *American Museum* also weighed in with its suggestion that a "Convention Hat, a Federal Bonnet, or a Congress Cap" would be more fitting for American women than any foreign designs.[69] President Washington expressed a similar desire. In a letter to Annis Boudinot Stockton he wrote, "And now that I am speaking of your Sex, I will ask whether they are not capable of doing something towards introducing federal fashions and national manners?" Washington deplored the fact that Americans purchased "foreign superfluities" and adopted "fantastic fashions." Clearly, for the nation's leader, women's fashions carried political implications.[70]

Some Philadelphia women chose to dress themselves in this stylized form of political attire, with caps that reflected Revolutionary origins, and garments that echoed the ideology of Napoleon's regime. Others chose a more overt sartorial demonstration of their political principles when they adorned their clothing with ribbons and cockades for ceremonies and celebrations. The arrival of the French minister Edmund Genêt in May 1793 evoked extensive celebration and display. Upon news of the minister's imminent appearance, women were encouraged to "decorate their elegant persons and adorn their hair with patriotic ribbands on the occasion." When Genêt landed in the capital on May 16 Philadelphia women turned out decorated in revolutionary red, white, and blue to honor him.[71] When the next French minister, Adet, issued the "Cockade Proclamation," calling on all Frenchmen in the United States to wear the tricolor, Americans again responded.[72] One British visitor to the capital in the summer of 1794 remarked on the number of men and women he encountered wearing the Revolutionary cockades: "the men with it in their hats, the women on their breasts."[73]

American women did not simply follow the lead of men in their sartorial political expression. In wearing their political allegiances on their sleeves, in the most literal sense, they pointed the way for American men to demonstrate their allegiances too. One "Fair Correspondent" to the *Albany Register* wished that she and others of her sex might be able to distinguish between the "Friends and Enemies of the RIGHTS OF MAN," and she urged republican bachelors to wear French and American cockades.[74] Thus, this thinly veiled threat to withhold approval, friendship, or even sexual favors could be used as a tool by politically minded women. As Lynn Hunt has observed of the clothing, colors, and adornments of the French Revolution, these seemingly mundane elements "constituted a field of political struggle." As political symbols, personal attire and adornments such as cockades, ribbons, and sashes endowed women with a political identity. This was as true for American women who expressed their political ideas about the French Revolution as it was for French women across the Atlantic.[75]

Such cultural politics on the part of women brought strong comment from those for whom all celebration of the French Revolution was anathema. Philadelphia editor William Cobbett, staunchly anti-French, saved his most venomous comments for women. Public display of French sentiments by "those bold, daredevil, turban-headed females" that he witnessed in the city was "a disgusting rencontre. For my part, I would almost as soon have a host of infernals in my house, as a knot of these fiery frenchified dames.—Of all the monsters in human shape, a *bully in petticoats* is the most completely odious and detestable."[76]

For Cobbett, political action, however informal, on the part of women was an unnatural act. He complained that women "began to talk about liberty and equality in a good masculine style," a blurring of roles that francophiles chose to ignore.[77]

It was not enough for some American women to merely clothe themselves in symbolic revolutionary garb. The proliferation of printed information about the French Revolution available to Americans enabled women to employ another symbol of support for the democratic principles espoused in France: the adoption of an egalitarian form of address. For men, "Mister" was abandoned in favor of "Citizen." Such a change begged the question of what to call women who felt similarly inclined. "Citizeness" was commonly used, though some favored the term "*citess*." Bostonians took to this new appellation with great enthusiasm.[78] In Virginia, sisters Judith and Nancy Randolph

[I think this is a pretty broad hint to thofe *Infidel Bucks,* of which we fee fuch num-bers.—How much more amiable do thefe young ladies appear, than thofe bold, dare-devil, turban-headed females, whom we fome-times meet with in this city; and in fami-lies too, where we ought leaft to expect fuch a difgufting rencontre.—For my part, I would almoft as foon have a hoft of infernals in my houfe, as a knot of thefe fiery frenchi-fied dames.—Of all the monfters in human fhape, a *bully in petticoats* is the moft com-pletely odious and deteftable.]

Porcupine's Gazette, July 27, 1798. Cobbett frequently ranted against all things French, but he took special exception to the way Phila- phia's women adopted not only the style, but also the politi-cal behavior, of French women. Courtesy of the Library Company of Philadelphia.

signed themselves "citizen" in their correspondence in the early 1790s.[79]

In the capital, the Democratic Republican newspapers announced marriages in this egalitarian fashion. Philadelphia women followed the lead of the many French female refugees living in the city, many of whom announced their marriages by identifying themselves as citizens in this revolutionary manner, even on sacramental documents at the city's Catholic churches. The *Aurora* reported the nuptials of "Citizen John Baptist Lemain and Citess Ann Lerre" in August 1794.[80] It also announced the marriage of "Citizen Jonathan Wild to Citess Mary Ridgeway, daughter of Citizen Samuel Ridgeway," and "Frederick W. Geyer, Jr., to Citess Rebecca Frazer, daughter of Citizen Nathan Frazer."[81]

The use of such titles for women drew criticism from many quarters. Vice President Adams lamented that "*Cit* and *Citess* is to come instead of Goffer and Gammer, Gooder and Gooden, Mr. and Mrs., I suppose."[82] But not all women wished to be identified as Cobbett's "fiery frenchified dames." One Bostonian submitted a poem to the *Columbian Centinel* rejecting these Revolutionary appellations:

> No citess to my name I'll have, says Kate,
> Tho' Boston lads about it so much prate;
> I've asked its meaning and our Tom, the clown,
> Says, *darn it*, 't means a Woman of the Town.[83]

At a meeting in Philadelphia, reported in the Federalist *Gazette of the United States*, women expressed alarm at this perceived evidence of the leveling principle: "The spirit of freemen is but poorly employed when it directs its researches to such frivolity as the nonsense of instituting terms of address, inconsistent with the *influence* and *power* of women—as *Citess*, for *Miss* or *Madam*, or *good woman*."[84] Women at this "meeting of the Fair ones" interpreted such innovative titles as a devaluation of their protected domestic status, not a vehicle for elevating them to a more egalitarian political plane.

Titles and names became one of the many battlegrounds between opposing political factions in the early republic, and the printed debates surrounding them underscored public concern over the democratizing tendencies that the French Revolution inspired. Pro-French American women intended their use of Revolutionary titles to declare their political sentiments and their participation in popular political culture. This practice, along with the "good masculine style" with which women began to discuss politics, was a result of a new ease many women felt in the political arena. Due to the encouragement they received from like-minded men, as well as from the examples of activist French women (at least prior to 1793), American women in the capital and other areas where a critical mass of support for the Revolution was evident took a further step into the political arena. On the other hand, opponents of the Revolution, specifically, and of women in politics, generally, were able in one stroke to denigrate the political power of these symbolic titles and dismiss the efforts of these women to claim a political identity. Opponents chose to recognize the sexual meaning of the term *femme publique*, a prostitute, and ignore the women's expression of their patriotism and civic identity. The French Revolution provided American women with a language to express their desire for a political identity, and although many were more interested in a nonpartisan rendering of "citess" than in its connection to Revolutionary ideology, the anti-French (and largely Federalist) segment of the public refused to give women the opportunity to be full-fledged, ideologically independent citizens.

Who were these "fiery frenchified dames"? The women who dressed in turbans, sashes, and cockades at balls and ceremonies were clearly part of Philadelphia's wealthy elite and burgeoning middle class. But just as French Revolutionary fashions borrowed from the politics of the street, the capital city's lower sort also wore the symbols of the Revolution: cockades and ribbons could be had from any dry goods shop or milliner. The streets were filled with the songs of the Revolution, sung in part by women unschooled in the French language, yet who understood the sentiments behind the words. Wives and relatives of the hundreds of sailors in the city were the first to adopt the red, white, and blue cockade. And though their support for France may have had as much to do with their dislike of American mercantile policies as with their promotion of democratic revolution, these women became political actors in the process.[85] Indeed, perhaps the women who lived along Front Street, shopped in the High Street market, and regularly negotiated the smells and tides of Dock Creek were better situated than their wealthy sisters uptown to hear the latest accounts from France.

Women's claim to a share in political culture went beyond the symbolic value of names and dress. They also took to the streets to participate in political rituals both for and against the French Revolution. But long before the French Revolution sparked ceremonies and celebrations in the capital and elsewhere, women were visible in the political culture of the fledgling nation. In 1783, for example, a torchlight procession through the streets of Philadelphia celebrating the peace included thirteen girls (one for each state) dressed in white.[86] Six years later another group of women and girls took part in the festivities surrounding President Washington's inauguration. In April 1789, Washington traveled from his home at Mount Vernon to the temporary capital in New York City to begin his presidency. Along the way, men and women prepared elaborate ceremonies to welcome Washington as he passed through their towns and cities. In Philadelphia, Washington was greeted at the western outskirts of the city at Gray's Ferry along the Schuylkill River. Artist Charles Willson Peale helped decorate the floating bridge crossing the river (a bridge built by the British during their occupation in 1777). Arches of laurel decorated each end of the bridge. Flags flew along the sides, one for each of the states. As Washington reached the western end of the bridge, a young girl, possibly Peale's daughter Angelica, lowered a laurel wreath onto the president's head. Philadelphia's citizens lined the shores, watching this ceremonial entry of the nation's first president into their city.[87] One observer, Mary Hewson, described for her sister in England Washington's demeanor: "He paid every polite attention with as much apparent ease as if he had been taking a common ride, yet sure no heart had ever cause for greater exultation. To be placed at the head of a free people is cause for triumph."[88]

By the 1790s, female political demonstrations began to reflect the partisanship of the times. In December 1792, two months before France declared war on England, Holland, and Spain, Democratic Republican Blair McClenahan led what was described as a procession of "citizens" and a number of girls, dressed in white with tricolor ribbons, to the British minister's residence in the capital. There "several signs of disrespect were manifested to his house."[89] It was a chilly December day on which George Hammond, His Majesty's minister plenipotentiary, received this unauthorized visit from Philadelphia's young women. They marched down Second Street, past the houses of working men and women, and close to many of the French refugees' lodgings.[90]

An east view of Gray's Ferry, near Philadelphia. Those Philadelphians unable to attend President Washington's entry into the city in April 1789 were able to view this sketch of the triumphal arch in the *Columbian Magazine* the following month. The sketch does not include the throngs of men and women who lined the bridge cheering for the nation's first president. Courtesy of the Library Company of Philadelphia.

Located in a heavily populated part of town, the protest at the minister's house was witnessed by many residents, some supportive, some indifferent, others angered by the political opinions displayed. This occasion was reminiscent of public punishments during the American Revolution, where women did their share of pelting or jeering at the target of their anger.[91] In the 1780s women and girls gathered to celebrate Washington as the defender of American womanhood. In the 1790s, it was partisanship that led young women to the streets. This rising generation of female political activists demonstrated that women claimed a central place in the political culture of the nation.

Accustomed to public political rituals, Philadelphia women participated in pro-French ceremonies closely modeled on those in France. In November 1793 a report direct from Paris described for readers a "Grand Festival dedicated to Reason and Truth" held at Notre Dame in Paris, that included girls dressed in white, surrounding an Altar of Reason, with "Liberty, coming out of the Temple of Philosophy, towards a throne made of grass, to receive the homage of the Republicans of both sexes, who sung an hymn in her praise."[92] The following August, Philadelphians echoed their French peers by celebrating in a similar manner. At ten o'clock in the morning, August 11, participants assembled at Center Square (the intersection of Market and Broad Streets). From there they paraded, accompanied by music, to Minister Fauchet's residence two blocks away on the corner of Twelfth and Market Streets. At Fauchet's, "Maidens dressed in white and tricolor costumes," surrounded an altar of liberty reminiscent of those constructed by Jacques-Louis David in Paris.[93] In Philadelphia, the symbolism of French street theater assumed an American form in which young women were performers who expressed their political opinions and asserted their rights as participants in the civic arena.[94]

Similar, though less staged, celebrations took place in other cities. Not long after the great civic feast held in Boston in January 1793 to celebrate the French victory at Valmy, women in Menotomy, Massachusetts, held their own demonstration of support for the Revolution. Fifty women gathered "to contribute their part in the late frequent celebrations of liberty and equality; and to felicitate their sisters in France upon the happy revolution in their nation." The women put on liberty caps and French cockades. They sang patriotic songs, drank toasts, and then ate "civic cake."[95]

A few months later in Charleston, South Carolina, two widows—one French, the other American—were publicly "married" to one another. According to the *City Gazette*,

> after having repudiated their husbands on account of their ill-treatment, [they] conceived the design of living together in the strictest union and friendship in order to give a pledge of their fidelity, requested that their striped gowns should be pinned together, that their children should be looked upon as one family, while their mothers shewed them an equal affection.

A Mr. Lee officiated, and explained the "reciprocal obligations" of the two women. A militia unit fired its guns to signal the completion of the contract, while the soldiers and spectators shouted "thousands of huzzahs." Each woman had a male representative: the American a Mr. Samuel Prioleau, the French one a Monsieur M. A. B. Mangourit, who urged the spectators to celebrate the *carmagnole* and to sing "Ça Ira."[96]

This highly staged street theater was a dramatization of the symbolic union between two nations, embodied by female representatives. Yet perhaps more was going on than meets the eye. The fact that the paper included the information that these two women "repudiated their husbands on account of their ill-treatment," suggests the line between celebration of the amity of nations and of the solidarity of women was somewhat blurry. France and America might form a more perfect union without Britain. Could women form a more perfect union without men?

One striking aspect of these celebrations is that women were the focus of attention—some ceremonies were explicitly conducted by women, for women, with the express purpose of honoring the *women* of France. These occasions marked the beginnings of a distinctive female political identity, fostered by transatlantic ideas and events. Indeed, by the mid-1790s, some American women, especially those in Philadelphia and other urban areas, were equipped with sufficient information and experience to begin to construct political identities for themselves that drew from America's revolutionary origins as well as those of France. The ideology that fostered this identity was thus republican rather than liberal, and emphasized women's contributions to the civic good, rather than their individual gain. As wives, mothers, sisters, and as public political actors, these women accomplished two things at once: they reinforced traditional roles, but they also fostered active political engagement in the public sphere. Creation of this new identity was aided by the wide dissemination of women's political activities through the nation's press. Descriptions of local and regional events were read hundreds of miles away. Such wide dissemination solidified this female political identity.[97]

Women's support for the French Revolution was by no means universal in the United States. Federalist Annis Boudinot Stockton, for example, circulated a critical poem about French minister Genêt after hearing a rumor that at his residence in Philadelphia he hung a print of the guillotine with President Washington's portrait directly underneath. She viewed Genêt (as many others did by late 1793) as a man "lost to diffidence / To prudence, policy, or Common Sense." If it was necessary to defend her beloved President Washington, Stockton wrote,

> Columbias *daughters* like the greecian dames
> Would grasp the helmet and enroll their name
> To be his guards and form a phalanx bright
> That soon would put your Sans Culottes to flight.[98]

Seventeen ninety-three marked a sea change in American public opinion about the Revolution. As refugees arrived in the capital, people heard about the horrors that followed in the wake of liberation. Moreover, ship seizures by the French as well as the British jeopardized Philadelphia's mercantile economy. By the late 1790s these circumstances, combined with the foreign policy issues entwining the fates of Britain, France, and the United States, provoked a very different public response from that of the early years of the decade. Partisan politics and competing visions of government had always generated competition between Federalists and Democratic Republicans to shape the meaning of political ceremonies and celebrations. By the end of the 1790s, the Federalists were prominently in control of popular political expression.[99]

The treaty between the United States and Great Britain, concluded by John Jay, accelerated a series of conflicts between France and the United States, culminating in April 1798 with the announcement by President Adams of the failure of negotiations with France and the subsequent XYZ Affair, in which three Parisian businessmen suggested to the American minister, Charles Pinckney, that bribery was the only way to ensure an audience with French foreign minister Talleyrand. Meanwhile, the Terror of Jacobin rule, with its wholesale bloodletting, had ended in 1794, but it continued to haunt many Americans. The national reaction to the XYZ Affair and the details of the level of carnage practiced by the Jacobins was fervent patriotism and a backlash against the American supporters of Republican France. Men and women of anti-Gallic opinions, many of them Federalist-minded, claimed the public political stage. The wife of the British ambassador noted the rapidity with which "a whole nation can change its sentiments with its politicks." She marveled at how opinions regarding the European powers had changed so quickly: "the different lights in which the French and English were viewed even when we arrived in America two years ago [in 1796], and that in which they are now respectively held, fills me with astonishment."[100]

From the beginning, many Federalists had not been happy about the French Revolution, with its challenge to constituted authority and privilege. France's struggle for democratic principles and the sovereignty of the people was dear to Democratic Republicans, but Federalists criticized the Revolution's power to undermine order and feared the consequences of such an ideology in the United States. In this climate of anxiety and accusation, Federalist women articulated their condemnation of the French. As one anonymous Philadelphia woman wrote in *Porcupine's Gazette*, France was the "enemy—a nation divested of every principle of morality and virtue."[101] Another Philadelphian, Mary Ridgely, privately expressed her fervent wish to see "every French *Demo*, at the bottom of the Sea or anywhere else in this world."[102] Elizabeth Hewson, expecting her brother to return to the

United States after an extended residence abroad, told him of her hope that "the French party will not be those whom you most associate with. I should be very sorry indeed to have you in the Democratic society."[103] Calling the French revolutionaries "barbarous democratic murderers," the president's granddaughter Eleanor Parke Custis, who lived with the president and his wife in Philadelphia, wrote to her friend Elizabeth Beale Bordley that she would not "trust the life of a *Cat* in the hands of a set of people who hardly know religion, humanity or Justice, even by *name*." Custis assured Bordley that she was ready "to lend a hand to extirpate the Demons if their unparellel'd impudence & thirst of conquest should make them attempt an invasion of our peaceable happy land."[104] Tired of the pro-French fervor and its affect on popular entertainment, Philadelphia poet Elizabeth Graeme Ferguson responded to Joel Barlow's "New Song," which was sung at July Fourth celebrations in 1796, by penning her own tongue-in-cheek revolutionary song (set to the music of "God Save the King")— "God Save the Guillotine."[105]

In the spring of 1798, Federalist crowds of young men roamed the streets of the capital, eager to confront Democratic Republican youth for a brawl.[106] When a group of Federalists marched through the streets to President Adams's house in May, William Cobbett reported in *Porcupine's Gazette* that "every female in the city whose face is worth looking at" (by which he meant every *Federalist* female face) graced the proceedings "with her smiles."[107] As in the Valmy celebration in Boston, some women lent their gaze in an approving fashion to the politics of partisanship.

Federalists were confident that their politics had won the day. Democratic Republican toasts now had to compete with those of the Federalists for space in the newspapers. Federalists, just as Democratic Republicans had done, called upon the "American Fair" to endorse their proceedings.[108] In Philadelphia, the gatherings had a martial spirit. The Second Troop of Cavalry toasted "the American Fair" and hoped that they might "despise the man who refuses to draw his sword in the defense of his country." The Philadelphia Volunteer Greens, dining at Bush Hill, asked that their "Fair Country Women [might] disdain the youth who will refuse to resent his country's wrongs."[109]

Political balls and dinners continued, but in the late 1790s the occasions for celebration were usually Federalist. Washington's birthday had been popular among the Federalists as a time of celebration since the early 1790s. One birthday ball in 1798, it was reported, owed its brilliancy to "the generous and patriotic spirit of our fair countrywomen."[110] Instead of red, white, and blue tricolor ribbons, women wore black silk roses (the color worn by Washington and the Continental army and adopted by the Federalists) to show their politics. At the July Fourth celebration in Princeton, New Jersey, the women all wore this "American cockade." It was Federalist occasions such as these, rather than pro-French festivities, that received attention in the newspapers at the end of the decade.[111]

Beginning in the summer of 1798, and continuing throughout the autumn of that year, women in Philadelphia and throughout the nation engaged in a new type of political behavior as they participated in the intensifying partisanship that characterized the political landscape in the closing years of the century. As the Federalists gained ascendency in the public political arena, they marshaled public opinion against France by stirring citizens to patriotic defense of the nation. Federalists took advantage of women's disgust and outrage at the excesses of the French by encouraging their organized participation in public activities designed to further a partisan agenda. When Federalist propagandists insisted that a French invasion was imminent, men and women gathered to support the militia groups formed to defend American shores. Throughout much of the nation, from the Ohio country into Virginia, women paid tribute to the militia units formed to protect the nation by presenting local militia troops with emblematic flags (sometimes done in needlework by the female presenters).[112]

There was a consistent format to these ceremonies: a militia company chose a particular woman (often the wife of the militia captain or another prominent, and politically supportive, female) to present the company standard. In 1797 the First Troop of Philadelphia City Cavalry, under Captain Dunlap's command, submitted a written request to Elizabeth Willing Powel, widow of the former mayor. She declined to actually present Captain Dunlap and the First City Troop of Cavalry with new colors, citing her age and infirmity, but she did send them a standard which she begged they would accept "as Evidence of her confidence in their valor and Patriotism." Powel was a symbol of Philadelphia's Federalist leadership, and a very appropriate choice.[113] On July Fourth the following year, Miss Sally Duane and Mrs. Joseph Hopkinson did agree to present an emblematical painting to MacPherson's Blues on behalf of the city's Federalist women.[114]

Flags as well as rhetoric expressed the women's patriotism in the militia presentations. Company flags were either purchased from local painters or made by the presenters themselves. For example, C. Gullager and George Rutter (rivals for the Philadelphia area's military business) both advertised their skills in "painting on silks for military purposes."[115] This was the case with the flag Elizabeth Powel paid for. The flag presented to MacPherson's Blues, on the other hand, was a needlework emblem, executed by Sally Duane. She impressed upon the assembly her contribution to their cause by likening her "art" of needlework to the militia's "art" of war.[116]

Militia presentations also included songs and toasts. On one occasion, after delivering the militia colors, the men and women together sang the Federalist song, "Adams and Liberty." They then gave several appropriate toasts. Philadelphia's *Country Porcupine* asked its readers, "what more liberal encouragement can the cause of Columbia have, than the sanction of her fair daughters. Even they are roused to expressions of political sentiment, which bear the plausible stamp of Federalism."[117]

The rhetoric of the militia presentation speeches also embodied the sentiments of republican motherhood with a public twist. Women spoke of "Spartan virtue," and claimed for themselves "the fortitude of a Roman Matron," which would "inspire true courage" in the soldiers. In turn, the militia commanders accepted the standards as emblems of "female patriotism and independence."[118]

Under the seemingly calm exteriors of the women who participated in these presentations lay fierce political sentiments. Eleanor Parke Custis complained about the principal individuals involved in the recently exposed XYZ Affair, finding Foreign Minister Talleyrand "an intolerable wretch. I could positively hang *him*, the five Directors, &

Monsieur le Philosophe Chasseboeuf de Volney—without the smallest remorse. I should glory in ridding this earth of such fiends." Nor were women, at least in theory, content with their designated role in the militia ritual. Custis at least entertained the notion of offering her services to defend the country by forming a "corps of *independent volunteers*" complete with helmets "ornamented with black bugles & an immense Plume of black feathers," while burnt cork was employed to give the women "*whiskers & mustachios* of uncommon magnitude, to strike with awe the beholders." Custis declared she felt "chok full of fight" at the thought of taking action. Her sex was no barrier to her feelings or her ambitions. "In such a cause," she exclaimed, "a Woman's vengeance tow'rs above her SEX!"[119] With sentiments such as these, it it not surprising that some Federalist women took a prominent role in the militia presentations and the subsequent celebrations.

Some militia presentations were elaborate affairs that included processions, picnics, and toasts. Men and women frequently drank toasts *together* after the ceremonies. In many instances, women led processions, initiated toasts, and were recognized in the newspaper accounts as the instigators and organizers of these occasions. These ceremonies were one of the activities that helped women attain a share in the public political sphere. Heretofore, women had assisted at male-directed public ceremonies. The crisis of 1798 evoked new political ceremonies which relied on women's participation and which were carried on in spaces traditionally reserved for male political activities of this kind.[120]

In addition to taking part in militia presentations, women continued to celebrate July Fourth as they had since 1777. As tensions grew between the United States and France over ship seizures, July Fourth celebrations turned into primarily Federalist affairs.[121] In Princeton, New Jersey, women wore "the American Cockade" at a gathering where men and women together sang the "President's March," and a toast to the "Fair of New Jersey" hoped that they might "never bestow their charms on Jacobins."[122] At a ball in Winchester, Virginia, an eyewitness reported that the "brilliant assemblage of ladies seemed to vie with each other in demonstration of patriotism." In the New Gardens of New Haven, Connecticut, women attending a tea wore "American Eagles or American cockades on their breasts or in their hats," while they joined the men in singing "Adams and Liberty."[123] In what seems to have been an instance of particularly strong female political assertion, one group of women in Middletown, Connecticut, drank July Fourth toasts to liberty, freedom, Mrs. Adams, and Mrs. Washington, and, finally, to "The daughters of America—May their applausive smiles reward the patriotic youth who step forward in defense of their country, and their frowns appall the traitor or coward who dares to betray or desert it." Afterwards, the women were joined by men. After more toasting, the entire group, led by the two eldest women present, processed "through the principal street, to a liberty tree."[124]

The militia presentations and July Fourth ceremonies demonstrate innovative female public behavior, but these occasions also retained elements of older rituals. The liberty tree harkened back to the American Revolution: Federalist women recreated a political role that women had played during the War for Independence, when, as exhorters, or firebrands, they had encouraged men to support the resistance to British tyranny. They had also publicly shamed cowardly soldiers. This was equally true in 1798: as the Connecticut women expressed it, "when the Fair exhibit such a spirit in their country's cause, who that is not a recreant, but would blush, to remain inactive."[125] The women who presented standards to militia troops took their political part in inciting men to action. This was a "detonating function" that, on the other side of the Atlantic, French Republican women also performed. But the public circumstances of such events, conducted by women (with men participating under female direction), added a new element to American political culture. The ceremonies and parades of the 1790s were public dramas of social relations. As such, these occasions illustrated the conditions under which women were defined as part of public political space.[126]

Partisan politics defined women's involvement in most of the public ceremonies conducted in the second half of the 1790s. Such partisanship was reinforced by newspaper editors (themselves usually supportive of one particular party) who rendered a partisan reading to their reports of such occasions.[127] The inclusion of women as the centerpieces in these new partisan ceremonies in the late 1790s, as well as the printed reports of them, demonstrate that if these occasions were powerful tools of political action, then women were consciously given a part in promoting political causes. Thus, as individuals or as a collective entity, invoked in absentia or present in ceremonies, American women performed an important political function—they were the civic glue that cemented political bonds between men.[128]

They were also pawns in the political partisanship between Federalists and Democratic Republicans. The conditions under which these women's ceremonies and celebrations gained acceptance say much about the dimensions of political party ideology and conscious political manipulation. Women's public presence helped assert competing notions of national identity: women were welcomed into public political space reinforce partisan principles, yet they were criticized for their public activities when it served the political opposition to do so.

As women participated in public events, they tested the waters of civic and political identity. Though Judith Sargent Murray might assert that women were "equally concerned with men in the public weal," not everyone agreed.[129] Deborah Logan's experience is an example of how the partisan press could deny women a role in political affairs. Logan was at the center of Federalist criticism of her husband's peace mission to France in the summer of 1798. Though a minor skirmish in the conflict between the Federalists and the Democratic Republicans, George Logan's visit elevated the tensions in the capital during his absence. As a Democratic Republican who publicly supported her husband's mission of conscience, Deborah Logan became a target of Federalist abuse and vituperation. Logan was a woman of strong character and determined convictions who actively participated in furthering the Democratic Republican political agenda, in an age when a woman's role in the social and political order was subsidiary, at best, to that of white middle-class males who could vote, hold office, and determine policy. As she herself stated, she was "as much interested in the welfare of the state as anybody, and fit to be intrusted with its secrets."[130]

Induced by the climate of fear and warmongering throughout the nation in the summer of 1798, and President Adams's disinclination to negotiate after Pinckney's failure with the French, George Logan chose to intervene personally in an effort to improve relations between the United States and France. With President Adams firmly resistant to negotiation with France, George Logan's decision to discuss affairs personally with the French ministers came as no surprise to his friends. Though no longer formally a Quaker, he was still a pacifist. His beliefs prompted him not to shrink from what his conscience told him was right. And so he jumped into the fray, regardless of personal consequences, in an attempt to decrease the tensions and misunderstandings between the United States and France. Whether George knew just how much public calumny the Federalists would heap on both himself and Deborah Logan is uncertain. He did make provisions for his wife's economic welfare should he meet either with accident or the Federalists' vengeance. He drew up a letter giving Deborah Logan power of attorney to manage their Germantown estate, Stenton, and all the family's affairs in his absence.[131] Armed with letters from Vice President Jefferson and Pennsylvania Chief Justice Thomas McKean confirming his citizenship and good character, George Logan embarked June 12 on a ship heading for Hamburg, Germany. The French consul in Philadelphia, Letombe, provided him with letters of introduction to Merlin, chief of the Directory of the French Republic, and to Talleyrand-Périgord, the minister of foreign affairs.[132]

No sooner was George Logan out of the harbor than Benjamin Rush and the others realized their quarry had eluded their surveillance. Deborah Logan clearly enjoyed Rush's chagrin: "As soon as his committee of surveillance missed their charge there was a prodigious stir in the city; they looked upon each other with blank faces, as having suffered an adroit enemy to escape their vigilance." Deborah Logan anticipated trouble once George had left. Among other things, there was a possibility that the government would search Stenton for evidence of his wrongdoing. A "friendly Federalist," whom Logan did not name, advised her to burn any incriminating evidence. But Logan's certainty in the justness of George's mission, and his complete lack of treasonous intent, made her proudly assure this friend that, "in case of a search, they would only have to regret that they had insulted a man of honor in his absence. I had nothing to secrete." Even Justice

McKean came under attack for having furnished George Logan with credentials. Deborah Logan later recalled that, "among other things, it was said in the Federal prints that it was believed to be 'the first instance where the chief judge of any place had furnished credentials to a traitor.'"[133] Despite these fears, the house was not searched. Her movements were not restricted. But all the same, George Logan's adversaries made the summer of 1798 very uncomfortable for his wife.

Deborah Logan was, as she put it, placed "under the ban of political excommunication." A Federalist surveillance committee watched her once George was gone. Worse still, any one who came into contact with her was automatically suspected of carrying messages or strategies between Logan and her Democratic Republican friends. Logan believed her not so covert observers marked anyone seen entering their gates. The Logans may have anticipated that Deborah would become the focus of Federalist ire and suspicion after George's departure. Nevertheless, her willingness to convey George's correspondence to his Democratic Republican friends and her attendance at political gatherings of allies indicate that Logan willingly undertook her role in the matter.

Shortly after George's departure, Thomas Jefferson offered Deborah Logan his support and advice. Jefferson took a circuitous route to get to Stenton, in an attempt to shake off the surveillance committee. His caution proved fruitless, however, as Logan shortly discovered. Jefferson was dismayed that the Federalists had turned their attention to Deborah Logan. He offered her a strategy for handling the rumors circulating throughout the city, rumors that implied that George Logan was too pro-French for his own good. In short, some suggested that he was a traitor. In the climate of political suspicion fostered by the Federalists, and with the newly passed Sedition Act to give their suspicions a legal bite, this suggestion was serious. Jefferson counseled Deborah Logan to go into Philadelphia and boldly face those who wished to persecute her, rather than hide away at Stenton. Such behavior, Jefferson assured her, would demonstrate Logan's "thorough consciousness of [her husband's] innocence and honor by showing [herself] in Philadelphia as one not afraid nor ashamed to meet the public eye."[134] She followed this advice, raising the eyebrows of some of her acquaintances, who rudely expressed their surprise at seeing her in public: "In a few days I put in [practice] the advice which Jefferson gave me, and went to the city, where some even told me they were surprised to see me! And many that did not notice it in this rude manner to myself, expressed to others their astonishment that I could look thus gay and cheerful in the circumstances in which I was placed."[135] Logan rode out this public scrutiny and social isolation with confidence. Unfortunately, there was worse to come.

From June 1798 until early into 1799, Deborah Logan was one of the Democratic Republican figures at whom Federalists aimed all their wrath. It was cantankerous William Cobbett, in the guise of Peter Porcupine, who made Deborah Logan a household name and identified her with the most radical form of Democratic Republicanism. The war hysteria fostered in 1798 was more fuel for Cobbett's raging anti-Democratic Republican fires. His editorial versatility even ran to catchy verses sung to the tune of "Yankee Doodle":

Yankee Doodle (mind the tune),
    Yankee Doodle Dandy,
If Frenchmen come with naked bum,
We'll spank 'em hard and handy.[136]

It came as a surprise to no one when he launched an attack on George Logan's mission to France. Soon after George Logan's departure, Cobbett, never one to understate his views, alerted his readers:

IMPORTANT.

It is well known that LOGAN, DOCTOR LOGAN, is just departed for *France!* Recollect his connections; recollect, that seditious Envoys from all the Republics that France has subjugated first went to Paris and *concerted measures* with the despots; recollect the situation of this country at this moment, and *tremble for its fate!*—The whole of this business is not come to light yet. We shall soon know it. In the mean time, watch Philadelphians, or the fire is in your houses and the *couteau at our throats.—A guard* should be mounted every night in this city.—Take care; or, when your blood runs down the gutters, don't say you were not forewarned of the danger.[137]

But he did not stop there. With George Logan on the high seas, and

Cobbett unable to obtain any reports of his activities for weeks, the Philadelphia press went in full cry after the next available target: Deborah Logan.

Deborah Logan's public career in the newspapers began with Vice President Jefferson's visit to Stenton in July. As Logan knew, keeping anything secret from the surveillance committee was difficult. And the press heard of her affairs almost as quickly. On July 21, Cobbett stepped up his attacks on Logan: "It is said that JEFFERSON went to his friend Doctor Logan's farm and spent three days there, soon after the Doctor's departure for France. *Query:* What did he do there? Was it to arrange the Doctor's *valuable manuscripts*?"[138] This sexual innuendo unleashed the rest of the Federalist papers to criticize both the Logans for their political stand.

Deborah Logan's responsibilities were manifold. As always in time of crisis, the Quaker community gathered around, visiting Logan daily. She was not always enthusiastic about these visits, however. Her guests were either like "Job's comforters," or else they interfered with the work Logan had to do in running a household for her immediate family as well as several relatives. At the close of one day she dryly wrote, "Nothing remarkable happened, only I was determined to be better and exerted myself, and as my comforters let me alone I succeeded." Her sons behaved as all children do, several times provoking Logan to call them "rude and unmanageable." Hardest of all, perhaps, were the political differences which distanced Logan from her brother, Joseph Norris, and George's uncle, James Logan, who was temporarily living at Stenton.[139]

Soon politics was eliminated from the topic of conversation at Stenton. Joseph Norris's visits from his nearby estate, Fairhill, during which he expressed his "aristocratic" opinions, forced Logan to refrain from discussing her own views. "I do not say a political word in his hearing, being but [as Norris had said of her] 'half informed.'" George's uncle James Logan was no more conciliatory. Living at Stenton, he observed all its visitors. On one occasion a Dr. Davy had the ill fortune to visit Logan while her uncle was present: "he [James Logan] understood Davy was a violent democrat, he is very cool to visitors he thinks of this class." Thus not only did Logan suffer from the pens of the Federalist press, but even her family opposed her. When the news reached Stenton that Benjamin Franklin Bache was dead, "Uncle made several reflections upon Bache which hurt my feelings, but I did not return them." It took a serious attack of yellow fever in the family to unite them in the face of adversity, at least temporarily. Logan wrote, "I am no longer consoled in order to be confronted, but I talk no politics."[140]

While Deborah Logan worried and waited, Talleyrand and Merlin received George with interest and attention. His mission to France was fortuitously timed to coordinate with the Directory's desires to avoid conflict with the United States. France never had any intention of going to war with its former ally the United States. And the government was having second thoughts about the embargo. It also considered releasing the imprisoned American sailors. The French newspapers declared that "It is virtually certain that war between the United States and France will not take place."[141]

At home, word of George's seeming success had preceded his return, and the tide turned against the Federalist warmongers. The citizenry was more than happy to have a war with France averted, to say nothing of their relief at the lifting of the embargo. Deborah Logan gauged how public opinion shifted in the Democratic Republicans' favor by how the members of the lower class responded to her: "I was early sensible myself of the change which public opinion was about to undergo by the kind inquiries and lively interest which the lower ranks of citizens expressed for my husband, for now, almost every day, wishes for his safety and speedy return greeted my ears."[142]

While waiting in Bordeaux the first week in September to board the ship *Perseverance* for his return home, George wrote to Deborah that he had accomplished what he set out to do. Because he feared that blame would be attached to his wife if it were known that she corresponded with him, he sent his letter to Governor George Clinton of New York, both a friend and a Democratic Republican. Deborah Logan showed George's correspondence to several Democratic Republican friends who agreed with her plan to publish an extract from one of George's letters in the Philadelphia papers, so that everyone would understand what his mission had accomplished.[143]

Her action placed Deborah Logan and her politics before the public eye again. Cobbett was joined by the other Federalist newspapers hungry for good copy. Deborah Logan first sent George's letter to Brown's *Philadelphia Gazette and Universal Daily Advertiser*, a Federalist paper. In part, the letter assured American readers that the American ships and prisoners had been released and that France was ready to enter into treaty to settle all disputes between the two nations. The editor, Deborah Logan pointed out, saw fit to add his own "very illiberal comment written in the spirit of that persecuting period," which denigrated George Logan's claims.[144]

This time attacks on her were more direct than a suggested sexual connection between the Quaker woman and the vice president. The Federalist press wanted it both ways: because Logan was the wife of a man at whom the papers wished to direct their attacks, it sometimes cast her in the role of helpless female, a victim of her husband's folly. At other times, the press targeted her as a political actor in her own right, equally deserving of the calumny that Cobbett and the other Federalists were eager to heap on their opponents. The *Philadelphia Gazette* ferociously attacked George Logan, claiming not only that the doctor was a traitor to his country, but that "his abandonment of wife, children, relatives and country, is a species of conspiracy, most fatal to freedom, and abhorrent to humanity." At the same time, Cobbett charged that Deborah Logan was deeply involved in this Democratic Republican conspiracy. With a large headline reading "LOGAN AND WIFE" he reprinted the letter from Brown's *Gazette* and added his own comments on the subject. He credited George's "too obedient wife" with having a hand in his mission. According to Deborah Logan, William Cobbett went further still. She remembered that "on one occasion it was recommended by Cobbett, in case of Dr. Logan's return, to put him in the pillory, in which I was to have the honor to accompany him."[145] Thus the newspapers seesawed back and forth in this manner, extracting maximum copy from Deborah Logan's position.

Although President Adams was determined to pursue good relations with France, thus leading ultimately to his break with the Hamiltonian Federalists, the Democratic Republicans chose to ignore

Adams's involvement in the turn of international affairs and viewed George Logan's mission as both a personal triumph and a boost for their own party. No longer would the Federalists be able to beat the war drum against France or argue that anyone who advocated friendship with that nation was a traitor to the United States. George Logan therefore made a triumphal tour upon his return, first to New Jersey, where "he was received with great cordiality in that neighborhood where Democratic Republicanism has a strong hold." Then, with Deborah Logan, he went on to Chester, Pennsylvania, to see Mary Parker Norris. They journeyed as far as Wilmington, Delaware, where George gave a detailed account of his mission to John Dickinson. The public was enthusiastic about the doctor even before his return. Its positive response continued as Logan and her husband traveled through the mid-Atlantic countryside. This response was what Deborah Logan had hoped for. She claimed not to be ambitious for herself, but "extremely desirous that my husband should deserve well of his fellow citizens and should on his return be received by them (if not by the men in power) with affectionate welcome." Her comment highlights the fact that Logan knew quite well that she played an important role in her husband's mission. The attention she received in the press kept before the public the issues and divisions between the Federalists and the Democratic Republicans. Though Logan did not see herself as a martyr to the Democratic Republican cause, she acknowledged that her participation had an impact on the public mind.[146]

Determined that no other private citizen would have the ability to negotiate with foreign powers, the House of Representatives passed the Logan Act on January 17 by a vote of 58 to 36. The Senate passed it a few days later with only two votes against it, and President Adams signed the bill into law at the end of the month. Deborah Logan's reflections on the incident twenty years later still were scornful. She dismissed the Federalists for their follies: "their censure fell innoxious on him, whilst the rebound made themselves (so much disappointed in not having a war on their hands) appear extremely ridiculous."[147]

The passage of the Logan Act did not silence Deborah Logan's detractors, however. Not only had George Logan's French visit fostered controversy throughout the nation, but Deborah Logan's part in the proceedings inspired men in other cities to elaborate on Cobbett's attacks. In the midst of the House debate on the bill, Richard Alsop of Connecticut published a poem about the Logans which not only was "widely circulated in other states," but made the rounds in the House of Representatives as well. According to one contemporary observer, "Congressmen quoted snatches from Alsop's verses on the floor of the House and sent many a reader scurrying to the poem to smack his lips over the references to the Doctor and his wife." The verse which readers found especially titillating referred to Cobbett's innuendo of the previous July:

> With joy we find thee rise from *coguing*[148]
> With Judge McKean and *foolish Logan,*
> And reeling down the factious dance,
> Send Deborah's husband off to France,
> To tell the Frenchmen to their cost,
> They reckoned here without their host;
> Whilst thou, to smooth the ills of life,
> Held sweet communion with the wife.[149]

William Duane, the new editor of the *Aurora*, staunchly defended George Logan's mission and condemned the Alsop poem. Several times he inserted criticisms of it in his paper: "The Connecticut poets have again from the press of Hudson and Goodwin, palmed upon the public *a vulgar ditty*—a specimen of the combined virulence of the party who direct that press, under the direction of President Dwight & Co." Two days later his criticism was more pointed. He claimed that not even the debauched city of London had ever produced "a greater libel upon public virtue or national morals." And he suggested that Philadelphia booksellers "hesitate to sell it, it is so replete with bagatelle, tete-a-tete, and private slander."[150] William Cobbett, of course, was not to be outdone. In early February 1799 he was still keeping the public interested in Deborah Logan with a reprint of a poem from the *Western Telegraph*. Cobbett supplied his own annotations to the verse.[151]

Deborah Logan became a symbol over which the Federalist and the Democratic Republican papers played out their hostilities. To counter the abuse and innuendo that Cobbett and others heaped upon her, the Democratic Republican press likened her to the heroines of the French Revolution. Some compared her to Madame Roland, who was known to have written many of her husband's political works and who ended her life on the guillotine. Others referred to the Logans "in the style of Louvet and his Ladouiskie," a reference to Jean-Baptiste Louvet de Couvrai's novel *Love and Patriotism*, published in Philadelphia in 1797. Louvet portrayed a faithful woman who, after suffering at the hands of her lover and being wronged by him, still followed him into political exile.[152]

The treatment of Logan in the press highlights the differences between the ways in which Federalists and Democratic Republicans dealt with political women. Federalists readily criticized Logan for her participation in the Democratic Republicans' efforts to come to a diplomatic resolution with France. Cobbett's advertisements of "LOGAN AND WIFE" placed blame for Democratic Republican activities on both George and Deborah Logan. The Democratic Republicans, on the other hand, never mentioned Deborah Logan in their reports of her husband's activities. Except for the one brief notice that Logan had sent George's letter to the Philadelphia papers, they simply ignored her. In the aftermath of Logan's mission, when it became clear that he may have had a hand in achieving an agreement with the French, Democratic Republicans praised Deborah Logan, but did so in ways that diminished her as a political actor. The Democratic Republican analogy of Logan to French revolutionary Lodoiska belittled her participation in the crisis: Lodoiska followed her lover out of faithful devotion to him, not because of her political principles. If Democratic Republicans approved of women taking political action, they did so only by highlighting their domestic role as good Democratic Republican wives or unnamed participants in public ceremonies. Federalists, on the other hand, were willing to credit American women with more initiative and independence of thought. Federalists *expected* women, at least when it suited the party agenda, to think and act for themselves.

But Federalists were also more than ready to dismiss unwanted women from the public political sphere by using traditional tactics.

Cobbett's poem "The Envoy of the People" accused Deborah Logan of being ugly, witchlike, and greedy for fame. Worse still, Cobbett's hint of Logan's sexual liaison with Vice President Jefferson guaranteed that gossip about the two would spread like wildfire. The response to Deborah Logan's entry into the harsh spotlight of party politics was certainly a cautionary tale for other women who may have had similar inclinations.

When Federalists took over the public political stage in the late 1790s, women were often included, and sometimes singled out, for recognition as members of the polity. And unlike Democratic Republicans, Federalists recognized female participants as women, not merely as a portion of "the nation."[153] Militia presentations emphasized the importance of women's civic activism to the republic: when Elizabeth Powel and Sally Duane were asked to present standards to the Philadelphia troops, it was expected that their speeches would explicitly refer to women's roles in the national community. Federalists could afford to be more inclusive in this respect because their conception of the political process included extralegal forms of political participation, whereas Democratic Republicans confined affiliation to the electorate, a body that encompassed white males regardless of class, but specifically barred all dependents, such as women. Yet this did not prevent Federalists from freely attacking women with opposing political views. As Cobbett said, "bearded or unbearded, whether dressed in breeches or petticoats," individuals who publicly challenged the Federalists' political agenda were fair game.[154]

Women's presence in this political public space clearly helped bolster first Democratic Republican, and then Federalist, aims. Yet at the same time, women's participation in partisan celebrations and ceremonies, the press's dissemination of information (as party propaganda) about female political activities, and the space given over to the political notices and opinions that women such as Logan posted in the newspapers also tacitly acknowledged women's place in public life. There were clear limits to this new public identity, however. When women entered the public political sphere they stepped into an arena that some men still considered an exclusively male province, and that others were willing to share with women, but only to a certain extent.

And if women promoted the opposition party's politics, as Logan did, they, no less than men, risked the full fury of the press.

By 1801, the resolution of the diplomatic crisis with France removed the French Revolution from the arena of popular political culture in America. Napoleon's meteoric rise, his foreign policies, and his eventual downfall were all chronicled in the letters and diaries of Philadelphia women. The newspapers reported at length on the situation in France and the rest of Europe. But the Revolution no longer occasioned public ceremonies and displays of women's political support. The phenomenon of the American public response to the events in France was contained within a space of roughly ten years. During that time, American women used the public and private occasions provided by the French Revolution to express their politics. They did so by recreating roles from their own country's revolution, but also through the invention of new female-focused political rituals. Ironically, while the French Revolution fostered new public roles for American women, in France the potential redefinition of women's roles and their relation to the state proved too threatening to the stability of the Republic. Women's organizations were shut down, outspoken activists were executed, and the Napoleonic Code negated any civil existence for women. In contrast, American women developed a political identity as necessary members of partisan displays, activism that was to be adopted by other political women in the years ahead.

Why did it take a revolution across the Atlantic to propel women into the American public sphere? Why hadn't the American Revolution accomplished this? Why didn't the Daughters of Liberty who spun, protested, and even fought for independence earn an acknowledged place in the polity upon independence? Why had politicians, the Constitution, and the public at large failed to translate female activism in the 1770s into political rights in the 1780s? Three things, which did not occur until later, were necessary: a consciousness on the part of women that they warranted a larger role in public life, the means of disseminating arguments for an expansion of women's roles, and a willingness on the part of men to create a space in public politics for women.

The development of a female consciousness has been amply documented by historians of the American Revolution. It took years of protest and war to push many women out of their traditional sphere, if only temporarily, and to prove to themselves and to men what they were capable of. It also took the creation of a language of rights, firmly promoted in the last quarter of the eighteenth century, that enabled women to articulate their desires. And it required an acknowledgment in the postwar years that the ladies had not been remembered, as the constitutional celebrations clearly demonstrated, either in custom or in law.

The communication developments in the 1780s and 1790s made a national forum available to the majority of Americans—more newspapers, more reprints of local stories (and international events) to a national audience, and magazines explicitly addressed to women all made possible the creation of a venue within which to circulate ideas about women. Finally, the French Revolution served as a catalyst to enhance women's place in public political culture by providing opportunities for their participation in a number of ways—as spectators, protestors, celebrants (official and otherwise), subjects of toasts, and leaders of ceremonies. Male politicians, especially Federalists, realized that their cause drew strength and legitimacy from the presence of like-minded women. In some ways this was a time-tested strategy used informally during the American Revolution, yet in the 1780s and 1790s the high degree of organization of many events, as well as attention from the press, guaranteed that women were recognized as political actors. These public women set a precedent for nineteenth-century female activists, who, as efficacious members of the civic body, promoted political candidates and challenged prostitution, alcoholism, slavery, and, ultimately, the condition of women themselves.

CHAPTER THREE

Women as Authors, Audiences, and Subjects in the American Theater

AS WOMEN gained a greater share in the social and political life of the nation, their presence was increasingly integral to the cultural sphere. Like the public streets, Philadelphia's playhouses were strongly contested, politicized spaces where women contributed to national political culture. The Democratic Republicans and the Federalists used performances to both demonstrate and encourage partisanship. They enjoined women to display their political opinions as audience members who supported the plays and songs favored by one party, they applauded actresses whose characters embodied party ideology, and they encouraged female playwrights who helped meet the demand for new plays with partisan content. Women used the opportunities that partisanship created to share in the formation of American cultural productions, to develop professional careers, and to sometimes express themselves on issues related to women's rights as well as politics.

They did so in a city which had the newest theatrical venues and the greatest number of theatrical productions in post-Revolutionary America. Only a handful of cities built or reopened theaters in the 1790s, but as the nation's capital, Philadelphia hosted a national elite who, when not concerned with affairs of state, demanded frequent and lavish entertainment. Drawing on the nation's largest urban population, great concentration of wealth, and cosmopolitan inhabitants, the city's theaters met the challenge of providing audiences with spectacles, plays, pantomimes, music, and dance. As the centerpiece of a developing national culture, Philadelphia provided the means and the opportunity for women to legitimate their public and professional lives.

Philadelphia's theatrical prominence was of recent origin in the 1790s. Pennsylvania's Quaker heritage prevented the establishment of theaters for almost eighty years after the colony's founding in 1689. But by 1766 the legislature responded to the interests of the growing majority of non-Quakers in the colony's government, especially the Anglicans, by lifting the ban against playhouses.[1] This new entertainment was shortlived, however, as the Revolutionary government, backed by the now politically dominant Scots-Irish Presbyterians, closed the city's theaters in 1779.[2] For ten years, Philadelphians went without theaters, with the exception of those theatricals staged by the British during their brief occupation of the city in 1777-78. By 1789 Philadelphia's Anglican elite, over the objections of both Quakers and Presbyterians, were successful in reestablishing legally sanctioned playhouses in the city.[3]

Once opened, the task of finding both plays and players forced theatrical managers to look overseas. Like many other aspects of American culture in the late eighteenth century, theater shared a transatlantic heritage with both Britain and France. When the playhouses reopened in the 1790s, managers sought experienced British actors and actresses for their companies rather than recruiting native talent. They did so not only because there were few Americans with theatrical experience, but also because it was advantageous to advertise the credentials of the actors and actresses with successful careers on the London stage. Some of the men and women who came to the United States were already known to Philadelphians who read the London magazine accounts of the British theater. Philadelphia magazines and newspapers began to include theatrical announcements, reviews, and profiles of individual performers as soon as the theaters opened. Musical performances in the theater were also largely the productions of British talent. In Philadelphia, immigrant Benjamin Carr composed and played much of the music heard at the New Theater. And as the

French Revolution forced many to flee both Continental France and the French islands in the Caribbean, Philadelphia audiences enjoyed the first ballet performance in the United States.[4]

The dearth of American plays and playwrights in the 1790s forced theater managers such as Thomas Wignell and Alexander Reinagle, of Philadelphia's Chestnut Street theater, to offer many of the tried and true British productions familiar to pre-Revolutionary audiences. The theater opened in 1794 with productions of Otway's Restoration drama *Venice Preserved* (1682), Garrick's farce *The Lying Valet* (1741), and Sheridan's comedy *The School for Scandal* (1777), the latter said to be among President Washington's favorites. In addition, the large number of British actors and actresses recruited to American companies in the late 1780s and early 1790s brought with them popular plays written and performed in Britain during the ten years when American theaters did not operate.[5]

The Philadelphia theaters built in the early republic were designed to accommodate, as well as segregate, all classes. The Chestnut Street theater (usually referred to as the New Theater) had a capacity of two thousand with almost half of its space reserved for the wealthy to sit in the boxes that lined the sides of the stage. It advertised that "The entrances are so well-contrived and the lobbies so spacious, that there can be no possibility of confusion among the audience going into different parts of the house."[6] The elegant draperies, chandeliers and decorative paneling along the boxes may have satisfied the refined tastes of the nation's elite, but the theaters did not exist solely on the patronage of Philadelphia's wealthy. The price of a ticket for a box, where individuals or parties sat in isolated splendor, was $1.25. The cheapest seats, in the gallery, cost 50 cents—making this form of entertainment more accessible to working people than either book purchases or circulating libraries. And servants apparently often attended as unpaid audience members. Many advertisements for plays included a warning to the wealthier patrons that their servants (who went ahead to reserve good seats) were forbidden to remain in the theater after the performance started, though clearly some did.[7] The president of the United States, who often visited the theater during his tenure, other members of the elite, artisans, shopkeepers, sailors, free African Americans, and streetwalkers all attended the theater, making it one of the most diverse public forums in the early republic.

The wide spectrum of theatergoers meant that managers needed to provide something for everyone. Hence, spectacle as well as theatrical productions filled the usual bill of fare for an evening's entertainment. Intervals, especially, catered to the less refined sensibilities of the audience. Anything from an "Occasional Address," such as Mr. Martin's recital of "Dr. Goldsmith's celebrated Epilogue in the character of Harlequin," to "Pantomimical Dance" might be offered. Especially popular was Monsieur Placide, a French tightrope walker who performed in Philadelphia and other coastal cities in the 1790s. And perhaps to offer competition to the more spectacular feats audiences witnessed at Ricketts' Circus (a building erected to house equestrian displays) one evening's entertainment at the New Theater promised to end with "a Leap through A Barrel of FIRE."[8] Theatrical performances also had an element of spontaneity to them; one commentator described the contribution of "a member of the legislature of the United States," whose performance "gave great satisfaction; it were to be wished that this son of S—e whoever he may be would make another digression from his political engagements and favor the public with a second specimen of his theatrical talents."[9]

Though Quakers, Presbyterians, and Universalists condemned the theater, not all of those whose religious views precluded attendance stayed away. When Judith Sargent Murray visited Philadelphia in 1790, she attended a performance of *The Contrast* incognito: "A large

Facing above: *Congress Hall and the New Theater on Chestnut Street, 1800.* William Birch's illustration not only shows the New Theater before its nineteenth-century renovations, but also conveys the proximity of the places where women congregated in the capital. Courtesy of the Library Company of Philadelphia.

Facing below: Interior of the New Theater. *New York Magazine.* As the biggest, most modern theater of the day, Philadelphia's New Theater was of interest to many Americans. Courtesy of the Library Company of Philadelphia.

black bonnet completely enveloped my face, and a scarf thrown over my shoulders sufficiently disguised me." Though an outspoken advocate for women, Murray was also the wife of a Universalist minister from Boston who would have been censured by his congregation for her participation in such a "school for vice."[10]

Such strictures on the part of her acquaintances, including Philadelphian Benjamin Rush, did not stop Murray from penning her own plays a few years later. She believed that there were moral lessons to be derived from "a good Play," and advantages to be gained from "reducing a system of ethics to practice, and adorning them with all that impressive action, and elegance of language." Neither did she subscribe to the opinion that performers, especially women, were "infamous" persons engaged chiefly on "idleness and debauchery." Indeed, she welcomed acquaintance with the actresses she met while visiting Benjamin Franklin's daughter, Sarah Franklin Bache, including "the celebrated Mrs. Henry" and her daughter, "a beautiful, and accomplished Girl, about thirteen years of age." Murray was thrilled to report that Mrs. Henry was "personally acquainted with, and thus often played with the celebrated Mrs. Siddons."[11]

Murray was not alone in her acceptance of actresses in polite society. Actresses were increasingly profiled in the magazines where their careers and specific performances were admired and critiqued, and their personal lives were praised for their virtue and propriety. For example, *Philadelphia Monthly Magazine* featured a "Biographical Anecdote" and full page portrait of the English actress Mrs. Merry in its April 1798 issue. Merry began her American career in Philadelphia in 1796 with Thomas Wignell's company, frequently playing leading roles in British and American plays. The editor noted that Mrs. Merry "is not less esteemed for her public talents than for the strict propriety of her conduct in private life."[12]

Despite the growing acceptance of women with professional careers, the theater was a place where audiences did not hesitate to express their approval or disapproval of what transpired on stage. "As soon as the curtain was down, the gods in the gallery would throw apples, nuts, bottles and glasses on the stage and into the orchestra. That part of the house being always crowded, it was always hard to discover the real perpetrators."[13] The most disreputable members of

Mrs. Merry as Honoria in *The Roman Father*. *Philadelphia Monthly Magazine*, April 1798. Popular actresses captured the interest of many Philadelphians. Much as in our own day, publications provided readers with details of the public and private lives of favorite performers. As acting became a legitimate career for women, the newspapers and magazines avidly followed their personal and professional exploits. Courtesy of the Library Company of Philadelphia.

the audience sat in the highest sections of the gallery. This included, according to French refugee Moreau de Saint Méry, "women [prostitutes] and colored people who can't sit anywhere else."[14] Performances were usually "boisterous" and the interludes between performances louder still. Saint Méry noted that "It is not unusual to hear such words as Goddamn, Bastard, Rascal, Son of a Bitch. Women turn their backs to the performance during the interludes."[15] Nonelite, though respectable, women, whom Méry described as "not of any social standing," sat in the pit, the area directly in front of the stage.

Women, like men, also talked continuously throughout performances, as one contributor to the *Aurora* complained:

I would wish to be indulged in one or two further, not on the players, but on two or three chattering females who sat in the stage box on the east side of the house. These ladies of the aspen leaf (particularly one of them) disturbed Pitt, Box, and Gallery with their incessant endeavors to attract attention and the perpetual motion of their tongues during the whole performance.[16]

The genteel part of the audience was not much more well behaved than the gallery, though they saved their altercations for the intermission. On at least one occasion two men with short tempers and slightly the worse for drink agreed to duel each other the following morning.[17] Despite this atmosphere of high spirits, incivility, and downright bad behavior, Philadelphia's elite women, including Martha Washington and Abigail Adams, regularly attended the theater. Though safely ensconced in a private box, rather than exposed to the liveliness of the pit or gallery, these women, along with those who did sit in the more public areas, shared in this new American entertainment.

These women participated in theatrical evenings that became increasingly political as events of the 1790s made partisanship a feature of public culture. The attendance of both President Washington and later President Adams while in residence lent a political flavor to theater attendance. Their presence served to inspire, or instigate (depending on which way the political wind was blowing) the men and women in the audience to express their political views. During Washington's presidency, the newspapers announced in advance, as a draw to audiences, when the president planned to attend a performance. The *American Daily Advertiser*, for example, reported in 1792, "We have authority to inform the Public, that the PRESIDENT of the UNITED STATES intended to honor the Theater with his Presence this Evening."[18] Thus, the President himself became a unpaid performer, ably filling his role as leader to an often admiring crowd. Reviewers sometimes included comments on the president's "performance." *The Federal Gazette and Philadelphia Daily Advertiser* described Washington's reaction to the Maid of the Mill: "the great and good Washington manifested his approbation of this interesting part of the opera by the tribute of a tear."[19]

The political atmosphere of the theater was often highly charged, prompting opprobrious cries or assenting cheers even before actors appeared on the stage.[20] This was especially true during the first years of the French Revolution, when Americans rejoiced at the creation of another republic and the overthrow of monarchy. In 1793, Democratic Republican editor Benjamin Franklin Bache announced that "the mountain" (the audience in the gallery, given the name of the Jacobin segment of the French National Assembly) demanded that the orchestra play the Revolutionary tune "Ça Ira." During this period of francophilia, Bache often printed "Vivat Republica!" at the bottom of theater advertisements in the *Aurora*.[21] Even when plays were politically neutral, the actors sometimes trod a fine line to keep all partisans content. When the actor Hodgkinson appeared on the Philadelphia stage wearing a British uniform, "The French [or pro-French] in the audience hissed. Hodgkinson, always ready to make an address, explained that his part was that of a coward and a bully. Immediately the English [and pro-British Americans] arose and threatened violence." This threat was not an idle one. In Boston in 1796 the performance of *The Poor Soldier* was interrupted when the audience objected to the portrayal of a Frenchman as "a libel on the character of the whole French nation." The aggrieved audience tore the theater apart.[22] On another occasion, New Yorkers "took offense at those parts in which the French are held up to ridicule," forcing the manager to alter the actors' lines.[23] After a performance of another play, *The Old Soldier*, at the Church Street theater in Charleston, the audience joined performers in singing the Marseillaise: "Everybody was French that night, and all the small boys beat tatoos in time."[24] French foreign minister Edmund Genêt's arrival in the capital in 1793, celebrated by Democratic Republicans, also occasioned political expression in the theater. When Genêt attended, he was greeted with huzzahs from the audience and the playing of the French political song "Ça Ira."[25]

Toward the close of the decade, Federalists used the theater to reach a large spectrum of the population with their political ideology. When the new frigate *Constitution* was launched from Boston Harbor in 1797, the Federal Street theater, performed a musical interlude, "The launch, or Huzza for the Constitution."[26] When the passage of the Alien and Sedition Acts and the imagined threat of French invasion boosted President Adams's popularity in 1798, "The President's March" and "Hail Columbia" were frequently played in theaters, supplanting the pro-French "Ça Ira." The audience responded with just as much "enthusiastic clamor and applause" for Federalist principles as they had for Democratic Republican ones earlier. On one occasion the orchestra was required to play "The President's March" six times before the audience was satisfied.[27] When President and Mrs. Adams attended the Chestnut Street theater in April 1798, the entire audience rose and sang "The President's March" in his honor.[28] It happened again at Adams's next theater appearance, only this time with greater fervor. The British ambassador's wife, Henrietta Liston, who witnessed this outpouring of enthusiasm for the Federalist president, told a correspondent that "nothing could equal the noise and uproar," and "The President's March" was repeatedly called for and "sung to, and danced to, [and] some poor fellow in the gallery calling for sa ira [*sic*] was threatened to be thrown over."[29]

The legitimation of theater as a space for women as performers and authors as well as audience members offered the possibility of literally "trying on" new public roles as well as enlarging old ones.

Through voice and body, actresses conveyed song, poetry, and ideas to their audiences. Actresses became Joan of Arc, Roman matrons, imperiled princesses, and thoughtful politicians. They embodied nations and political principles: in Alexandre Placide's original pantomime *American Independence, or the 4th July, 1776,* Mrs. Placide portrayed America, "dressed as an Indian, her face covered with a black veil as a token of mourning and grief, and her hands in chains." Mrs. Val represented England, in "grand Court dress, holding in one hand a standard, bearing the armorial of Great Britain, and in the other hand a naked sword," and Mrs. Douvillier, dressed in white, played Liberty.[30]

Actresses could also speak for the nation, and for the women of the nation. On the Charleston stage, Mrs. Marriott recited her original poem "Ode to Liberty." In Boston, Mrs. Harper delivered the eulogy for George Washington.[31] Actresses readily combined politics and patriotism on the public stage. Women of the audience became active participants in this political arena as well. They could be directly appealed to for partisan displays, such as when Joseph Hopkinson's new song "Hail Columbia" was first performed at the Chestnut Street Theater in 1798. Reporting on its reception, the Federalist *Gazette of the United States* extended the wish that "the ladies will practice the music and accompany the words at its next repetition." Such participation went beyond the discreet female entertainments in the parlor. Women were expected to voice their support for this patriotic, and decidedly partisan, public display.[32] Yet women could not expect to be shielded from attack. Inevitably, a woman's politics also drew fire from the opposition. On opening night of *Tammany, or the Indian Chief*, Mrs. Melmoth, who had performed on the English stage before arriving the United States in 1793, was scheduled to speak the epilogue. But she refused to do so "because of the patriotic [and anti-British] sentiments contained in it." As a result, a boycott was staged for the evening of Melmoth's next performance. The *New York Journal* warned, "She is to appear on the stage this night. I hope she will be convinced, by the absence of republicans when she appears that the people resent her impertinence."[33] Women's political views became an acceptable part of theatrical display, but their sex did not protect them from the ferocity of partisanship.

The desire for plays with American themes, and the Federalists' and Democratic Republicans' use of the theater as a venue to promote their politics, provided an opportunity for female authors to stage their plays. This was especially evident in Susanna Rowson's *Slaves in Algiers* and Anne Kemble Hatton's *Tammany, or the Indian Chief*, both performed in Philadelphia in 1794. Rowson's work dealt with a politically timely issue for Americans—the plight of men and women captured by Algerian pirates in the North Atlantic. The play promoted the freedom of America against the tyranny of foreign powers, a message that should have gratified the Federalists (who were not only furious with the Algerians but by this time openly hostile to the French as well) but in fact pleased the Democratic Republicans instead. The Democratic Republicans, who were in the midst of their heated campaign against the Jay Treaty between the United States and Great Britain, blamed the British for allowing the Algerians free reign in the Atlantic. They took Rowson's message as anti-British. At the same time that Rowson's play stirred up the conflict between the two political parties, Hatton's *Tammany, or the Indian Chief,* "seasoned high with spices from Paris," had been deliberately written at the instigation of the Tammany Society, a Democratic Republican organization. One reviewer wrote: "The Prologue and Epilogue were brim full of the present popular notions of liberty; and of course went down with great éclat."[34]

Hatton's production demonstrated that it was not only possible for women to succeed as playwrights, but also to contribute to the partisan political culture of the era. Rowson's play *Slaves in Algiers* worked as a political piece, but at the same time it contained a message about male dominance and the slavelike position of women in their domestic relationships and in the larger society. Her play affirmed Mary Wollstonecraft's arguments for female independence.

Since Rowson specifically wrote the play for her benefit night (which meant she kept all the profits after paying the house expenses), her play was intended to be a box office draw. Its subject, the imprisonment of Americans at the Court of the Dey of Algiers, would have evoked a strong response from the audience. The United States had refused to negotiate with the pirates, perceived as the eighteenth-century version of terrorists, and therefore American ships, seamen, and passengers were easy prey for Algerian pirates. This was particularly true after a British agreement with the Portuguese in 1793 gave the Algerians free access from the Mediterranean to the Atlantic.[35] The captured passengers were held for ransom, and it was rumored that women were sometimes placed in harems.

Thus Rowson's play appealed to American patriotism. *Slaves in Algiers* involves much speechmaking about liberty and freedom, and claims these principles as the right of all true Americans. The subplot depicts strong American women standing up for both their sexual and political virtue and hoping for their liberation. The theme of tyrants and slavery functions in two ways. Not only do the captive women

NEW THEATRE.

Mr. & Mrs. Rowson's
NIGHT.
This Evening,

JUNE 30.

Will be Presented,

A NEW COMEDY, in three acts, interspersed with songs, written by Mrs. Rowson, called

Slaves in Algiers;
OR

A struggle for Freedom.

The Music composed by Mr. Reinagle.

Muley Moloch,	Mr. Green
Frederick,	Mr. Moreton
Henry,	Mr. Cleveland
Constant,	Mr. Whitlock
Sebastian,	Mr. Bates
Ben Hassen,	Mr. Francis
Mustapha,	Mr. Bailey, jun.
Sadi,	Master Warrell
Selim,	Mr. Blisset
Zorianna,	Mrs. Warrell
Fetnah,	Mrs. Marshall
Rebecca,	Mrs. Whitlock
Selima,	Mrs. Cleveland
Olivia,	Mrs. Rowson
Slaves,	Messrs. Warrell, De Moulin, Lee, &c.

The Prologue by Mr. Fennell—the Epilogue, by Mrs. Rowson.

End of act 2d, (Song) The heaving of the Lead, by Mr. Rowson.

End of the Comedy, a Characteristic Pantomimical Dance, called

The Sailor's Landlady;
Or, JACK IN DISTRESS.

Jack,	Mr. Francis
Ned Haulyard, (with a song)	Mr. Darley jun.
Sailors,	Messrs. Warrell, Blisset, Warrell jun. Lee, Bason, and De Moulin.
Lasses,	Mrs. Cleveland, Mrs. Bates, Miss Rowson, and Miss Willems.
Landlady,	Mr. Rowson
Orange Girl,	Mrs. De Marque

To conclude with a double Hornpipe by Mr. Francis and Mrs. De Marque

To which will be added,

A FARCE, called

Announcement of the first performance of *Slaves in Algiers*, *Gazette of the United States*, June 30, 1794. Courtesy of the Library Company of Philadelphia.

want their physical freedom, they discuss their desire for women's freedom and equality in marriage and society. Hence the play's subtitle *A Struggle for Freedom*. Rebecca, an American held for ransom, conveys her own ideas of women's roles to her Algerian companion, Fetnah, who has been sold by her father to the Dey's harem. Fetnah credits Rebecca with nourishing in her a "love of liberty [she] taught me woman was never formed to be the abject slave of man." Thus Rowson evoked a sense of nationalism in which women's independence was a critical part.[36]

Rowson's female characters exhibit heroism and patriotism, for as Fetnah says, "in the cause of love or friendship, a woman can face danger with as much spirit, and as little fear, as the bravest man amongst you." It is in the epilogue, however, that female rights are most conspicuously advocated. At the conclusion of the play, Rowson stepped out on the stage, not in her role as the play's heroine, Olivia, but as herself, the author. She addressed the female members of the audience, and solicited their opinion. Rowson asked, "Well, Ladies, tell me—how d'ye like my play?" She then spoke the imaginary replies of the women in the audience:

"The creature has some sense," methinks you say;
"She says that we should have supreme dominion,
"And in truth, we're all of her opinion.
"Women were born for universal sway,
"Men to adore, be silent, and obey."

Rowson had her own reply to these women, which at first reading seems to contradict the audience's desire for the supremacy of women:

True, Ladies—bounteous nature made us fair,
To strew sweet roses round the bed of care.
A parent's heart, of sorrow to beguile,
Cheer an afflicted husband by a smile.
To bind the truant, that's inclined to roam,
Good humor makes a paradise at home.

To raise the fall'n—to pity and forgive,
This is our noblest, best prerogative.
By these, pursuing nature's gentle plan,
We hold in silken chains the lordly tyrant man.

Her epilogue nicely illustrates the issues at work in the discussion of women's public roles in the 1790s. Rowson's fictional female audience, like Wollstonecraft, pressed for a reevaluation of woman's status in the economic, political, and domestic spheres. Rowson's reply to her female audience retreated from this position to a more traditional one: women in control of the domestic sphere. Rowson claimed, in effect, that women held power in the political sphere through their subtle influence, or manipulation, of the men in their domestic circle.[37] It is impossible to know how Rowson's audience, some of them only a few feet away from her, responded to her message. Much would have depended on how she delivered her lines—were they sarcastic? Playful? All that remains are the words she spoke, not how she spoke them. But the fact that the play became an often performed piece in the New American Company's repertoire indicates that it met with approval long after the Algerian crisis had faded away.[38]

Rowson's politics and her arguments for women's rights pleased some Philadelphians but angered others. William Cobbett, the fiercely pro-British Philadelphia newspaper editor, and always a bellwether of the most reactionary politics, was appalled at the use of the Algerian issue. In *A Kick for a Bite: or Review Upon Review: with a Critical Essay on the Works of Mrs. Rowson: in A Letter to the Editor, or Editors of the American Monthly Review* (1795), he attacked Rowson's play. Cobbett criticized Rowson for the political position evinced in *Slaves in Algiers.* But he spent most of his venom on the matter of women's place in the republic. In his acerbic way, he acknowledged that there were already signs that Rowson's ideas on women's power had been carried into action: "Sentiments like these could not be otherwise than well received in a country, where the authority of the wife is unequivocally acknowledged." He feared that women would continue to achieve more autonomy, especially in the political sphere; he expressed his dismay at, but acknowledged the existence of, a "whole tribe of female scribblers and politicians," possibly linking her with Woll-stonecraft and Murray, the "tribe" to which Rowson belonged.[39] Cobbett's invective illustrates the limits of acceptance for women who questioned the status quo, especially when the message came packaged in partisan sentiments.

Yet this very partisanship earned Rowson a champion in the form of newly elected Democratic Republican congressman John Swanwick, who defended Rowson against Cobbett's attack in *A Rub from Snub*, a pamphlet in which he chiefly ranted against Cobbett's reactionary, pro-British politics. By the time Cobbett's pamphlet appeared, the nation was engaged in a heated debate over the Jay treaty, an agreement designed to improve U.S.-British relations at the expense of U.S.-French relations. In Philadelphia, Swanwick was a leading opponent of the treaty. He personally organized two protests against it in July 1795 after the Senate voted approval in June. The parade and burning of Jay in effigy in the capital on July 4, 1795, were both promoted and funded by the congressman. Swanwick clearly had political reasons to confront Cobbett. But he had women in mind as well. He served on the board of the Young Ladies Academy of Philadelphia, and was an active proponent of women's education. Swanwick had already expressed his ideas on the future for women's education in his 1787 essay *Thoughts on Education Addressed to the Visitors of the Young Ladies Academy of Philadelphia*, in which he advanced sophisticated views on the potential for women in society. He believed, for example, that it was merely inferior education that accounted for women's subjugation, and he challenged his readers, "But can you prove that a male education would not qualify a woman for all the duties of a man?"[40] Swanwick took Rowson seriously. And his defense of her on political grounds was significant: these warring pamphleteers treated Rowson as a political peer. For her own part, Rowson briefly responded to Cobbett in the preface to *Trials of the Human Heart* (1795), calling him a "loathsome reptile," and left it at that.[41]

Slaves in Algiers showed how politics and women's issues could be strongly intertwined. Rowson deliberately used political language to address women's concerns: freedom and slavery could be understood metaphorically as well as literally. This intimate connection between gender and politics was precisely what made many people uncomfortable with the discussion of women's roles in the late eighteenth century. Republican rhetoric, intended to emphasize the independence of men, was employed to promote the cause of those it was meant to exclude: women.

Slaves in Algiers was not the only play to challenge American audiences to compare the rights of man to the rights of woman. Just as Wollstonecraft's writings spread quickly from Britain to America in this transatlantic world of ideas, many of Englishwoman Elizabeth Inchbald's works were familiar to Americans, and were frequently performed in Philadelphia in the 1790s. Inchbald was a popular actress turned novelist and playwright whose plays were broad farces in the tradition of Restoration comedy.[42] Inchbald was by no means as strident in her championship of women's rights as Wollstonecraft, yet some of her plays ventured into the same territory. *Everyone Has His Fault*, performed in Philadelphia, New York, Boston, and Baltimore in the same season as *Slaves in Algiers*, advanced the notion of companionate marriage, a frequent topic in the periodicals of the day. Thus the discussion of women's roles reached across a variety of public forums. [43]

Even more pointed in its content than the play itself, the the prologue for the play, written especially for the Philadelphia performances, reminded the audience that the play they were about to see was by a woman, an authoress whose plays the Philadelphia audience had seen with pleasure more than once before. Having noted that women are successful playwrights, the speaker then made an oblique reference to Wollstonecraft and reminded his audience that at that moment, French women were fighting counterrevolutionaries and foreign enemies:

> The Rights of Women, says a female pen,
> Are, to do every thing as well as Men.
> To think, to argue, to decide, to write,
> To talk, undoubtedly—perhaps to fight.
> (For females march to war, like brave Commanders,
> Not in old Authors only—but in Flanders.)

The audience would have been familiar with such reports in the American newspapers. As if he sensed the disapproval these claims might evoke in the audience, the speaker retreated to the traditional viewpoint, that "Men should rule, and Women should obey." Yet he also conceded that

> since the Sex at length has been inclin'd
> To cultivate that useful part—the mind;—
> Since they have learnt to read, to write, to spell;—
> Since some of them have wit,—and use it well;—

then women should not be "Confin'd entirely to domestic arts, / Producing only children, pies and tarts."[44] This deliberate evocation of the ongoing debate on women's roles in the early republic suggests that theatergoers were familiar (as indeed many of them would have been if they were also magazine or novel readers) with the topic and with the arguments used in the debate. These theatrical speeches were constructed for their entertainment value. Yet this fact illustrates the pervasiveness of women's roles as a topic of interest for audiences of the day, and the prologue to Inchbald's play indicates that Philadelphians wished to hear women's roles discussed in a variety of settings.

Clearly, the presence of women as actors, authors, and observers in this politicized theatrical space was neither unusual nor unwelcome. Just as female audience members were expected to be political, female characters freely expressed themselves on political matters too. This was the case in John Burke's 1797 production *Bunker Hill, or The Death of General Warren*. Burke's play quickly became a popular July Fourth piece (and thus more popular among Democratic Republicans rather than Federalists) often performed in Philadelphia, Boston, and New York. Though historically inaccurate, the play is a rousing celebration of the Revolution. The two main characters are a British soldier, Ambercrombie, and his American sweetheart, Elmira. Though love unites them, political loyalty keeps them apart. Like many real women in the war, Elmira does not share the politics of her man. She tries to persuade Ambercrombie to "forsake the hateful standard of oppression," and abandon a cause which is not an honorable one. She argues that he owes no allegience to a king who instigates a civil war among his people. Despite her attempts to reason with him, Ambercrombie insists that he cannot dishonor himself by refusing to fight. Elmira's tale does not have a happy ending. There can be no reconciliation of the couple's political differences. Despite her feelings for her lover, Elmira cannot approve his actions. Her politics—as much as his—keep them apart. Love is not powerful enough to persuade Elmira to abandon her political principles. Like the Philadelphia women who invoked their identification with the women of Rome and Sparta at militia presentations, Burke's Elmira steadfastly asserts her patriotism and commitment to the nation.[45]

Likewise, Philadelphian John Murdock's 1798 play *The Politicians; or, A State of Things*, written as an examination of the various responses to the Jay Treaty, depicts women unwilling to compromise their political principles. Murdock intended to show the multiplicity of opinions which divided the nation over this issue. Presented in a matter-of-fact manner, two of his most politically heated characters are Mrs. Turbulent and Mrs. Violent. Mrs. Violent is a staunch Federalist, who defends Washington as "A man, who is an honour to his God, a credit to his country, and an ornament to human nature." Mrs. Turbulent declares, on the other hand, that, "[Washington] was never equal to the situation he was placed in: vastly has his talents been overrated; he possesses none beyond that of being an overseer to a Virginia plantation, or the superintendence of a horse-stable: he is an excellent judge of horses." As for the treaty, Mrs. Turbulent wishes that President Washington's hand "had withered" before he signed the "cursed treaty." Mrs. Violent declares she is bitter towards "your party," and accuses Mrs. Turbulent of Jacobinism. Speaking to her as a member of the hated Democratic Republican party, Mrs. Violent says, "you have been abetting the French tyrants from the first to the present moment." She predicts that Mrs. Turbulent and her fellow "demos" will reap the fruits of their labor. Using curses very reminiscent of newspaper editor William Cobbett, she says, "time will unfold your mole-workings; and, like that animal, you will be dragged forth before your country, with dirt upon your heads."[46] Their political sentiments are not confined to debates with each other. The women also discuss politics in mixed company: Mrs. Turbulent engages two members of the Senate, Mr. Timid and Mr. Anticipate, in political conversation.

As casually as Murdock presents these characters, he also makes use of them for comic effect. The opening scene of the play shows Mrs. Turbulent's servant, Cato, a stereotypical black character, shaking his head over the constant political debates between the two women: "I wonder what e debil woman have do we poletic, dere my miss and miss Violent, talke, talke, talke, bout treaty, bout Masse Jay, bout president, bout congree, bout English, bout French, it mak me sick, dere two tongue go like mill clap."

The idea of women talking too much was often repeated in plays. As Inchbald's prologue says, among the rights of women is "To talk, undoubtedly." Although Mrs. Turbulent and Mrs. Violent are fictional characters, broadly drawn, the assumptions made about their political involvement, as well as their acceptance by male politicians ready to engage in political conversation with women is important. The assumption in Murdock's play is that such behavior was not extraordinary. Murdock presented his audience with a familiar situation. They could laugh about it, perhaps disapprove of it, yet recognize it as a real life occurrence nonetheless.[47]

If Burke's and Murdock's plays simply assumed that women could be just as political as men, other plays written in the 1790s showcased the public discussion of women's roles and abilities. Several authors, including Judith Sargent Murray, carried their arguments about women's roles from one public medium to another. Like her didactic essays, Murray's two plays, *Virtue Triumphant* and *The Traveler Returned*, first performed in Boston and then read by Philadelphians in her 1798 collection *The Gleaner*, argue for women's education and marital equality. Both have strong, articulate female characters.[48]

The central plot in *Virtue Triumphant* is the obstacle to a marriage between Eliza Clairville and Charles Maitland. Eliza, orphaned and penniless, refuses the proposal of the wealthy Charles because she cannot meet him "on equal terms." Even the eventual approval of Charles' father does not sway her from her belief that marriage to Charles would not be a marriage of equality: "Nor will I enter a family whose every attention I should regard as a condescension which would tinge my cheek with the hectic of conscious inferiority." Eliza views her conclusion as reasonable and realistic. She counters her lover's passionate disregard for impediments, quelling his blithe assumption that all will turn out right in the end. She tells him: "That hope is not the offspring of probability; it may serve to illumine the pages of a novel, or produce a happy denouement to the fifth act of a play; but as it conflicts with reason, let us not indulge it." Lest Eliza seem to be indifferent to Charles, Murray takes pains to show that Eliza returns his love with equal fervor, but refuses to let passion rule her head. Instead, Eliza's sense (as opposed to sensibility) is one of her virtues. Nor is she portrayed as helpless, despite her lack of family or fortune. Among her virtues is her use of an education, as she says, "which secures my independence."[49] Eliza is the fictional embodiment of Murray's prescriptions in her *Massachusetts Magazine* essays. Murray cannot let her virtue go unrewarded. Virtue does triumph in the play, and Eliza and Charles do marry, thanks to the timely revelation that Eliza is an heiress. Yet Murray reminds her audience that Eliza earned the love and admiration of the other characters long before her monetary reward enabled her to accept Charles on equal terms. Murray reinforces Eliza's example of checking passion in favor of reason with another female character, Eliza's friend and employer, Augusta Bloomfield. When Augusta confesses to her aunt, the appropriately named Matrimonia, that she does not love her husband, Col. Bloomfield, Matrimonia assures her that "ungovernable ardours" are not the basis of a good marriage. "Friendship is still the *ne plus ultra* of every married pair." [50]

Mrs. Montague in *The Traveler Returned* is a learned woman who spends her days pouring over scientific treatises. We first encounter her, as the stage directions state, in the library, "Table covered with Books—Mrs. Montague making Extracts," and murmuring to herself about theories of phlogiston.[51] Mrs. Montague, abandoned by her husband twenty years before because of her flirtatious behavior, has spent the intervening time in studious retirement. Her intellectual pursuits are presented as an appropriate occupation for a woman. Even after her husband's return and the reuniting of their family, there is no indication that Mrs. Montague will abandon her studies. Yet Murray does use Mrs. Montague's thirst for knowledge to comic effect. Though she tries to concentrate on her studies, household affairs force themselves on her attention. In one scene her servant tells her, "the cook has left open the door of the larder, and the grey cat has helped herself to the partridges." An absorption in her books also prevents her from seeing the true state of affairs existing between her daughter, Harriot, her niece, Emily, and Major Camden. Mrs. Montague does admit that "perhaps, books engross too much of my time." As Murray argued in her essays, women have the right to educate themselves, but their domestic responsibilities and maternal duties should not be neglected.

Mrs. Montague has raised her daughter, Harriot, as an independent-minded woman of the republic. Certain of her own virtues and accomplishments, Harriot openly welcomes the chance to appear before the public eye. In an exchange with her cousin, who in contrast to Harriot prefers to "slide through life, performing my little part without observation," Harriot claims, "why I would rather be paragraphed in the newspaper, than not distinguished at all." When Emily cautions Harriot that such notoriety could easily damage her reputation, the following exchange takes place:

HARRIOT: Why, child, a single scribbler, scratching his malicious noodle, may fabricate his abuse, and the cynic has only to preface his invidious production by the little comprehensive monosyllable *we* think and *we* wish, while he thus hands my name to thousands, who would not otherwise have known *that I had an existence*.

EMILY: Well, but with the knowledge of *your existence*, they would at the same time receive an impression *that would not be to your honour*.

HARRIOT: Yes, Emily; but their *curiosity* would be called into action —it would impel them to *inquire*; I should come out an *innocent sufferer*, be allowed *my full share of merit*, and acquire a *prodigious deal of consequence*; ha! ha! ha! I protest the very idea is enchanting.[52]

As in *Slaves in Algiers*, *The Traveler Returned* shows the new American woman who asserts her right to freedom from domestic domination.[53]

When critic Thomas Paine (Robert Treat Paine) described the play as "tedium of uninterested solemnity," Murray appended an "Apology for the Author" which was spoken at the next performance by Mrs. Powell (a member of the company who had not appeared in the play):

Women, perhaps, were born a match for men:
But natal rights by education crampt,
The sex's inequality is stampt.
Yet sure in this celebrious age design'd,
To crown the struggles of the opening mind,
To equal efforts you will point the way,
Nor e'en the emulative wish betray.[54]

Echoing her *Massachusetts Magazine* essays, Murray defended this work by "a female pen," asking only for a level playing field in which an author's sex would not be a legitimate point of criticism.

Women on both sides of the stage played a larger role in public life as a result of the opportunities created for them by theaters reopening in the 1790s and by political partisans encouraging them to participate in the battle for control of the nation's identity. The Federalists and Democratic Republicans, who encompassed women in their demonstrations of political ideology in the street, also expected female audience members to contribute to demonstrations of party sentiment. As performers, they often embodied the symbols of Federalist conservatism or Democratic Republican democracy and played female politicians, patriotic revolutionaries, and bright, strong-willed women. As playwrights, they wrapped political messages in artistic representations and articulated their support for recognition of women's place in the intellectual and social, as well as political, life of the nation. Men of both political parties were more interested in recruiting loyal, vocal members regardless of their sex. Women could be just as useful and perhaps, as talented actresses conveying party sentiments, even more so than men. Their recognition of women's political identity did not extend to a recognition of women's political rights. Yet Federalist and Democratic Republican encouragement of female political activity lent tacit approval and perhaps even encouragement for women to expand their public identity.

CHAPTER FOUR

The Creation of the American Political Salon

THE AMERICAN response to the French Revolution afforded women the opportunity to participate intermittently in public political activities. The theater offered them a public presence and a profession. At the same time, the creation of a federal government in 1788 fostered yet another public role for American women. The emergence of a national elite, based in the capital city, afforded women a new place in the cultural, social, and political life of the developing nation. Unlike the political culture of the street and the theater, the salon was not a contested space. The Federalists' dominance of official functions and the president's control of both formal and informal occasions ensured that Federalist women would hold sway, establishing for themselves avenues to political power and influence throughout the 1790s. The American salon was a part of the public sphere where gender, politics, and society intersected. This nexus of social and political functions provided women with access to public political space through the vehicle of social occasions for the nation's political elite.

This new public existence was made possible by the formal roles created by both the first president and his wife. George and Martha Washington hosted official dinners, celebrations, and weekly levees, all of which were attended by the capital's elite residents, political associates, and foreign dignitaries. In turn, the formal and semiformal political occasions provided women who had access to this circle with an opportunity to court political figures and establish a reputation for

elegant entertainment and polite intercourse, simultaneously participating in political culture and helping to make politics an accepted
part of women's public lives. No one did this better than Anne Willing Bingham. As a close friend of the President and First Lady, and
wife of a wealthy, prominent Federalist senator, she was able to create
a social space where congressmen, senators, and cabinet members
could discuss politics, consolidate alliances, and lobby colleagues in an
informal setting. Though Martha Washington had the official
Philadelphia salon, Bingham's was the most lavish, and the most
talked about.

The American salon was a product of American culture, but not
exclusively so. It owed some of its features to French influence as well.
It is worthwhile to begin an examination of American salon culture in
the 1780s and 1790s by explaining how French salons functioned,
who hosted them, and who participated in them.[1] The salons of Old
Regime France were not political in nature. Their very existence
depended upon the fact that salons were removed from politics.
Groups of men and women came together for the purpose of furthering cultural and intellectual pursuits in an atmosphere of sociability.
To discuss politics, or to assemble individuals because of their political affiliations, would have done violence to the nature of salon culture. The role of the salonnière was as a "civilizing force" in a female-
centered, mixed-gender setting. The need for women at the heart of
these gatherings was based on the philosophical notion of "comple-
mentarity," a neo-Platonic theory which implied that "autonomous,
rational beings (gendered male) were not sufficient to the attainment
of the ends they sought by nature, whether philosophical, social, or
political."[2] Hence, women were essential, not peripheral, to this enter-
prise. Salonnières did not create their meeting places to achieve power through their association with men. It was women who were central to salon culture, not men.[3] The Enlightenment salonnières instead
strove first and foremost to meet their own intellectual and educational needs. Their task was to bring order to "the variety of views
expressed by [their] guests. Such harmonizing was necessary both
because different views were expressed, and because strong egos were
involved."[4]

In England the salon was particularly important as a source of literary patronage as well as a public space for serious conversation. Hostesses such as Elizabeth Montague used their wealth not only to create a physical space for the gathering of the London intelligentsia, but also to provide financial support in the form of unofficial pensions, gifts, and living accommodations for struggling authors. Hester Thrale's care and feeding of Dr. Samuel Johnson in the 1760s is a case in point. Her attentions allowed Johnson the freedom from poverty and domestic cares necessary for him to write.[5]

The English salon was a social space for the dissemination of new ideas in a polite social setting, an informal academy one of whose aims was to shape public opinion.[6] The salon that most fulfilled this ambition in the late eighteenth century was the Bluestocking Club, which included among its female members Elizabeth Montague, Elizabeth Vesey, Hester Thrale, Hannah More, and Fanny Burney. More so than in France, English salonnières nurtured the talents of younger women writers and established a sororal network for the private as well as public exchange of ideas and creative work.[7]

Salons were an important part of the life of Enlightenment society on both sides of the Atlantic. In America, this institution, though drawn from both British and French progenitors, assumed a character unique to the time and place. In colonial salons a handful of articulate, well-educated women consciously gathered together groups of like-minded friends and acquaintances for good conversation and entertainment.[8] One of the most prominent of these women was Philadelphian Elizabeth Graeme Ferguson. The daughter of a wealthy physician, Ferguson was encouraged to develop her intellectual and literary talents. As a young woman she visited England, where in 1764 she was introduced to several literary salons. There she met figures such as Samuel Johnson and Laurence Sterne. Borrowing from this English model, Graeme formulated her own American version of the salon. Saturday evenings were reserved, according to her friend Dr. Benjamin Rush, for entertainment "of the Attic kind," recalling the simple elegance and delicate wit associated with the ancient Athenian city-state. Graeme charmed her guests "by a profusion of useful ideas, collected by her vivid and widely expanded imagination."[9]

Ironically, as salon culture became a more prominent part of American society in the late 1780s, it was already waning in pre-Revolutionary France, where men had begun forming masculine societies in which women did not play a role."[10] In France, the salon was in competition with Masonic lodges and male-centered intellectual coteries. In America, the salon did not compete with, but rather complemented, homosocial meetings. Taverns, bookshops, and Masonic lodges existed side by side with the salon. It was one among many public spaces within which men could gather for political, social, or intellectual purposes, and one of the few places where women held a prominent position. It also profited from the sororal networks of the day: women such as Elizabeth Graeme, Hannah Griffitts, and Elizabeth Boudinot sustained intensive intellectual and emotional relationships with other Philadelphia-area women, exchanging their poetry, essays, and commentaries. Such conversational exchanges among women overflowed into the heterosocial gatherings of these women, and laid the path to more pointedly political gatherings.[11]

The uniquely defining feature of salon culture as it was practiced in the early republic was its political dimension. American salons, as they existed after 1788, were different from the social and intellectual gatherings that existed in the colonial era. Whereas British and French salon culture explicitly rejected politics and political affiliations as a unifying characteristic of gatherings, the American salons that developed in conjunction with federal society were intentionally political.[12] This was first apparent in New York City in 1789 and 1790. As the first, though brief, seat of the federal government, New York society took on a decidedly political cast. The social season was no longer determined by the onset of summer heat or the beginning of cooler fall weather. Rather, the social agenda was regulated by congressional sessions, a practice that continued when the capital moved to Philadelphia and then on to Washington.[13]

When Martha Washington arrived in New York City soon after the president's inauguration, the first couple set about constructing their official social life. Their style and mode of hospitality shaped the activities and participation of the women associated with congressmen, senators, and cabinet members. The president assigned certain hours in the week for the official reception of visitors by the president of the United States. His wife designated Friday evenings as a time when she would entertain local society and visiting dignitaries. This was the nation's first political salon. Martha Washington's Friday evenings set a precedent for the role of the president's wife. These occasions were "select and courtly" with full evening dress required.[14] Abigail Adams noted that Washington was "plain in her dress, but that plainness is the best of every article. Her manners are modest and unassuming, dignified and feminine, not the tincture of hauteur about her." Judith Sargent Murray, on a visit from her home in Gloucester, Massachusetts, recorded a description of one of these Friday evenings:

The apartments are always crowded—The Lady is introduced by some gentleman in waiting—she curtsies low to Mrs. Washington, who returns the ceremony—but not a single word is exchanged—the Lady then steps back[,] mixes in the rooms, takes her share of tea, Coffee, and Cakes, in their variety—fruits, ices, Lemonade, wines etc etc and at the close of the visit, she is again led up, makes her silent obeisance as before, and departs.[15]

Like her husband, Martha quickly became, in Adams's words, an "object of veneration and respect." But she could be far less formal and forbidding on private occasions. Murray had the pleasure of dining with both the president and his wife in New York City, as well as a surprise morning visit from Martha Washington. With great pleasure Murray described the "inborn benevolence," and informality of the first lady: "so much of friendship did her salutations connect, so interesting and animated was our conversation, that a bystander would not have entertained an idea of the distance between us, would hardly have supposed, that we met but for the second time, thus benignly good, and thus adorned with social virtues is our Lady Presidentess."[16]

In addition to weekly social evenings, the Washingtons included several ceremonial days in their social calendar. Martha hosted a Christmas Eve entertainment, a New Year's Day reception, and a celebration of the president's birthday on February 22.[17] All official and private entertainments and activities of the first couple were meticulously reported by Federalist John Fenno in his *Gazette of the United States*. The levees, parties, and theater attendances were described for any interested reader, whether in New York City or elsewhere.

Political opponents took advantage of this reportage to criticize the Washingtons and their circle for flirting with aristocratic, even monarchical tendencies. The president's personal demeanor did nothing to dispel these criticisms. Generally untalkative among strangers, the president preserved a rather severe countenance and, when introduced to visitors at his weekly afternoon levees, did not shake hands. As Murray described one such occasion, Washington stood the entire time, "and of course no one else takes a seat nor is the smallest refreshment offered."[18] He was no more friendly at his wife's salon, preferring to let her take center stage as hostess. With the nation's critical eyes upon her, Martha devoted attention to her clothes, manners, and social obligations. Despite her critics' accusations, Martha's levees were neither ostentatious nor pretentious. Her style and personality created a formal setting within which the national elite assembled for sociability and conversation.

This republican salon was a place where the national elite was consolidated through acquaintance and friendship.[19] Important alliances between legislators could be strengthened or initiated through casual meetings of like-minded individuals. Pennsylvania senator William Maclay, perhaps less savvy about the circuits of power than his fellow congressmen, complained that his colleagues seemed more eager to attend the levees than to stay in Congress Hall and discuss important bills. In his opinion this "empty ceremony" did little more than "interfere with the business of the public." Yet for all his complaining, Maclay attended every single one, and usually wore his best suit. He worriedly confided to his diary that he was the recipient of malignant glances from his political antagonists.[20] Maclay, who remained at odds with his fellow Federalists throughout his brief term, was not reelected to his seat.[21] Massachusetts congressman Theodore Sedgewick was no more convinced than Maclay that such receptions were necessary. In a letter to his wife he described attending "Mrs. Washington's rout" in Philadelphia. "I staid about an hour and returned home satiated with the stupid formality of a great number of well dressed people assembled together for the unmeaning purpose of seeing and being seen."[22]

This first political salon, with its brief tenure in New York City, did not fully realize its potential because the Washingtons curtailed many of their public engagements. The death of Washington's mother, and then his own ill health, prevented both Martha and her spouse from hosting or attending many formal and informal social occasions. Despite these setbacks to the development of a national social forum, this first republican salon was able to provide a few American women with a public space where they conversed with men on social and political matters. Alexander Hamilton's wife, Elizabeth, held receiving days, and Mary Morris, wife of wealthy financier Robert Morris, a senator from Pennsylvania, provided entertainment and hospitality to her husband's colleagues and acquaintances. Described by one senator as "the second female Character at Court," Morris and her husband were close friends of the president and first lady.[23]

Simultaneous with the beginnings of this political salon culture was the equally important practice of political sociability between the women of New York City and the resident legislators. Paying calls on the wives of important legislators was part of political business. Mary Morris was the recipient of attentions from her fellow Pennsylvanians. Martha Washington and other congressional wives also received such courtesy calls from congressmen. William Maclay recalled making three calls in one day, first to Mrs. Morris, then to Mrs. Langdon and Mrs. Dalton, the wives of Maclay's fellow senators from Massachusetts and New Hampshire. The ladies, in turn, paid calls on the legislators.[24]

These seemingly social occasions frequently served a political purpose as well. Visits provided women with an opportunity to convey their political sentiments to the men who could act on their behalf. While congressmen and senators sat in session all day, many of their wives and relations did likewise. In addition to the ceremonial occasions when women took part in political ritual, such as the opening of Congress during which the first lady and wives of prominent legislators and diplomats sat with their husbands at the front of the room, women attended the House of Representatives so frequently that a space was reserved for them.[25] Although the Senate held closed meetings for its first six years, the House allowed observers to view its proceedings from the beginning. During Judith Sargent Murray's visit to New York City in 1790, she attended the Congress, sitting in the upper gallery, which was "appropriated to the ladies." Prepared to listen with "enraptured veneration," Murray was disappointed to observe that many members spent their time "walking to and fro—their hats occasionally on, or off—reading the newspapers—lolling upon their writing stands—picking their nails, biting the heads of their canes, examining the beauty of their shoe buckles, ogling the gallery."[26] Despite the inattention of its members, business did get done, and women were able to watch important bills debated.[27]

Some women put the information they gleaned from these visits to good use. Maclay's friend and relative by marriage Isabella Plunket Bell, after having observed Congress in action, was not shy about using her acquaintance with Maclay to tell him how she felt about the proposed removal of Congress to Pennsylvania: "She took occasion to tell me that Mr. Morris, was not sincerely attached to the Pennsylvania interest. That his commercial arrangements were calculated for this place. That the Yorkers depended on him but were lately staggered by an oath which (it was said) he had sworn. That he would have Congress away." Maclay "endeavored to perswade" Bell that Senator Morris was sincere. She caustically replied that Morris had "good reason, now to wish for popularity in Pennsylvania."[28] Some women lobbied hard to persuade their legislative acquaintances to vote a certain way. In what Maclay came to call "the campaigns of Mrs. Ricketts," he described Sarah Ricketts's determination to persuade Maclay and anyone else who would listen that Congress should retain the capital in New York.

Despite the efforts of Mrs. Ricketts and others, Congress voted to move the capital to Philadelphia in 1791. Philadelphians, as the hosts of both the State Assembly and the national capital for nearly a decade between 1791 and 1800, had a greater opportunity than New Yorkers to foster this new, prominent public setting for elite women. Despite its Quaker heritage, the city boasted some of the most elegant architecture, lavish gardens, and varied social occupations—hunting, balls, dancing assemblies—in short, sufficient luxuries, entertainments, and stimulations to dazzle the spartan New Englander and satisfy the wealthy southern planter.[29]

In contrast to New York, Philadelphia was the nation's capital for an extended period. As a result, full complements of official and unofficial social occasions developed that afforded several key women the opportunity to establish themselves as salonnières to the political elite. These included Mrs. Robert Morris, whose husband was a personal friend to the president and the leading financier of the Revolution; Mrs. Henry Knox, wife of the Secretary of War; and Elizabeth Powel, wife of a state senator and former mayor and member of one of Philadelphia's most important families. The most eminent of these women was Anne Willing Bingham (1764-1801), the wife of William Bingham, a wealthy and well-placed Federalist senator. She was the daughter of a rich and socially prominent Philadelphia merchant family and the niece of Elizabeth Willing Powel, wife of Philadelphia's mayor in the 1770s and 1780s. Morris, Powel, and Bingham had already established themselves as intimates of Washington and many prominent Federalists during the Convention in the summer of 1787. All three quickly renewed social ties with the president in the early 1790s and expanded their circle to include senators and congressmen.[30]

The men and women who frequented the social gatherings at the Washingtons' official residence, the Morris or Powel houses, and the Binghams' elaborate mansion were consciously aware that these occasions functioned to smooth over the variety of political and personal differences among guests. As novelist Charles Brockden Brown wrote in the *Ladies Magazine* in 1792, female moral superiority had the power to "teach our sex politeness and affability," and could "render us worthy members of society."[31] French visitors, themselves familiar with the salons at home, remarked favorably on American women's similar abilities. The Marquis de Chastellux noted of Elizabeth Powel that she was "well read and intelligent; but what distinguished her most is her taste for conversation, and the truly European use that she knows how to make of her understanding and information."[32] In Philadelphia, Powel and her niece Anne Bingham brought together men of different parties and political sentiments and encouraged them to converse with each other in a serene setting, removed from the floor of Congress, where tensions ran high and civility was stretched to its limits. And as the wives of prominent Federalists, they also provided an informal setting for members of Congress and the administration to strengthen political ties within the party.

It was no accident that Philadelphia women knew how to employ European ways. Some hostesses and many of their guests had some directly familiarity with French social customs. The Binghams, Adamses, Jefferson, and Major William Jackson (who was President Washington's secretary from 1789 to 1791 and married Anne Bingham's sister Elizabeth Willing in 1795) all visited France in the 1780s.

Some Americans clearly derived more from this European education than did others. The Adamses, for example, were suspicious of the opulent display, and lack of "modesty and delicacy" in women such as Franklin's friend Madame Helvétius, whose salon welcomed the many Americans visiting Paris.[33] Likewise, Nabby Adams suspected that Anne Bingham, who with her husband spent three years in Europe, learned all too well the ways of these women: Adams thought that Bingham rouged more than was "advantageous to her," and showed her lack of taste by wearing the latest fashions designed by Mlle. Bertin, dressmaker to Marie Antoinette. Even worse, like Madame Helvétius, Bingham exhibited "an exuberance of sprightliness and wit" that taken together, to Nabby's mind, meant Bingham had become "quite a French woman."[34] On the other hand, Nabby reported favorably on Bingham's skills in polite conversation: "She joins in every conversation in company; and when engaged herself in conversing with you, she will, by joining directly in another chit chat with another party, convince you, that she was all attention to every one."[35] Anne Bingham learned an essential quality of a true salonnière: harmonizing disparate political opinions and characters and facilitating political business in an informal setting. As Bingham herself recognized in many of the French women she encountered, "their education is of a higher cast, and by great cultivation they procure a happy variety of genius, which forms their conversation to please either the fop or the philosopher."[36]

In addition to the worldly education she received in Europe, Bingham had been tutored in the social graces by her paternal aunt, Eliz-

abeth Powel, herself a practiced salonnière.[37] Married to a twice-elect-
ed mayor of Philadelphia who served as a state senator from 1790
until his death in 1793, Powel was a particular favorite of the president, often "eagerly and passionately" arguing politics with Washington during his tenure in the city.[38] In recognition of her progressive
thinking on instruction for girls, her friend Dr. Benjamin Rush dedicated his essay "Some Thoughts on Female Education" to her. Indeed,
young Anne Willing could not help but benefit from the instruction
as well as example provided by Powel. She grew to be an articulate,
gracious hostess, well placed through family and marriage to become
the premiere salonnière of the capital city.

Bingham earned this prominence in the capital city due to a combination of circumstances and intention: because of her close relationship with her Aunt Powel, she enjoyed an intimate friendship with the
president and first Lady. Her husband was a senator for Pennsylvania
and a leading Federalist with financial ties to men like Robert Morris.
And with great wealth at their disposal, Anne and William Bingham
deliberately sought to recreate the type of social environment they had
encountered in London and Paris in order to attain preeminence
among the political elite.[39] With these social and political connections, education and knowledge of European salons, and wealth, Anne
Bingham was the unchallenged leader of national society in the capital city.

The Binghams built their residence, known as the Mansion House,
in 1786, just after their return from Europe. It was spacious, elegant,
and furnished with the finest of British and French furniture and
accoutrements. Modeled after the Duke of Manchester's London
mansion, it had ample space for entertaining, a feature particularly
desired by the Binghams. Visitors to the Mansion House entered into
a large central hall, elaborately decorated with marble. Spaced around
the hall on pedestals were busts of Voltaire, Rousseau, Benjamin
Franklin, and several other stone and bronze figures. The ground floor
had two formal parlors, and upstairs on the first floor was a ball-
room.[40] From the outset, the Binghams intended to entertain visitors
on a grand scale—the dining room contained twenty-four "leather-
bottom mahogany" chairs, a French dining set of three hundred and

fifty pieces, two hundred pieces of silver tableware, and two hundred and six drinking glasses. Most of the interior furnishings were purchased in Europe, including a glass chandelier for the dining room and several mirrors.[41]

The Binghams' affairs were held in large rooms, brightly lit by devices whose employment was designed to facilitate "entertainment and display."[42] The downstairs rooms had candlesticks, but also several girandoles, which provided brighter light reflected from mirrors mounted behind them. There were mirrors everywhere, reflecting light as well as the visages of guests. Although the effect must have been brilliant, their mode of formal entertainment met with mixed responses from Americans. Virginian Arthur Lee remarked that "The vanity and nonsense, is nothing worse of French parade. [T]hey are more fit subjects of ridicule than admiration."[43] Lee probably had in mind the Binghams' introduction of the practice of a footman announcing guests as they arrived, a practice they abandoned after a series of misadventures. Americans happily adopted some European manners while quite definitely rejecting others.

The Binghams invited three types of guests to their home: family members and close friends, Federalist associates of William Bingham, and celebrities (like Washington, as well as foreign dignitaries and visitors). Washington dined there frequently, and remarked on the "great splendor" of the food to be found at the Binghams' table. In December 1798 he dined with the family every night between the second and the thirteenth.[44] Thomas Jefferson, already a close enough friend to Bingham that he was willing to purchase her Parisian face cream for her, was also welcomed into this Federalist enclave. Even William Maclay, ostensibly a Federalist, but usually at odds with his party, and particularly with William Bingham, enjoyed an evening of dinner and conversation. Like everyone else, Maclay was impressed with the style and scale of the Bingham's abode: "I cannot say barely that he affects to entertain in a Stile beyond every thing in this place, or perhaps in America. He really does so. There is a propriety a neatness a Cleanliness that adds to the Splendor of his costly furniture, and elegant Apartments."[45]

Many contemporary observations of Anne Bingham's behavior,

character, and entertainments come from the letters, diaries, and memoirs of her guests and acquaintances. Abigail Adams noted that from the first reception held by Martha Washington in the new capital in 1791, Anne Bingham had "certainly given laws to the ladies here, in fashion and elegance; their manners and appearance are superior to what I have seen."[46] Another visitor remarked that, in her own home, Bingham's "conversational cleverness in French and English, graceful manners, and polite tact in doing the honors of her splendid establishment, rendered it exceedingly attractive."[47]

Anne Bingham's role as a salonnière was cemented by her quali-

View in Third Street from Spruce Street, William Birch and Sons, 1800. This street scene shows the imposing scale and grandeur of the Bingham mansion. Courtesy of the Library Company of Philadelphia.

fications in conversation, elegance, and elaborate dinner-giving. Whereas Martha Washington's salon was reputedly cold and uncomfortable, Bingham had the ability, according to Nabby Adams, "to keep several conversations going at once and still appear to give attention to everyone, and to politely and subtly flatter others."[48] Despite the disparity in their hostessing skills, Washington and Bingham shared a participation in a distinctly American cultural environment.

Unlike French salon culture, which was removed from the political sphere, American salons were an arena for national political society. Bingham entertained politicians of opposing ideologies such as Thomas Jefferson and Alexander Hamilton, as well as foreign dignitaries such as Sir Robert Liston, British minister to the United States, and political refugees such as the Viscount Noailles, Louis Philippe, the oldest son of Louis XVI. Furthermore, Bingham's ability to be "all attention to every one" meant she joined in conversations on politics as well as on dress, food, entertainment, and reading. John Adams remarked after sitting next to Bingham at one of her dinner parties that he had carried on "something of a political conversation with her." She "had more ideas on the subject" than he supposed, "and a corrector judgement."[49] John Adams was perhaps surprised at Bingham's knowledge. His own wife and daughter continually criticized both Binghams for their ostentation and social climbing, occupations which should have left little time for keeping up with political issues. Adams did not seem disapproving of her political conversation. Nor, considering whom he was married to, would he have been unused to women speaking their minds on political subjects.

The experience of conversing with women on political topics, in a gathering of top government leaders, had become accepted behavior. As the French Revolution took a bloody turn in 1793 with the execution of the king, many Americans expressed their revulsion. Jefferson reported the reactions of men and women at a dinner that included Anne and William Bingham where both "the warmest Jacobinism" as well as "the most heart felt aristocracy" were represented. Jefferson noted that the wives present, women "of the first circle" of Philadelphia society, were "all open-mouthed against the murderers of a sovereign, and they generally speak those sentiments which the more cautious husband smothers."[50] Another eyewitness to Anne Bingham's political expression was more tolerant in his opinion of her publicly spoken anti-French views than Jefferson. While Anne Bingham and her daughter visited the Knox family at Montpelier in Maine, the Reverend Paul Coffin paid a call. His impression of Bingham was that she was "sensible." She "had been in France, could talk of European politics, and give the history of the late King of France, etc."[51] Though we do not know what Bingham said on either of these occasions, from the response of her audiences, we can infer that she took a Federalist line on the radical stage of the Revolution, and perhaps like many of her sister Americans, she, too, felt outrage at the treatment of the queen. These were sentiments that Jefferson would not have shared, though Coffin and the Knoxes may have.

Bingham's political acuity was not merely for the benefit of pleasing her guests. Her correspondence with Thomas Jefferson, of which only one letter has survived, clearly shows her belief in women's right to involve themselves in politics. Jefferson described for her the atmosphere in Paris in 1788 where "all the world is run politically mad. Men, women, children talk nothing else; and you know that naturally they talk much, loud and warm." This political fervor interfered with the polite social intercourse Jefferson expected to enjoy in salons. Perhaps more to reassure himself rather than Bingham, Jefferson assumed that "our good ladies, I trust, have been too wise to wrinkle their foreheads with politics." He credited American women with "the good sense to value domestic happiness above all other." He went on to describe the political activities of the women of Paris, assuring Bingham that such women were "Amazona" compared to the American "Angels," who were wise enough to know that politics was beyond their designated sphere. He refused to give her details of "political news of battles and sieges, Turks and Russians, because you would be less handsome after reading them."[52]

Bingham disagreed with Jefferson and told him so. His comment that politics rendered her "less handsome" did not stop Bingham from declaring her opinions: "The candor with which you express your sentiments, merits a sincere declaration of mine." Perhaps thinking of her own role in the American capital she remarked, "In what other country can be found a Marquise de Coigny, who, young and handsome, takes a lead in all the fashionable dissipation of life, and at more serious moments collects at her house an assembly of the Litterati, whom she charms with her knowledge and her *bel esprit*." As to Jefferson's complaints about French women interfering in politics and his assurance that American women knew better, Bingham corrected him. She praised French women who, "either by the gentle arts of persuasion, or by the commanding force of superior attractions and address," had "obtained that rank and consideration in society, which the sex are entitled to, and which they in vain contend for in other countries." Bingham declared that American women were therefore "bound in gratitude to admire and revere them, for asserting our privileges, as much as the friends of the liberties of mankind reverence the successful struggles of the American patriots."[53] The language of rights clearly affected Bingham's prose. Like others of this era, she easily made the transition from general to particular—from abstract political theory to the concerns of women.

Anne Bingham is well remembered in the various memoirs and reminiscences of Philadelphia society in the late eighteenth century. Her ability to facilitate political sociability by bringing together a wide variety of individuals at her balls, dinners, and theater parties, as well as her patronage of rising authors such as Susanna Rowson, marked her success as a true salonnière. The most remarkable thing about Bingham's achievement is that she elevated social occasions to a new level. The combination of her well-learned lessons at home and abroad, with her presence at the center of the national political community, provided Bingham the opportunity to help create a public political space for women which had not previously existed in America. The intermingling of social and political groups, and their presence at the homes of prominent women such as Bingham allowed women to be a visible part of political society. As the focus of attention, Anne Bingham's opinions were remembered by her observers. But Bingham was not the only woman present on these occasions (indeed it was generally other *women* such as the Adamses who were her most acute observers and harshest critics), and all of them freely articulated their ideas and opinions on topics of the day.

It is perhaps not a coincidence, then, that in the print culture of the era the salon became a prime vehicle for commenting upon women's political engagement. Benjamin Franklin Bache printed the reported conversation of several young women, all actively involved in political issues, in the *Aurora* in 1791.[54] And Charles Brockden Brown's novel *Alcuin* presented the most extended example of the uses of the salon for the discussion of women's rights. Brown may never have set foot in the Bingham mansion, but he would certainly have known of Anne Bingham's hospitality, and perhaps even of her opinions.[55]

Bingham's career as the leading salonnière of national society was cut short when she died of pneumonia in the spring of 1801. Her daughters possessed the upbringing, wealth, and social status to have followed in their mother's footsteps, but both left America, along with William Bingham, to reside in England soon after her death. But the political salon culture she fostered during the capital's Philadelphia years continued to flourish when the federal government removed to the banks of the Potomac.

A seamless transition from scattered pre-Revolutionary nonpolitical salons to the consolidation of a national elite in the capital cities of New York, Philadelphia, and then Washington, enabled women to talk politics, further the agendas of spouses and friends, and sometimes lobby on their own behalf for political outcomes. How was this possible? Did no one notice that women were far more visible in political settings? That they more frequently discussed politics in public gatherings of men and women? For the most part, this increased public presence went unremarked because women were already in charge of a vehicle for sociability that readily lent itself to a political environment in which elites could function. Women had always talked politics—at the tea table, in the bedchamber, at dancing assemblies. What transpired in the 1790s was not a break with the past, but rather a widening of scope, an increasing of opportunities, and a raising of the stakes. The creation of a national elite in the capital cities allowed women, those who accompanied their spouses to the capital as well as those who were permanent residents there, to learn firsthand about the process and politics of government. They sat in the gallery of Congress in the federal building in New York or the statehouse in

Philadelphia, where they had a seating area designated for them. They listened to husbands, friends, and visitors discuss strategies. In the process women themselves became more acute politicians. Women spoke openly to the chief officers of the land. They expressed their thoughts in public settings—Elizabeth Powel argued with the president over the tea table, Anne Bingham told Vice President Adams of her views at dinner, and Mrs. Ricketts lobbied senators to keep the capital in New York.

Just as women's presence at militia presentations and their presence in the theater singing "Hail Columbia" aided the Federalist cause, the establishment of political salons facilitated the informal workings of the political elite.

Women's participation in political culture expanded because it met the needs of those in power. Men who interested themselves in the government sought out the salons of the women who brought together the right people for conversation, the establishment of alliances, or simply the acknowledgment of common interests. Though not the only venue for informal politicking, salons were an acknowledged part of political society. And as Senator Maclay's grudging attendance indicates, even the most reluctant understood the benefits such occasions conferred on their careers and political agendas. Like the salons of Enlightenment France, American salons depended on women to facilitate polite discourse. Unlike salonnières of the Old World, however, American women carved for themselves an accepted place in political as well as intellectual culture. The informal networks of power that quickly established themselves in New York, Philadelphia, and finally Washington permitted American women to achieve a foothold in the world of politics.

Conclusion

ON JULY FOURTH, 1800, a group of New Jersey women publicly assembled to celebrate the day. Democratic Republican newspapers reported that the women drank toasts to "the female Republicans of France," and to "the rights of women—may they never be curtailed."[1] Despite the Federalists' dominance of the public stage in the late 1790s, some Democratic Republicans continued to claim July Fourth as a day to celebrate their political views, and, in this particular case, to assert the ties that bound American and French women together. Like the public "marriage" of the widows in South Carolina, these New Jersey women saw themselves not only as members of the political nation, but also as members in an international female community. Women in the 1780s and 1790s were consciously given a role in partisan political displays—celebrating French victories, urging militia troops to defend American shores—thereby becoming political actors in their own right. When the Middletown, Connecticut, women toasted Martha Washington and Abigail Adams at their July Fourth celebration in 1798, they, like the New Jersey Democratic Republicans two years later, championed the role of women in the public life of the nation. The official vision of the new republic as constructed by the Grand Federal Procession in 1788 excluded most women, yet, as these examples and the others presented in this volume demonstrate, during the following decade the opportunities provided by the extensive political partisanship allowed American women to claim a place for themselves in the public life of the nation.

The task of this book has been to examine the avenues through which women's presence became important or even central to the

competition for control of the nation's political culture, and to understand how the conservative political ideology of the era, which has
generally been construed as reinforcing the identity of women with
the private sphere, was at least in part responsible for propelling them
into the public sphere. Despite a lack of change in women's legal or
economic status in this era, this study has shown that our categories of
female identity for this time period require a reassessment. Women's
lives *were* changed by the political and cultural developments of the
late eighteenth century.

What I have confirmed through the course of this study is that
women clearly were part of the public sphere in this era—more so
than they had been previously—largely as a result of political, social,
and cultural developments in the late 1780s and 1790s. The political
ideologies of both the Democratic Republicans and the Federalists
permitted women to expand their public roles, thus further blurring
the line between public and private that in theory limited women's
activities within the public sphere, but in practice was already under
attack. Moreover, the concept of republican womanhood, a construction intended to prescribe essentially private behavior for women, in
reality was taken beyond the domestic sphere to allow women to gain
entry into the public political world. This happened as a result of both
the Federalists' and Democratic Republicans' need to claim the alle-
giance of women in order to promote the legitimacy of their claim to
represent the best interests of the nation. This conscious appeal to
women facilitated their public activities in the form of intellectual, literary, and theatrical pursuits, participation in ceremonies and celebrations, and the development of informal political networks. Some
women's historians deny that there was significant change for women
in this era, based on their (correct) assessment of the lack of innovation in terms of women's legal, economic, or political status, and their
assumption that this fact confirms that separate spheres ideology was
as true in practice as in theory. Yet the undeniable presence of women
in the public sphere forces us to reassess how we categorize female
experience and identity.

Women did not enter the public sphere on the same terms that men
did, however. They carried with them the attributes traditionally

assigned to them in their role in the private sphere. But women's ability to promote moral behavior did not confine them to a domestic setting; instead, this talent made them perfectly suited to the needs of society as a whole. Women could promote the welfare of the nation in the public sphere because they were responsible for the welfare of their families in the private sphere. But what did this do to the public-private dichotomy? For women in the late eighteenth century, the personal became political and the once-private became public. Acknowledged as a necessary ingredient in the development of a good society as well as the creation a good family, women expanded their place in public life through a variety of venues.

Print culture, replete with arguments, ideas, and contradictions, provided a contextual framework for the activities of many of the women who participated in the public political culture of the era. The writings of Mary Wollstonecraft and Judith Sargent Murray epitomized the breadth of the discussion over women's authority and responsibilities in marriage, their economic self-sufficiency, and their participation in public political life. Though the range of American opinion on these topics was wide, an enthusiasm for increased female autonomy was expressed in many essays, plays, novels, letters, and diaries. By creating a new public forum that addressed the needs, desires, and abilities of women, the magazines, novels, and didactic essays of the day became the agents of change.

As literacy and readership expanded and print production became less expensive in the early nineteenth century, magazines and novels proliferated, many of them authored by women. Women wrote short stories, religious tracts, and children's books as well. Susanna Rowson, for example, retired from life on the stage to found her own female academy and produce textbooks. Other women also wrote grammars, biographies, and histories, beginning with Mercy Otis Warren's *History of the Rise, Progress and Termination of the American Revolution* (1805).[2] Most dramatic was the increase in magazines that catered to a female readership. Some, like *The Port Folio*, though not explicitly a women's magazine, championed female equality. Others, such as Mary Clarke Carr's *Intellectual Regale or Ladies Tea Tray*, and *Godey's Lady's Book*, catered to a rapidly expanding female audience. *Philadelphia*

Repository and Weekly Register was a forum for the talents of James Neal's pupils at the Young Ladies Academy; it regularly published essays, addresses, and poems composed by these "fair daughters of America."[3] Female readers were also catered to by the circulating libraries of the nineteenth century. Many of the smaller ones were run by women, who sometimes combined their libraries with millinery stores or fancy good shops—public spaces where women would feel welcome. Larger establishments sometimes provided separate entrances for women, or maintained separate reading rooms for them. For example, Joseph Robinson advertised that his circulating library contained a women's room with reading tables, writing desks, and a piano on which they could try new music before making a purchase.[4]

Many of the well-read eighteenth-century women had used the public and private occasions provided by news of the French Revolution to express their political sentiments. Collectively and individually, women involved themselves in political events and political controversies. William Cobbett may have been irritated by the "whole tribe of female scribblers and politicians" he encountered in public, but the activities of such women reflected a sophisticated political consciousness that resulted from women's exposure to the ideas and arguments of the day, as well as careful thought and conversation, wide reading, and the experience of revolution. Women in the 1780s and 1790s recreated roles from the American Revolution, but they also innovated female-focused activities. Women's choice of clothing, forms of address, their participation in political rituals and celebrations, and the widespread reportage on these activities in the nation's press, all helped expand women's civic identity. Women's public participation in politics in the nineteenth century drew upon the legacies of the early republic. In the Whig campaign of 1840, for instance, women participated in party events such as public processions, the presentation of standards, picnics, and balls.[5] In addition, they were a strong presence in electioneering, using their traditional female power bases—home, kin, and neighbors—to promote Whig candidates. This "Whig Womanhood" drew on the experiences of Federalist women in the 1790s, and assumed that women would take a public role in promoting partisan politics.[6] Just as the Democratic Republicans had commissioned

Anne Kemble Hatton to write a play expressing their partisan principles, fifty years later the Whigs hired Lucy Kenney to author political
pamphlets. And the great Daniel Webster employed his rhetorical
powers to persuade an audience of twelve hundred women in Richmond, Virginia, to support the Whig cause.[7] It is difficult, however, to
draw a direct line from the activities of women in the late eighteenth
century to those involved in the political and social causes of the nineteenth century. Though precedents were set, this did not immediately
produce any consistently accepted public political role for women. It
was in areas of American life less avowedly political that women more
systematically increased their public presence.

Women's participation in the cultural life of the nation included the
creation and performance of American plays. Political issues dominated Hatton's *Tammany* and Susanna Rowson's *Slaves in Algiers*, but
women's roles were considered as well. Female performers portrayed
American women as strong, self-reliant, and heroic. Rowson and
Judith Sargent Murray deliberately wrote female parts which highlighted women's strength, self-reliance, and courage. The audiences
for these plays included increasingly greater numbers of women, many
of whom were also magazine and novel readers. They were the women
who sent their daughters to the new female academies, and those who
most likely read Wollstonecraft's *Vindication* and Judith Sargent Murray's *Gleaner*. In the early nineteenth century women increasingly
wrote for, performed in, and attended the theater. More American-
born actresses took to the stage, although British imports like Fanny
Kemble still dazzled audiences. Strong female roles continued,
emphasizing women's courage and patriotism. *She Would Be a Soldier*,
for example, written at the end of the War of 1812, depicted a
woman's successful masquerade during the conflict. As female theatergoers became an increasingly valued part of the audience, the theaters began to cater to their comfort. William Warren, manager of the
Chestnut Street theater, announced the opening of the "Ladies Coffee Room" in December 1808, a space where men were welcome only
if they were "in the party of Ladies."[8] As theaters increasingly catered
to their female audience, attendance began to include young women
as well. In 1805, the parents of future author Catherine Sedgwick first

took her to a New York theater when she was eleven years old. Believing that the theater could be instructive as well as entertaining, instructors such as Mrs. Gibson, who ran a girls' school in Richmond, Virginia, took her young charges to the theater there in 1811.[9]

Armed with education, wealth, and for some, a firsthand knowledge of French and English society, the salonnières of Philadelphia had promoted a central role for women in political culture by fostering the interconnection between social and political relationships. The salons created under Washington's presidency offered elite women in the inner circles of national power a place in political culture that they did not have before 1789. Salons such as Anne Bingham's owed much to a transatlantic culture of civility and social intercourse, but defined itself within a developing American national political elite.

After Jefferson's election in 1800, Democratic Republicans, rather than Federalists, controlled much of the political scene. Their ideology, which allied slaveholders, farmers, and urban artisans, officially left no space for black males or white or black women. But women had already attained a foothold in political culture, and their influence expanded, even within the Democratic Republican party. Washington City's sole reason for existing was politics. There, society and government continued to blend as they had in Philadelphia. Jefferson's Democratic Republican party held sway between 1801 and 1824, giving the leading social center a different partisan cast than the capital had during the Philadelphia years. And the president's refusal to hold levees such as those of Washington and Adams fostered alternative sociopolitical gatherings rather than quelling them. Margaret Bayard Smith, wife of Samuel Harrison Smith, a close ally of Jefferson, was one of the first Washington salonnières. She spent much of her early life in Philadelphia, and, as the daughter of a Federalist, she may have witnessed firsthand the social practices of Bingham, Powell, and Washington. Men and women gathered at her home to discuss both political and intellectual topics of the day. Here, to an even greater extent than in Philadelphia, and much to Jefferson's dismay, women were part of the political scene. As Smith noted, women continued to attend the House of Representatives and the Supreme Court: "On every public occasion, a launch, an oration, an inauguration, in the court, in the representative hall, as well as the drawing room, they are treated with mark'd distinction."[10]   When James Madison assumed the presidency in 1808, his wife, Dolly, or "Queen Dolly" as her contemporaries called her, reinstituted the White House salon and took firm command of Washington society. Through at-homes, state dinners, and personal calls on Washington society, Madison not only facilitated political alliances, but actively participated in the system of political patronage presence.[11]

In addition to the extension of practices established in the early republic, women continued the transformation of private roles into public, and often political, ones. One of the ways that they broadened their public activities was through the creation of benevolent organizations. Taking their cue from the Ladies' Association in 1780, nineteenth-century women created permanent organizations and drew on their identities as moral watchdogs of the nation. Women used their privately run benevolent organizations to lobby state legislatures and seek public funds for their causes. They sometimes combined these new activities with practices from the 1780s and 1790s, such as the July Fourth rallies staged by female temperance societies in the 1820s.[12] Thus the innovations begun in the late eighteenth century fostered a generation of young women with the intellectual tools to make good choices, develop their talents, and ultimately, assert their right to fuller participation in the life of the nation.

This study was designed to explore the crucial years of the early republic when the achievement of a capital city made it possible for politics, society, and culture to develop and thrive on a national scale. Philadelphia served this purpose well for almost ten years at the end of the eighteenth century. The events and developments of this particular time and place contributed to ideas and practices that became a watershed in the historical evolution of women's roles. Women's public presence was one of the defining features of the American community in the early republic. And the foothold women gained in political and cultural arenas laid the foundation for even greater female participation in the century ahead.

Notes

INTRODUCTION

1. Report of event from November 1793 in the *Independent Gazette*, Wednesday, February 26, 1794. See Lynn Hunt, *Politics, Culture and Class in the French Revolution* (Berkeley: University of California Press, 1982), 63–65.

2. *Aurora*, August 9, 28, 1794.

3. Though explicitly copied from French ceremonies, Americans already had their own highly staged rituals as models. In 1790 Judith Sargent Murray described this July Fourth ceremony at Philadelphia's Schuylkill Gardens: "The Arms of America and France entwined by Liberty—a rich display of Fire works, exhibited from the Lawn, in front of the Federal temple—Thirteen Boys, and an equal number of Girls, issuing from the Grove, habited as shepherds, and shepherdesses, and proceeding to the Federal Temple, chanting responsively, an Ode to Liberty, with a number of songs, Odes, and Choruses, in honour of the auspicious event, which the day commemorated." Judith Sargent Murray to her parents, July 10, 1790, *From Gloucester to Philadelphia in 1790: Observations, Anecdotes, and Thoughts from the Eighteenth-Century Letters of Judith Sargent Murray*, ed. Bonnie Hurd Smith (Cambridge, Mass.: Judith Sargent Murray Society, 1998), 175.

4. Barbara Welter first described this new definition of gender roles which developed in the early nineteenth century, known as separate spheres ideology, in "The Cult of True Womanhood: 1820–1860," *American Quarterly* 18 (1966), 151–174. Also see Nancy F. Cott, *The Bonds of Womanhood: "Woman's Sphere" in New England, 1780–1835* (New Haven: Yale University Press, 1977). For recent thoughts on how historians should move beyond this conceptual framework see Linda Kerber et al., "Beyond Roles, Beyond Spheres: Thinking About Gender in the Early Republic," *William and Mary Quarterly* 46, no. 3 (1989), 565–585.

The concept of Republican Womanhood is treated extensively in Linda Kerber, *Women of the Republic: Intellect and Ideology in Revolutionary America* (Chapel Hill: University of North Carolina Press, 1980), and Mary Beth Norton, *Liberty's Daughters: The Revolutionary Experience of American Women,*

1750–1800 (Boston: Little, Brown, 1980). These are two careful studies of women during the American Revolution and the years immediately following. Both demonstrate how political events affected women's consciousness about their domestic position and encouraged society as a whole to question the traditional status of women.

For arguments against the idea that the post-Revolutionary era brought significant change for women the following works are important: Joan Hoff, *Law, Gender, and Injustice: A Legal History of U.S. Women* (New York: New York University Press, 1991); Elaine F. Crane, "Dependence in the Era of Independence: The Role of Women in a Republican Society," in *The American Revolution: Its Character and Limits*, ed. Jack P. Greene (New York: New York University Press, 1987); Jan Lewis, "The Republican Wife: Virtue and Seduction in the Early Republic," *William and Mary Quarterly* 44 (1987); Rosemarie Zagarri, "Morals, Manners, and the Republican Mother," *American Quarterly* 44, no. 2 (June 1992); Jan Lewis, "'Of every age sex and condition': The Representation of Women in the Constitution," *Journal of the Early Republic* 15, no. 3 (fall 1995), 359–388.

5. In recent years, historians have relied on variations or emendations to the ideas of Jürgen Habermas. According to Habermas, the public sphere consisted of elite and middle-class individuals possessing enough education and opportunity to read, write, and converse. Implicitly, the eighteenth-century public sphere was inclusive: "anyone with access to cultural products—books, plays, journals—had at least a potential claim on the attention of the culture-debating public." Craig Calhoun, introduction to *Habermas and the Public Sphere* (Cambridge, Mass.: MIT Press, 1992), 13. It included "all private people, persons who—insofar as they were propertied and educated—[could be] readers, listeners, and spectators." Jürgen Habermas, *The Transformation of the Public Sphere*, trans. T. Burger and F. Lawrence (Cambridge, Mass.: MIT Press, 1989), 37, quoted in Calhoun, *Habermas and the Public Sphere,* 13. The existence of this public sphere enabled the articulation and validation of "processes that promote open discussion among a wide spectrum of social actors on a wide range of concerns." In other words, the public sphere had the "capacity to bring citizens together to rationally present, discuss, and reach a consensus about the general good." Most historians take their definition from Habermas, "The Public Sphere: An Encyclopedia Article (1964)," *New German Critique* 5, no. 2 (1974), 49–55. But as Habermas explains, this inclusiveness only extended to the propertied and the well educated, a group almost exclusively composed of men. The antithesis, the private sphere, had long been identified with women.

6. Rosemarie Zagarri, "The Rights of Man and Woman in Post-Revolutionary America," *William and Mary Quarterly* 55, no. 2 (April 1998).

7. See Nancy Fraser, "Rethinking the Public Sphere: A Contribution to the Critique of Actually Existing Democracy," in Calhoun, *Habermas and the*

Public Sphere, 116, for a discussion of such counterpublics.

8. Linda K. Kerber, "The Republican Mother: Women and the Enlightenment—An American Perspective," in *Toward an Intellectual History of Women* (Chapel Hill: University of North Carolina Press, 1997), 41–62. The most extensive treatment of the topic of sensibility is G. J. Barker-Benfield, *The Culture of Sensibility: Sex and Society in Eighteenth-Century Britain* (Chicago: University of Chicago Press, 1992).

9. Three important works on this subject have recently been published: Simon P. Newman, *Parades and the Politics of the Street: Festive Culture in the Early American Republic* (Philadelphia: University of Pennsylvania Press, 1997); Len Travers, *Celebrating the Fourth: Independence Day and the Rites of Nationalism in the Early Republic* (Amherst: University of Massachusetts Press, 1997); and David L. Waldstreicher, *The Making of American Nationalism: Celebrations and Political Culture, 1776-1820* (Chapel Hill: University of North Carolina Press, 1997).

10. Judith Sargent Murray, letter to her parents, June 12, 1790. *From Gloucester to Philadelphia in 1790*, 106.

11. These population figures come from Travers, *Celebrating the Fourth*, 118, and Ethel E. Rasmusson, "Capital on the Delaware: The Philadelphia Upper Class in Transition, 1789–1801" (Ph.D. diss., Brown University, 1962), 39–40.

12. Linda K. Kerber, "The Republican Ideology of the Revolutionary Generation," in *Toward an Intellectual History of Women* (Chapel Hill: University of North Carolina Press, 1997), 131–156.

13. Linda K. Kerber, "'I Have Don much to Carrey on the Warr': Women and the Shaping of Republican Ideology After the American Revolution," in *Women and Politics in the Age of the Democratic Revolution*, 232.

14. Norton, *Liberty's Daughters*, 219.

15. Ibid., 223–224.

16. Hoff, *Law, Gender, and Injustice*, 81; Crane, "Dependence in the Era of Independence."

On divorce, see Kerber, *Women of the Republic*, chapter 6; Nancy F. Cott, "Divorce and the Changing Status of Women in Eighteenth-Century Massachusetts," *William and Mary Quarterly* (October 1976).

17. Karin Wulf, *Not All Wives: Women of Colonial Philadelphia* (Ithaca: Cornell University Press, 1999).

18. This decision was finally made twenty-one years after Grace Galloway's death. The Pennsylvania Supreme Court declared that "Joseph Galloway's attainder for treason vested no claim to the real estate of his wife." Elizabeth Evans, *Weathering the Storm: Women of the American Revolution* (New York: Charles Scribner's Sons, 1975), 244; Carol Berkin, *First Generations: Women in Colonial America* (New York: Hill and Wang, 1998), 164–168.

Jane Bartram had far less property than did Grace Galloway, but much more clearly articulated her political views. Bartram, when ordered to leave Pennsylvania in 1782 because of her husband's loyalism, petitioned the state to allow her to return, arguing that she should not be punished "'merely from a fault of her husband's.' She claimed to have always 'manifested a friendly and warm desire for the Liberties and rights of the United States of America.'" Wayne Bodle, "Jane Bartram's 'Application': Her Struggle for Survival, Stability, and Self-Determination in Revolutionary Pennsylvania," *Pennsylvania Magazine of History and Biography* 115, no. 2 (1991), 200–201.

19. Joan R. Gundersen, "Independence, Citizenship, and the American Revolution," *Signs* 13, no. 1 (1987), 59–77, 66; Judith Apter Klinghoffer and Lois Elkis, "'The Petticoat Electors': Women's Suffrage in New Jersey, 1776–1807," *Journal of the Early Republic* 12 (summer 1992), 161–193. Joan Hoff credits liberal Quakers in the Garden State for maintaining rather than innovating a practice. *Femes soles* in the colonial era had participated in local property and tax matters and as litigants in county court systems. Hoff, *Law, Gender, and Injustice*, 99.

20. Lewis, "The Republican Wife," 689–721. Kerber, *Women of the Republic*. Republican ideology was not the only influence on American's thinking. As Rosemarie Zagarri has shown, the Scottish Enlightenment thinkers also considered women's roles. Republican motherhood "was actually part of a broad, long-term, transatlantic reformulation of the role and status of women." "Morals, Manners, and the Republican Mother," 193.

21. Lewis, "'Of every age sex and condition'," 371, 377.

22. Kerber, "The Republican Ideology of the Revolutionary Generation," 148.

23. Ibid., 707.

24. *Lady's Magazine and Repository of Entertaining Knowledge* (Philadelphia), 1 (1792), 64–65.

25. The play was performed Monday, October 20, at the New Theater in Philadelphia. This review appeared in the *Theatrical Censor and Critical Miscellany* (1806), 123.

26. Lewis, "'Of every age sex and condition,'" 703. Margaret Nash, "Rethinking Republican Motherhood: Benjamin Rush and the Young Ladies' Academy of Philadelphia," *Journal of the Early Republic* 17 (summer 1997), 171–191.

27. Norton, *Liberty's Daughters*, 68; see all of chapter 9 on female education in eighteenth-century America. Benjamin Rush, *Thoughts upon Female Education, Accommodated to the Present State of Society, Manners and Government in the United States of America* (Philadelphia, 1787).

28. August 13, 1783, Abigail Adams, *The Book of Abigail and John: Selected Letters of the Adams Family, 1762-1784*, ed. Lyman H. Butterfield, et al. (Cambridge, Mass.: Harvard University Press, 1975), 360.

29. Ironically, this new sensibility occurred simultaneously with the retreat

of middle-class women from making economic contributions to the household. See Jeanne Boydston, "The Woman Who Wasn't There: Women's Market Labor and the Transition to Capitalism in the United States," *Journal of the Early Republic* 16, no. 2 (summer 1996), 183–206.

30. The Young Ladies' Academy of Philadelphia included these two topics. For more information on female education in the early republic, see Kerber, *Women of the Republic*, chapter 7; Thomas Woody, *A History of Women's Education in the United States*, vol. 1 (New York, 1929), and Jill K. Conway, "Perspectives on the History of Women's Education in the United States," *History of Education Quarterly* 14, no. 1 (spring 1974), 1–12.

31. Nancy F. Rosenberg, "The Word Within, the World Without: Quaker Education in Philadelphia, 1682–1837" (Ph.D. diss., University of Michigan, 1991). On Philadelphia Quaker education, see George S. Brookes, *Friend Anthony Benezet* (Philadelphia, 1837); Nancy F. Rosenberg, "An Uncommon Language: Education and Social Perceptions in Eighteenth and Early Nineteenth Century Philadelphia," paper presented to the 1987 Annual Meeting of the American Historical Association, Washington, D.C. On non-Quaker female education in Philadelphia, see Ann D. Gordon, "The Young Ladies' Academy of Philadelphia," in *Women of America: A History*, ed. Carol Ruth Berkin and Mary Beth Norton (Boston: Houghton Mifflin, 1979), 69–91.

32. Caleb Bingham, "Oration upon Female Education, Pronounced by a Member of One of the Public Schools in Boston" (September 1791), reprinted in Bingham's *American Preceptor* (Boston, 1813) 48–50.

33. The announcement of the intention to publish the *Lady's Magazine and Repository of Entertaining Knowledge* in 1792, quoted in B. M. Stearns, "Early Philadelphia Magazines for Ladies," *Pennsylvania Magazine of History and Biography* 64 (1940), 480.

34. "Nitidia's Defence of Women and White-Washing," *Columbian Magazine*, 1 (1787), 375.

35. "Rights of Woman," *Philadelphia Minerva*, October 17, 1795. The song was intended to be sung to the tune of "God Save the King."

36. Whitfield Jenks Bell, Jr., "The Federal Processions of 1788," *New York Historical Society Quarterly* 66 (1962).

37. Francis Hopkinson, *An Account of the Grand Federal Procession, Performed at Philadelphia on Friday, the 4th of July 1788* (Philadelphia: Mathew Carey, 1788).

38. Cynthia J. Shelton, *The Mills of Manayunk: Industrialization and Social Conflict in the Philadelphia Region, 1787–1837* (Baltimore: Johns Hopkins University Press, 1986), 28–29.

39. Boydston, "The Woman Who Wasn't There." Lewis, "'Of every age sex and condition,'" 363.

40. Young says white women in skilled trades were also excluded from the Boston celebration. "Mechanics on Parade: Measures of Artisan Conscious-

156   *Notes to Pages 18–22*

ness in Boston, 1784–1789," paper presented at the Festive Culture and Public Ritual in Early America Conference, American Philosophical Society, April 1996, 6.

Information on Stewart, Sage, and Middleton comes from a comparison of the 1785 and 1791 city directories. There were no directories published between those years. Francis White, *The Philadelphia Directory* (Philadelphia: Young, Stewart and McCulloch, 1785); Clement Biddle, *The Philadelphia Directory* (Philadelphia, 1791). Jeanne Boydston suggests that the proportion of female-headed households in the postwar years, many run by war widows, may have been large. "The Woman Who Wasn't There," 193.

41. John P. Kaminski and Gaspare J. Saladino, eds., *The Documentary History of the Ratification of the Constitution* (Madison: State Historical Society of Wisconsin), vol. 18, 288–289.

42. Kaminski and Saladino, *Documentary History*, 403. Kaminski's table in appendix 2 states the frequency of circulation of items relating to the ratification of the Constitution.

CHAPTER 1. WOMEN AND THE DEVELOPMENT OF AMERICAN PRINT CULTURE

1. *Only for the Eye of a Friend: The Poems of Annis Boudinot Stockton,* ed. Carla Mulford (Charlottesville: University Press of Virginia, 1995), 6, 8. These female authors, though not appearing in print, were "public" nonetheless. As David Shields notes of Graeme Ferguson, Stockton, and Griffitts, they became "literary celebrities without participating in the hurly-burly of print." *Civil Tongues and Polite Letters in British America* (Durham: University of North Carolina Press, 1997), 319.

2. George W. Boudreau examines the colonial origins of this developing readership in his dissertation, "The Surest Foundation of Happiness: Education and Society in Franklin's Philadelphia" (Ph.D. diss., Indiana University, 1998).

3. Robert B. Winans, "The Growth of a Novel-Reading Public in Late Eighteenth-Century America," *Early American Literature* 9 (1975), 273.

4. Rosalind Remer, *Printers and Men of Capital: Philadelphia Book Publishers in the New Republic* (Philadelphia: University of Pennsylvania Press, 1996), 71–73. Philadelphia City Directory; *The Boston City Directory* (Boston: Manning and Loring, 1796); *Nelson's Charleston Directory and Strangers' Guide for 1801* (Charleston: John Dixon Nelson, 1801).

Printers contracted with booksellers from Boston to Savannah. Books and magazines were distributed throughout the country from the major printing centers of Boston, New York, and Philadelphia. See Remer for a full discussion of this process.

Robert Winans suggests that southerners purchased most of their books from England rather than from northern booksellers. This would account for the paucity of booksellers south of Pennsylvania. Book catalogues from the South sometimes advertised the origins of their stock. For example, Ross & Douglas advertised they had books "from both Europe and Philadelphia." They carried Mathew Carey's *American Museum* for 1798. Hearn's Book Store in Savannah, Georgia, carried the *Columbian Magazine* as well as a large assortment of English novels, essays, and histories. Robert B. Winans, *A Descriptive Checklist of Book Catalogues Separately Printed in America, 1693–1800* (Worcester: American Antiquarian Society, 1981), xviii; Ross & Douglas *Catalogue of Books* (Petersburg, Va., 1800); *A Catalogue of Books to be sold at Hearn's Book Store* (Savannah, Ga., 1790).

5. Winans, "The Growth of a Novel-Reading Public," 268. *Rules of the Carlisle Library Company with a Catalogue of Books* (Carlisle, Pa.: 1797). Given the expense involved in purchasing sufficient volumes to attract members, social libraries were also quite protective of their books. The Carlisle Library Company rules for members stipulated that readers take care "not to hold the books too near the fire, nor permit children to have them nor will they suffer any scribbling in them." *Rules of the Carlisle Library Company*, 6.

6. Information on libraries was derived from Winans, *A Descriptive Checklist of Book Catalogues.*

7. Cathy Davidson refers to all these libraries in "The Novel as Subversive Activity," in *Beyond the American Revolution: Explorations in the History of American Radicalism*, ed. Alfred F. Young (Dekalb: Northern Illinois University Press, 1993), 289.

8. Cathy N. Davidson, *Revolution and the Word: The Rise of the Novel in America* (New York: Oxford University Press, 1986), 27; Jesse H. Shera, "The Beginnings of Systematic Bibliography in America, 1642–1799," in *Essays Honoring Lawrence C. Wrath*, ed. Frederick Richmond Goff et al. (Portland, Me.: Anthoesen Press, 1951), 274.

9. Davidson estimates that the average day laborer in Massachusetts earned fifty cents a day. Davidson, "The Novel as Subversive Activity," 289. *Catalogue of the Annapolis Circulating Library*, 1783.

10. *Literary Magazine and American Register* (Philadelphia), 3 (May 1805), 359.

11. For a quantitative study of the magazine articles concerning women, see Karen K. List, "The Post-Revolutionary Woman Idealized: Philadelphia Media's 'Republican Mother,'" *Journalism Quarterly* 66 (1989), 65–75.

12. Amy Beth Aronson, "Understanding Equals: Audience and Articulation in the Early American Women's Magazine" (Ph.D. diss., Columbia University, 1996), 5. Mary Beth Norton claims that the magazines were the most important forum for expressing a "new Approach to women." *Liberty's Daughters: The Revolutionary Experience of American Women, 1750–1800* (Boston:

Little, Brown, 1980), 246–247.

13. Haywood's magazine is discussed extensively in Kathryn Shevelow, *Women and Print Culture: The Construction of Femininity in the Early Periodical* (London: Routledge, 1989), 167–175. The antecedents for these eighteenth-century publications included the writings of Mary Astell and other early English feminists. Astell helped create a seventeenth-century female audience wide enough that a few British periodicals of the time addressed the issue of women's mental capacities and intellectual interests. By the beginning of the eighteenth century a handful of British writers argued from a feminist viewpoint in some of their publications. Daniel Defoe's essay, *Conjugal Lewdness; or Matrimonial Whoredom* (1727), for example, argued for more egalitarian relationships within marriage. His novels *Moll Flanders* and *Roxana* spoke to the issue of the discriminatory social conditions faced by a laboring-class English woman. Both works illustrate women's ability to meet the demands of circumstances with intelligence and fortitude. American readers were familiar with this English literature. *Moll Flanders* and *Roxana* were available before the Revolution.

14. Hazel Garcia's systematic study of colonial American magazines noted that of all extant issues of all the magazines, totaling 8,300 pages, 429 pages concerned women in some way, and only 68 pages were written by women. "Of Punctilios Among the Fair Sex: Colonial American Magazines, 1741–1776," *Journalism History* 3, no. 2 (summer 1976), 49.

15. Mathew Carey advertised the *Massachusetts Magazine* for 1789–1791 in a sale catalog inserted into the *American Museum, or Universal Magazine*, 12, no. 4 (October 1792). This copy is in the Library Company of Philadelphia. My thanks to James Green for showing it to me.

The southern states did not begin to produce magazines until the end of the century. Charleston's *South Carolina Weekly Museum* was published between January 1797 and July 1798. Baltimore's first magazine, the *Weekly Museum*, lasted for only two issues in 1797. The *National Magazine* of Richmond, Virginia, was published from 1799 to 1800. Frank Luther Mott, *A History of American Magazines, 1741-1850* (Cambridge, Mass.: Harvard University Press, 1938), 790–791.

16. Mott, *A History of American Magazines, 1741-1850*, 788. Not until Mrs. Mary Clarke Carr introduced the *Intellectual Regale, or Ladies' Tea Tray* in November 1814 did American women have a female directing the contents of a periodical. And Carr's venture was not smooth sailing by any means. She claimed that in addition to her editing responsibilities, at times she was forced to even take the printing into her own hands. The *Intellectual Regale* lasted only a year, even with Carr's valiant efforts.

B. M. Stearns, "Early Philadelphia Magazines for Ladies," *Pennsylvania Magazine of History and Biography* 64 (1940), 479–491; Mott, *History of American Magazines*, vol. 1, 787–799.

To get an idea of the national proliferation of women's periodicals, see

James P. Danky, ed., *Women's Periodicals and Newspapers from the Eighteenth Century to 1981* (Boston, 1982).

17. *Gentleman and Lady's Town and Country Magazine*, May 1784.

18. February 1789. Quoted in Bertha Stearns, "Early New England Magazines for Ladies," *New England Quarterly* 2 (1929), 421.

19. *American Magazine* (New York), December 1787.

20. Preface to *Massachusetts Magazine*, vol. 5, 1793, quoted in Mott, *History of American Magazines*, vol. 1, 65.

21. August 1796. Quoted in B. M. Stearns, "Before Godey's," *American Literature* 2 (1930), 250.

22. Winans, "The Growth of a Novel-Reading Public," 267.

23. David Paul Nord, "A Republican Literature: Magazine Reading and Readers in Late-Eighteenth-Century New York," in *Reading in America: Literature and Social History* ed. Cathy N. Davidson (Baltimore: Johns Hopkins University Press, 1989), 114–139.

24. Mathew Carey, *American Museum, or Universal Magazine* 12, no. 4 (October 1792), 221–226.

25. *Ladies Magazine and Repository of Entertaining Knowledge*, 1793, under "Notes to correspondents." The British *Lady's Magazine or Entertaining Companion for the Fair Sex*, which began publication in the 1770s, was in many ways the model for the Philadelphia *Lady's Magazine*. It included essays on female education and advocated that women cultivate the qualities of reason, virtue, and good sense rather than coquetry and empty social entertainments. The many plays the *Lady's Magazine* printed for its "fair patronesses" were usually cautions against coquettish behavior. See for example "The Unreserved Young Lady," and "The Reformed Coquette: A Farce in Two Acts" in the *Lady's Magazine*, 19 (London, 1788).

26. *Lady's Magazine and Repository of Entertaining Knowledge*, I (July 1792), 64–65, "On Matrimonial Obedience." *Lady's Magazine and Repository of Entertaining Knowledge* 2 (1793), inside back cover.

Almost twenty years earlier than this, Thomas Paine linked natural rights theory to domestic relationships. Ten months before writing his revolutionary pamphlet *Common Sense*, he argued in the April 1775 issue of the *Pennsylvania Magazine* that marriage was not intended to be an economic contract. Love between husbands and wives was a necessary, not optional, component to a good marriage; only the laws of affection could be considered binding.

27. *Philadelphia Minerva* 1, no. 3 (Saturday, February 21, 1795); "On the happy influence of Female Society," *The American Museum or Repository of Ancient and Modern Fugitive Pieces* 1 (1787), 74–78.

28. *Lady's Magazine and Repository of Entertaining Knowledge*, 1 (1792), 127. Copy owned by the Historical Society of Pennsylvania, stored at the Library Company of Philadelphia.

29. See "Letters to a Young Lady" by Rev. John Bennet, in *American Museum or Universal Magazine* (May 1792), 195; *Philadelphia Minerva*, Saturday,

July 18, 1795; *Philadelphia Minerva*, 3, no. 109 (March 4, 1797); *Philadelphia Minerva*, 3, no. 110 (March 11, 1797).

30. Stockton's poem was written ca. 1756. *Only for the Eye of a Friend*, 74–75. Mulford cites Alexander Pope's *Rape of the Lock* as the most prominent piece of eighteenth-century literature in this tradition. *Only for the Eye of a Friend*, 34.

31. August 1796. Quoted in Stearns, "Before Godey's," 250.

32. The announcement of the intention to publish the *Lady's Magazine and Repository of Entertaining Knowledge* in 1792. Quoted in Stearns, "Early Philadelphia Magazines for Ladies," 480.

33. *Weekly Magazine of Original Essays* (Philadelphia, May, 1798). This piece also demonstrates that the magazine was aimed at a middlebrow rather than a highbrow audience. In contrast, Joseph Dennie's *Portfolio* was definitely produced for Philadelphia elites. See William C. Dowling, *Literary Federalism in the Age of Jefferson: Joseph Dennie and The Port Folio, 1801-1812* (Columbia: University of South Carolina Press, 1999).

34. Martha C. Slotten, "Elizabeth Graeme Ferguson: A Poet in 'The Athens of North America,'" *Pennsylvania Magazine of History and Biography* (1984), 267–268.

35. Judith Sargent Murray to Winthrop Sargent, November 23, 1791. Letterbook, 5:362. Judith Sargent Murray Papers, Mississippi Department of Archives. This is quoted in Sheila L. Skemp, *Judith Sargent Murray: A Brief Biography with Documents* (Boston: Bedford Books, 1998), 51.

36. Murray was not alone in her dislike of Rousseau's opinions on women. The magazine selections often promoted ideas contrary to those of the French philosopher. Privately, women sometimes expressed their antipathy as well. After reading Rousseau's *Confessions* Elizabeth Drinker commented: "I like him not, nor his ideas." September 13, 1800, *The Diary of Elizabeth Drinker*, ed. Elaine F. Crane, 3 vols. (Boston: Northeastern University Press, 1991), 2:1371.

37. John Gregory, *A Father's Legacy to His Daughters* (1774; reprint, New York: Garland, 1974), 31–32; Jean-Jacques Rousseau, *Emile*, trans. Barbara Foxley (London: Everyman, 1993), 419. According to Rousseau, "A female wit is a scourge to her husband, her children, her friends, her servants, to everybody." Rousseau's ideal woman was embodied in his fictional character Sophie, envisioned by Rousseau as Emile's perfect mate. Sophie is weak, pliable, and submissive. She is educated solely in the art of pleasing a man. Her talents do not extend beyond baking and sewing. *Emile*, 445. Rousseau's views are clearly presented in chapter 1 of Mary Seidman Trouille, *Sexual Politics in the Enlightenment: Women Writers Read Rousseau* (Albany: State University of New York Press, 1997). Both Gregory's and Rousseau's works were frequently among books for sale in American catalogs in the 1790s.

38. Murray was not alone in her opinions. The *Rudiments of Taste in a Series*

of Letters from a Mother to Her Daughters (Philadelphia: William Spotswood, 1790) took it for granted that women's intellectual powers were acknowledged: "The Moahometan sentiment which prevailed some years ago, of the inferiority of the female mind, seems exploded in this age of universal refinement; and a woman of cultivated understanding is no longer a phenomenon" (31).

39. "On the Equality of the Sexes" was written in 1779 and published in the *Massachusetts Magazine* in 1790. Judith Sargent Murray, *Selected Writings of Judith Sargent Murray*, ed. Sharon M. Harris (Oxford: Oxford University Press, 1995), 3–14.

40. Murray had William Alexander's *History of Women from the Earliest Antiquity to the Present Time* (London, 1782) to draw on for her examples.

41. Murray to Sally Wood, November 25, 1800. Judith Sargent Murray Papers, Mississippi Department of Archives. Reprinted in *From Gloucester to Philadelphia in 1790, Observations, Anecdotes, and Thoughts from the Eighteenth-Century Letters of Judith Sargent Murray*, ed. Bonnie Hurd Smith (Cambridge, Mass.: Judith Sargent Murray Society, 1998), 51.

42. Murray, *Selected Writings*, 44. Originally published in the *Gentleman and Lady's Town and Country Magazine: or, Repository of Instruction and Entertainment*, 6 (October 1784), 251–253.

43. June 16, 1782, letter to Anna (Hannah), an orphan whom Murray (then Judith Sargent Stevens) and her husband had taken in. Murray, *Selected Writings*, 92; 39.

44. Ibid., 39.

45. Ibid., 48–49.

46. Ibid., 37.

47. Rosemarie Zagarri, "The Rights of Man and Woman in Post-Revolutionary America," *William and Mary Quarterly* 55, no. 2 (April 1998), 211.

48. Gary Kates, "'The Powers of Husband and Wife Must Be Equal and Separate': The Cercle Social and the Rights of Women, 1790–91," and Dominique Godineau, "Masculine and Feminine Political Practice during the French Revolution, 1793-Year III," in *Women and Politics in the Age of the Democratic Revolution*, ed. Harriet Branson Applewhite and Darline G. Levy (Ann Arbor: University of Michigan Press, 1990); Gita May, *Madame Roland and the Age of Revolution* (New York, 1970); Joan Wallach Scott, "French Feminists and the Rights of 'Man': Olympe de Gouges's Declarations," *History Workshop Journal* (fall-winter 1989), 1–21; Lenora Cohen Rosenfield, "The Rights of Women in the French Revolution," *Studies in Eighteenth Century Culture* 7 (1976), 117–137; Jane Abray, "Feminism in the French Revolution," *American Historical Review* 80, no. 1 (February 1975), 43–62.

49. Mary Wollstonecraft, *A Vindication of the Rights of Woman* (London, 1792), 112.

50. Ibid., 134.

51. Ibid., 320.

52. Ibid., 283. See Murray's "Desultory Thoughts upon the Utility of Encouraging a Degree of Self-Complacency, Especially in Female Bosoms," in *Selected Writings*, 44.

53. Wollstonecraft, *Vindication*, 139.

54. Ibid., 284.

55. Ibid., 285.

56. Ibid., 158, 148.

57. Ibid., 288.

58. Margaret Murphey Craig (1761–1814) to Marianne Williams, no date [after 1798]. Rush-Biddle-Williams Family Papers, series 2, box 17, Rosenbach Museum and Library.

59. Aaron Burr to Mrs. Burr, Philadelphia, February 16, 1793. *Memoirs of Aaron Burr*, ed. Matthew L. Davis (1836; reprint, Freeport, N.Y.: Books for Libraries Press, 1970), 363.

60. Mary Moody Emerson to Mrs. Ruth Emerson, January 20, 1799, *Selected Letters of Mary Moody Emerson*, ed. Nancy Craig Simmons, (Athens: University of Georgia Press, 1993), 23–24.

61. April 22, 1796, *The Diary of Elizabeth Drinker*, vol. 2. 795.

62. Karin A. Wulf, "'My Dear Liberty': Quaker Spinsterhood and Female Autonomy in Eighteenth-Century Pennsylvania," in *Women and Freedom in Early America* ed. Larry D. Eldridge (New York: New York University Press, 1997), 83–108.

63. Adams wrote this to his wife sometime in 1794. See Charles W. Akers, *Abigail Adams, An American Woman* (Boston: 1980), 116. Mary Beth Norton provides examples of women's private responses to Wollstonecraft in other American cities. See *Liberty's Daughters*, 251–252.

64. See the bill from Colerick and Hunter to Mathew Carey, September 17, 1794, Carey Papers, American Antiquarian Society. My thanks to James Green at the Library Company of Philadelphia for providing this information.

Carey advertised *A Vindication* at the back of the 1794 edition of Rowson's *Charlotte Temple* as selling for one dollar. This would have confined the purchase of the book to Philadelphia's middle and upper classes.

65. Elizabeth Meredith to David Meredith, Philadelphia, September 24, 1796. Box 5, folder 6, Meredith Family Papers, Historical Society of Pennsylvania. Linda Kerber points out that *A Vindication* confirmed what Americans were already experiencing, or at least willing to hear. See *Women of the Republic: Intellect and Ideology in Revolutionary America* (Chapel Hill: University of North Carolina Press, 1980), 222–224. In contrast to this view, Mary Beth Norton claims that Wollstonecraft's book received a largely negative reception. See *Liberty's Daughters*, 251.

66. *Ladies Magazine*, 1 (July 1792), 190.

67. Ibid., 195. For a discussion of the possibility that Brown was editor of the magazine, see B. M. Stearns, "A Speculation Concerning Charles Brockden Brown," *Pennsylvania Magazine of History and Biography* 59 (1935), 99–105.

68. *Ladies Magazine*, 1 (July 1792), 189.

69. J. A. Neal, *An Essay on the Education and Genius of the Female Sex. To Which is Added, An Account of the Commencement of the Young Ladies' Academy of Philadelphia, Held the 18th Day of December, 1794* (Philadelphia, 1795), 18.

70. *Philadelphia Minerva*, October 17, 1795.

71. Annis Boudinot Stockton, Morven, March 22 [no year]. Rush-Biddle-Williams Family Papers, series 1, box 5, Rosenbach Museum and Library, Philadelphia. The entire letter appears in appendix 3 of *Only for the Eye of a Friend*, 304-307.

72. Annis Boudinot Stockton, "To the Visitant *from a circle of Ladies, on reading his paper* No. 3 *in the* Pennsylvania Chronicle." March 14, 1768, *Pennsylvania Chronicle*, reprinted in the *American Museum*, December 1788, and in *Only for the Eye of a Friend*, 89.

73. Annis Boudinot Stockton, Morven, March 22 [no year].

74. Elizabeth Hewson to Thomas Hewson, November 30, 1795. Microfilm reel 103, Hewson Family Papers, American Philosophical Society.

75. Elizabeth Hewson to Thomas Hewson, November 6, 1796, Microfilm reel 103, Hewson Family Papers, American Philosophical Society.

76. Elizabeth Hewson to Thomas Hewson, July 11, 1796, Microfilm reel 103, Hewson Family Papers, American Philosophical Society.

77. *The Rise and Progress of the Young Ladies' Academy of Philadelphia* (Philadelphia, 1794), 90–95.

78. Hogan, *City Directory* (Philadelphia, 1795), 45.

79. "An Oration," delivered at Elizabeth Town, New Jersey, July 4, 1793 (Special Collections Department, Rutgers University Library, New Brunswick, N.J.), quoted in Judith Apter Klinghoffer and Lois Elkis, "'The Petticoat Electors': Women's Suffrage in New Jersey, 1776–1807," *Journal of the Early Republic* 12 (summer 1992), 159–193.

80. For Rowson's career see Eve Kornfield, "Women in Post-Revolutionary American Culture: Susanna Haswell Rowson's American Career, 1793–1824," *Journal of American Culture* 6 (winter 1983), 56–62, Patricia L. Parker, *Susanna Rowson* (Boston: Twayne, 1986); and Doreen Alvarez Saar, "Susanna Rowson: Feminist and Democrat," in *Curtain Calls: British and American Women and the Theater, 1660-1820,* ed. Mary Anne Schofield and Cecilia Macheski (Athens: Ohio University Press, 1991).

81. The "Rights of Women" appeared in the *Weekly Magazine of Original Essays, Fugitive Pieces, and Interesting Intelligence* vol. 1 (March 17, 31, April 7, 1798). See Cathy N. Davidson, "The Matter and Manner of Charles Brockden Brown's *Alcuin*," in *Critical Essays on Charles Brockden Brown*, ed.

Bernard Rosenthal (Boston: G. K. Hall, 1981), 71–86.

82. Brown, "Rights of Women," 231.

83. Ibid., 233.

84. Ibid., 300.

85. Ibid., 234.

86. Ibid., 272.

87. Ibid., 299.

88. Ibid., 299–300.

89. Ibid., 300.

90. William Godwin, *Memoirs of Mary Wollstonecraft Godwin, Author of "A Vindication of the Rights of Woman"* (Philadelphia, 1799).

See *Porcupine's Gazette*, Friday, July 20, 1798, for a letter reprinted from the *Gentleman's Magazine* from a reader who had just finished the *Memoirs* and lamented Mary Wollstonecraft's irreligiousness as well as her suicide attempts.

Elizabeth Drinker, *Diary*, reading list for 1799. For the reaction to Wollstonecraft in Britain after 1798 see G. J. Barker-Benfield, *The Culture of Sensibility: Sex and Society in Eighteenth-Century Britain* (Chicago: University Press of Chicago, 1992), 368–382. For further information on America's response to Wollstonecraft, see R. M. Janes, "On the Reception of Mary Wollstonecraft's *A Vindication of the Rights of Woman*," *Journal of the History of Ideas* 39 (April–June 1978), 293–302; and Marelle Thiebaux, "Mary Wollstonecraft in Federalist America: 1791–1802," in *The Evidence of the Imagination: Studies of Interactions Between Life and Art in English Romantic Literature*, ed. Donald H. Reiman, et al. (New York: New York University Press, 1978), 195–245. Thiebaux discusses much of the negative criticism of Wollstonecraft and her work. More recently, Chandos Michael Brown has looked at New Englander Benjamin Silliman's attack on Wollstonecraft in the *Letters of Shahcoolen, a Hindu Philosopher* (1801–1802) in his article "Mary Wollstonecraft, or The Female Illuminati: The Campaign Against Women and 'Modern Philosophy' in the Early Republic," *Journal of the Early Republic* 15 (fall 1995), 389–424.

91. This parody was included in *The American Ladies Pocketbook for 1802* (Philadelphia: John Morgan). The song had been sung by a Mrs. Franklin at the Vauxhall Gardens (located on Broad Street).

Simon Newman has pointed out that the controversial political songs of the 1790s had their parodies as well, for example, the Republican "God Save the Rights of Man" had its Federalist parody of the same name. See *Parades, Festivals, and the Politics of the Street: Popular Political Culture in the Early American Republic* (Philadelphia: University of Pennsylvania Press, 1997).

92. Margaret Murphey Craig (1761–1814) to Marianne Williams, no date [after 1798]. Rush-Biddle-Williams Family Papers, series 2, box 17, Rosen-

bach Museum and Library.

93. Rev. Samuel Miller, "The Appropriate Duty and Ornament of the Female Sex," in *The Columbian Preacher, Or, A Collection of Original Sermons, from Preachers of Eminence in the United States. Embracing the Distinguishing Doctrines of Grace* (Catskill, N.Y.: 1808), 253.

94. *Philadelphia Repository and Weekly Register*, vol. 1, no. 2; vol. 1, no. 35; vol. 1, no. 18, March 14, 1801. *Lady's Magazine and Musical Repository* vol. 1, May 1801; 3, January 1802. Amy Beth Aronson discusses the "embedded questions" often found in these writings in "Understanding Equals," 119.

95. See Murray, *From Gloucester to Philadelphia*, 50–51.

CHAPTER 2. AMERICAN WOMEN AND THE FRENCH REVOLUTION

1. Report of a dinner in Alexandria, Virginia, December 27, 1792, to celebrate the French victory over the Duke of Brunswick. *Dunlap's American Daily Advertiser* January 3, 1793.

2. John Bach McMaster, *A History of the People of the United States from the Revolution to the Civil War*, 6 vols. (New York, 1896), 2:93.

3. *General Advertiser* advertisement for July Fourth celebration at Gray's Gardens, July 1, 1791.

4. *Freeman's Journal*, July 13, 1791.

5. Mary Meredith to David Meredith, January 2, 1795. Meredith Family Papers, box 2, folder 9, Historical Society of Pennsylvania.

6. Advertisement for the Merchants Coffee House at the City Tavern in *Dunlap's American Daily Advertiser*, January 1, 1793.

7. Elizabeth Drinker, *The Diary of Elizabeth Drinker*, ed. Elaine F. Crane, 3 vols. (Boston: Northeastern University Press, 1991), February 3, 1795.

8. Catherine Anne Bieri Hebert, "The Pennsylvania French in the 1790s: The Story of Their Survival" (Ph.D. diss, University of Texas at Austin, 1981), 50.

9. C. A. Moré [Chevalier de Pontibaud, Comte de Moré], *Mémoires du Comte de Moré, 1758-1837* (Paris, 1898), cited in Francis Sergeant Childs, *French Refugee Life in the United States, 1790-1800: An American Chapter of the French Revolution* (Baltimore: Johns Hopkins University Press, 1940), 103.

10. John F. Watson, *Annals of Philadelphia and Pennsylvania* (Philadelphia: Edwin S. Stuart, 1905), 1:181. He must have read Moré's description.

11. Edmund Hogan, *The Prospect of Philadelphia* (Philadelphia, 1795).

12. Jefferson to Anne Bingham, Paris, May 11, 1788, *The Papers of Thomas Jefferson*, ed. Julian P. Boyd et al., 28 vols. to date (Princeton: Princeton University Press, 1950–1996), 11:392.

13. Bethia Alexander and Isabelle Alexander Hankey to Marianne Williams, July 10–12[15], 1791. Rush-Biddle-Williams Collection [Rush II:6:05], Rosenbach Museum and Library, Philadelphia.

14. Bethia Alexander and Isabelle Alexander Hankey to Marianne Williams, July 10–12[15], 1791.

15. "Washington's Household Account Books, 1793–1797," *Pennsylvania Magazine of History and Biography* 29 (1905), 30 (1906). Washington subscribed to the *Leyden Gazette* as well as all the Philadelphia papers.

16. *National Gazette*, September 4, 1793; September 7, 1793.

17. "Plan of a French & English Periodical Paper," 1794, Historical Society of Pennsylvania.

18. "June 30 [1797] Cash paid to Suey Hatton to take to son James [Gibbons] to pay for the French NewsPaper 4 dollars." James Gibbons Account book, 1797–1816. Gibbons Collection Manuscripts 1760–1837, Historical Society of Pennsylvania.

19. Gary Kates, "'The Powers of Husband and Wife Must Be Equal and Separate': The Cercle Social and the Rights of Women, 1790–91," in *Women and Politics in the Age of the Democratic Revolution*, ed. Harriet Branson Applewhite and Darline G. Levy (Ann Arbor: University of Michigan Press, 1990), 164, 167. The Cercle Social advocated more liberal divorce laws for women. The Marquis de Condorcet's *Outline of an Historical View of the Progress of the Human Mind* was published in Philadelphia in 1796. In it, he argued for improving women's status.

20. Thomas Jefferson to Angelica Schuyler Church, Paris, September 21, 1788. *The Papers of Thomas Jefferson*.

21. *Independent Gazette*, October 2, 1793; R. B. Rose, "Women and the French Revolution: The Political Activity of Parisian Women, 1789–94," *University of Tasmania Occasional Paper* 5 (1976).

22. Dominique Godineau, "Masculine and Feminine Political Practice During the French Revolution, 1793 Year III," in *Women and Politics in the Age of the Democratic Revolution*, 70; Olwen H. Hufton, *Women and the Limits of Citizenship in the French Revolution* (Toronto: University of Toronto Press, 1992), 25–32. *American Star* Saturday, February 15, 1794, no.7, vol 1, 53. This information is from *Le Moniteur* from 1793. French news was often considerably delayed in reaching the United States.

23. The Jacobins, hoping to push the Girondists from power, encouraged these women. Ironically, once in power, the Jacobins quickly banned women's clubs. Aware of the efficacy of women's collective political force, Jacobins did not want their political opponents to reap the same benefits.

24. Another political activist, Théroigne de Méricourt, even proposed to organize an armed "phalanx of Amazons." Darline G. Levy and Harriet B. Applewhite, "Women, Radicalization, and the Fall of the French Monarchy," in *Women and Politics in the Age of the Democratic Revolution*, 102–103, 89.

25. *Philadelphia Gazette*, July 20, 1798.

26. Elizabeth F. Ellet's work contains many accounts of these patriot women. *The Women of the American Revolution*, 2 vols. (1848–50; reprint, Philadelphia, 1900). It is not a coincidence that a female hero of the American Revolution received mention in the newspapers at this time. Deborah Gannett had petitioned Congress for a military pension following her service, disguised as a man, in the Continental army. A poem by Philip Freneau described this "gallant Amazon" in the *Philadelphia Gazette*, July 19, 1798.

27. *American Star*, February 4, 1794. Roland belonged to the Brissotins, who were replaced by the Jacobins and their leader Robespierre.

28. *Independent Gazette*, January 25, 1794; *Dunlap and Claypoole's American Daily Advertiser*, February 26, 1794.

29. Madelyn Gutwirth, *The Twilight of the Goddesses: Women and Representation in the French Revolutionary Era* (New Brunswick, N.J.: Rutgers University Press, 1992), 245.

30. *American Star* 1, no. 2 (February 4, 1794), 20.

31. *American Star* 1, no. 14 (March 4, 1794); Joan Wallach Scott, "French Feminists and the Rights of 'Man': Olympe de Gouges's Declarations," *History Workshop Journal* (fall-winter 1989), 1–21; Lenora Cohen Rosenfield, "The Rights of Women in the French Revolution," *Studies in Eighteenth Century Culture* 7 (1976), 117–137; Jane Abray, "Feminism in the French Revolution," *American Historical Review* 80, no. 1 (February 1975), 43–62; Gutwirth, *Twilight of the Goddesses*, 248. De Gouges had Wollstonecraft's *Vindication of the Rights of Woman* to draw from. It was translated into French shortly before De Gouges's *Declaration* appeared.

32. *National Gazette*, September 25 and October 2, 1793.

33. However, even Podgson found it difficult to combine Corday's actions with her femininity. She has Corday proclaim: "I sacrifice—I quit—myself / And all the softness of a woman's name." Amelia Howe Kritzer, *Plays by Early American Women: 1794-1844* (Ann Arbor: University of Michigan Press, 1995), 19–20, 159, 147.

34. *American Star* 1, no. 17 (March 11, 1794).

35. The *Independent Gazette* (September 28, 1793) carried the first notices of the queen's pretrial treatment. The transcript of her trial was printed, with the British report that she was brought "like the meanest malefactor from the vile prison of the Conciergierie and placed at the criminal bar of the Revolutionary Tribunal." *Independent Gazette*, January 11, 1794.

36. *Independent Gazette*, January 11, 1794.

37. *Independent Gazette*, January 11, 1794, reprint of letter to editor from London, October 26–28, 1793.

38. Elizabeth Colwill, "Just Another Citoyenne? Marie Antoinette on Trial 1790–93," *History Workshop Journal* 28 (September 1989).

39. Rufus Wilmot Griswold, *The Republican Court; or American Society in*

the Days of Washington (New York: D. Appleton, 1867), 393; *Gazette of the United States,* January 29, 1794.

In late January 1794, American papers carried a vivid account of the execution. *Gazette of the United States,* January 27, 1794; also January 11, 13–17.

40. Abigail Adams to Abigail Smith, February 9, 1794, Charles Francis Adams, *Letters of Mrs. Adams* (Boston, 1840), 422.

41. Mary Norris to Deborah Logan, Chester, January 20, 1794, Maria Dickinson Logan Family papers, box 3, Mary Parker Norris folder, 1792–1795, Historical Society of Pennsylvania.

42. Drinker, *Diary,* January 11, 1794.

43. Scharf and Westcott, *The History of Philadelphia, 1609–1884,* 3 vols. (Philadelphia: L. H. Everts, 1884), 2:912. Mentioned in Charles Downer Hazen, *Contemporary American Opinion of the French Revolution* (Baltimore, 1897; reprint Gloucester, Mass., 1964), 258, citing La Rochefoucauld, *Travels,* 3:488, 489.

44. William Cobbett, in his edition of William Playfair's *History of Jacobinism, Its Crimes, Cruelties and Perfidies* (Philadelphia: for William Cobbett, 1796), 25.

45. Carey's advertisement, *Independent Gazetteer,* January 25, 1794; *Independent Gazetteer,* January 29, 1794; the *Aurora* of March 15, 1794, advertises that the *Aurora* office is selling the new French calendar for 1794. This ad appeared in both English and French.

46. *Aurora,* August 19, 1794. Also for sale at Stewart and Cochran's, no. 34 South Second Street, were copies of the French Constitution (1793) and the U.S. Constitution; *Dunlap's American Daily Advertiser,* January 3, 1793.

47. Advertised in the *Aurora,* January 1, 1798, and in *Porcupine's Gazette,* January 2, 1798.

48. Entry for April 23, 1793, in "Washington's Household Account Books, 1793–1797," *Pennsylvania Magazine of History and Biography* 29 (1905), 394. This may have been Rabaut's history of the Revolution advertised in the *Aurora.* Martha Washington also bought a pamphlet, "Prophetic Conjectures on the French Revolution." Entry in "Washington's Household Account Books," for March 8, 1794.

Both Martha Washington and Elizabeth Drinker read Moore's *Journal in France.* See "Washington's Household Account Books," entry for September 13, 1793; and Drinker, *Diary,* June 26, 1794.

49. "Washington's Household Account Books," entries for November 7, 1794, and February 3, 1796.

50. Drinker, *Diary,* reading list for 1801.

51. Susanna (Dillwyn) Emlen to William Dillwyn, January 15, 1799. Dillwyn Family Papers, Historical Society of Pennsylvania.

52. Moreau de Saint Méry, *Moreau de Saint Méry's American Journey: 1793–1798,* ed. and trans. Kenneth Roberts and Anna M. Roberts (Garden City,

N.Y.: Doubleday, 1947), 204 (September 23, 1795).

Charles Willson Peale also displayed a piece of the Bastille in his museum. Judith Sargent Murray mentioned it among the many objects of wonder she viewed there on her visit in 1790. Judith Sargent Murray to her parents, July 3, 1790, *From Gloucester to Philadelphia in 1790: Observations, Anecdotes, and Thoughts from the Eighteenth-Century Letters of Judith Sargent Murray*, ed. Bonnie Hurd Smith (Cambridge, Mass.: Judith Sargent Murray Society, 1998), 165.

53. *Aurora*, March 5, 1794.

54. Cobbett, *History of the American Jacobins* (Philadelphia, 1795), in *Peter Porcupine in America*, ed. David A. Wilson (Ithaca: Cornell University Press, 1994), 200.

55. *National Gazette*, April 13, 1793; Elizabeth Graeme Ferguson, Commonplace Book, 1796, Historical Society of Pennsylvania.

56. "Washington's Household Account Books," entries for March 24, 1794, and April 5, 1794.

57. *Aurora*, March 14, 1794; *American Star* 1, no. 14, March 4, 1794. The automatons were exhibited below Mr. Poor's Ladies Academy at no. 9 Cherry Alley, between Third and Fourth Streets. The price was fifty cents.

58. Watson, *Annals of Philadelphia* 1, 181–182. See *National Gazette*, June 28, 1792, June 5, 1793; *National Advertiser*, July 17, 1793.

59. A "Federal Hat for ladies" was advertised in the *Carlisle Gazette* (Pennsylvania) in time for July Fourth celebrations in 1788. The connection between fashion, politics, and society is an intimate one. As Fernand Braudel noted, dress is "an indication of deeper phenomena—of the energies, possibilities, demands and *joie de vivre* of a given society, economy and civilization." It is also "a search for a new language to discredit the old." Fernand Braudel, *The Structures of Everyday Life*, trans. Siân Reynolds (New York: Harper and Row, 1979), 323, 324.

60. Lynn Hunt, *Politics, Culture and Class in the French Revolution* (Berkeley: University of California Press, 1982), 75–86.

61. Méry, *American Journey*, 284.

62. Anne Bingham, letter to Jefferson, June 1787. *The Papers of Thomas Jefferson*, 11:392. Reproduced in Robert C. Alberts, *The Golden Voyage: The Life and Times of William Bingham, 1752-1804* (Boston: Houghton Mifflin, 1969), 464–466.

63. Not that this innovation freed women from the tyranny of the corset. It merely changed the form of the figure-shaping undergarments to fit the new design. For David's organization of Revolutionary festivals see Mona Ozouf, *Festivals and the French Revolution*, trans. Alan Sheridan (Cambridge, Mass.: Harvard University Press, 1988), 76–79.

64. Jennifer Harris, "The Red Cap of Liberty: A Study of Dress Worn by

French Revolutionary Partisans 1789–94," *Eighteenth-Century Studies* 14, no. 3 (spring 1981).

65. There were many representations of this cap in ancient Greek art. The cap was already being worn by male revolutionaries at the time the women adopted it. Bonnie G. Smith, *Changing Lives: Women in European History Since 1700* (Lexington, Mass.: D. C. Heath, 1989), 109.

66. *Journal des Dames et des Modes*, November 10, 1797. Quoted in Aileen Ribeiro, *Fashion in the French Revolution* (New York: Holmes and Meier, 1988), 134.

67. *Journal de la Mode et de Goût*, December 5, 1790. Quoted in Ribeiro, *Fashion in the French Revolution*, 58.

68. Benjamin Rush, *The Rise and Progress of the Young Ladies' Academy of Philadelphia* (Philadelphia, 1794), 90–95.

For American Revolution boycotts by women, see Linda K. Kerber, *Women of the Republic: Intellect and Ideology in Revolutionary America* (Chapel Hill: University of North Carolina Press, 1980), chapter 2, and Mary Beth Norton, *Liberty's Daughters: The Revolutionary Experience of American Women, 1750–1800* (Boston: Little, Brown, 1980), 161–163.

69. "Address to the Ladies of America" signed "Frank Amity," *American Museum*, November 1787, II, 481.

70. Stockton, *Only for the Eye of a Friend: The Poems of Annis Boudinot Stockton*, ed. Carla Mulford (Charlottesville: University Press of Virginia, 1995), 216–217, n. 251.

71. *National Gazette*, April 10, 1793.

72. Hazen, *Contemporary American Opinion*, 286. As of July 1792, all French men were required by law to wear the tricolor cockade.

73. Henry Wansey, *An Excursion to the United States of North America in the Summer of 1794* (Salisbury, England, 1798), 175.

74. *Albany Register*, March 17, 1794. Quoted in Alfred F. Young, *The Democratic Republicans of New York* (Chapel Hill: University of North Carolina Press, 1967), 362.

75. Hunt, *Politics, Culture and Class*, 53, 54.

76. *Porcupine's Gazette*, July 27, 1798. Though Cobbett was quick to articulate his antipathy to the French Revolution, his first occupation after arriving in Delaware in the early 1790s was as a tutor of English to the French refugees.

77. William Cobbett, in his edition of Playfair, *The History of Jacobinism*, 25. This intentionally unflattering masculinity credited to women who were political was a carryover from the American Revolution. Kerber, *Women of the Republic*, 279.

78. Bostonians were not quite sure how to feminize the word "citizen." One writer suggested a compromise: styling the men "*cits*," and the women "*citizens*." *National Gazette*, February 6, 1793.

79. Cynthia A. Kierner, *Beyond the Household: Women's Place in the Early South, 1700-1835* (Ithaca: Cornell University Press, 1998), 120.

80. *Aurora*, August 2, 1794. Women even signed themselves *"citess"* on sacramental documents. "Sacramental Registers at St. Joseph's Church, Philadelphia, Pa.," *American Catholic Historical Society Records* 16 (Philadelphia, 1905), 66.

81. *Aurora*, August 2, 1794, January 29, 1793.

82. Charles Francis Adams, ed., *Letters to Mrs. Adams*, 2:123.

83. *"Citess," Columbian Centinel*, March 16, 1793.

84. "At a meeting of the Fair ones," *Gazette of the United States*, February 9, 1793.

85. Simon P. Newman, *Parades and the Politics of the Street: Festive Culture in the Early American Republic* (Philadelphia: University of Pennsylvania Press, 1997), 154, 156–157. For a profile of the economic situations of Philadelphia's laboring people during this era see Billy G. Smith, *The "Lower Sort": Philadelphia's Laboring People, 1750-1800* (Ithaca: Cornell University Press, 1990), 63–91.

86. Drinker, *Diary*, July 4, 1783, n. 3. The centerpiece of this procession was a large sofa embellished with portraits of Generals Washington, Rochambeau, and Gates.

87. Douglas Southall Freeman, *George Washington, A Biography*, 7 vols. (New York: Scribners, 1948–1957), 6:172.

88. Mary Hewson to Barbara Hewson, Philadelphia, April 22, 1789. Microfilm reel 103, Hewson Family Papers, American Philosophical Society.

89. *National Gazette*, December 26, 1792. John Fanning Watson reported the event in his *Annals of Philadelphia*, 1:180. It is clear from Watson's account that it was Americans who participated.

90. James Hardie, *The Philadelphia Directory and Register* (Philadelphia, 1794).

91. Young, *The Democratic Republicans of New York*, 192.

92. Report of event from November 1793 in the *Independent Gazetteer*, February 26, 1794. See Hunt, *Politics, Culture and Class*, 63–65.

93. *Aurora*, August 9, 28, 1794.

94. Though explicitly copied from French ceremonies, Americans already had their own highly staged rituals as models. In 1790 Judith Sargent Murray described this July Fourth ceremony at Philadelphia's Schuylkill Gardens: "The Arms of America and France entwined by Liberty—a rich display of Fire works, exhibited from the Lawn, in front of the Federal temple—Thirteen Boys, and an equal number of Girls, issuing from the Grove, habited as shepherds, and shepherdesses, and proceeding to the Federal Temple, chanting responsively, an Ode to Liberty, with a number of songs, Odes, and Choruses, in honour of the auspicious event, which the day commemorated." Judith Sargent Murray to her parents, July 10, 1790, *From Gloucester to*

Philadelphia in 1790, 175.

95. *New York Journal and Weekly Register,* May 1, 1793. The article is titled "Rights of Women."

96. *City Gazette and Daily Advertiser* (Charleston, S.C.), July 20, 1793. My thanks to Robert Alderson for sharing this remarkable source with me. His dissertation, "'This Bright Era of Happy Revolutions': M.-A.-B. de Mangourit in Charleston, S.C., 1792–1794" (University of Georgia), details the experiences of the French refugees in that city.

97. As a result of the Postal Act of 1792, the press became truly national in scope. Every newspaper editor in the country could send one copy of their paper to every other editor and receive one copy in return. Thus the news in Philadelphia was quickly spread across the nation, and events in other locales made their way into the Philadelphia papers within a matter of days. David Kaser, *A Book for a Sixpence: The Circulating Library in America* (Pittsburgh: Beta Phi Mu, 1980), 73.

98. "Impromptu On hearing that a print of the Guliteene [*sic*] with our beloved presidents figure under it was executed in Mr. Genets family—under his Sanction." Stockton, *Only for the Eye of a Friend,* 178.

99. Details of the foreign policy issues directly affecting relations with France and Britain are lucidly presented in James Sharp, *American Politics in the Early Republic: The New Nation in Crisis* (New Haven: Yale University Press, 1993), and in Stanley Elkins and Eric McKitrick, *The Age of Federalism: The Early American Republic, 1788-1800* (New York: Oxford University Press, 1993), 303–375. For Philadelphia in particular, see Albrecht Koschnik, "Political Conflict and Public Contest: Rituals of National Celebration in Philadelphia, 1788–1815," *Journal of the Early Republic* 68, no. 3 (July 1994), 209–248.

100. Henrietta Liston, letter, June 11, 1798. "A Diplomat's Wife in Philadelphia: Letters of Henrietta Liston, 1779–1800," ed. Bradford Perkins, *William and Mary Quarterly* 11, no. 4 (October 1954), 617.

For details on the difficulties of the United States with both France and Britain in the 1790s see Jerald A. Combs, *The Jay Treaty: Political Battleground of the Founding Fathers* (Berkeley, 1970); Alexander De Conde, *Entangling Alliance: Politics and Diplomacy Under George Washington* (Durham, N.C.: Duke University Press, 1958).

101. *Porcupine's Gazette,* October 22, 1798. Now Federalists feared a wild Jacobin joining the Irishman under every bed.

For a discussion of the anti-French attitudes prevailing in late 1790s the following are useful: Alexander De Conde, *The Quasi-War: The Politics and Diplomacy of the Undeclared War with France, 1797-1801* (New York, 1966), Hebert, "The Pennsylvania French in the 1790s, and Newman, *Parades and the Politics of the Street,* chapter 7.

102. Mary Ridgely to Henry M. Ridgely, Philadelphia, April 27, 1798.

Mabel L. Ridgely, ed. *Ridgelys of Delaware and Their Circle: What Them Befell in Colonial and Federal Times: Letters 1751-1890* (Portland, Me., 1949), 118.

103. Elizabeth Hewson to Thomas Hewson, Bellemeade, June 5, 1797. Microfilm 103, frame 65, American Philosophical Society.

104. Mount Vernon, November 23, 1797. Patricia Brady, ed., *George Washington's Beautiful Nelly: The Letters of Eleanor Parke Custis Lewis to Elizabeth Bordley Gibson, 1794-1851* (Columbia: University of South Carolina Press, 1991), 41.

105. Elizabeth Graeme Ferguson, 1796 Commonplace Book, Historical Society of Pennsylvania. Cited in Martha C. Slotten, "Elizabeth Graeme Ferguson: A Poet in 'The Athens of North America,'" *Pennsylvania Magazine of History and Biography* 1984, 277n41.

106. Drinker, *Diary*, May 9, 1798. William Drinker reported that a company of Butchers from Spring Garden, with white cockades in their hats had attacked another group of men (perhaps wearing black cockades—the symbol of the Federalists).

107. *Porcupine's Gazette*, May 7, 1798.

108. *Porcupine's Gazette*, October 31, 1798.

109. *Gazette of the United States*, July 9, 1798. For information about the political and social influence of these city troops, see Koschnik, "Political Conflict and Public Context," 239–245.

110. *Claypoole's American Daily Advertiser*, February 27, 1798.

111. *Philadelphia Gazette*, July 6; *Gazette of the United States*, July 11, 1798.

112. There is some precedent for these female militia presentations from the early eighteenth century and the American Revolution. *Pennsylvania Gazette* reported a presentation on January 12, 1748. Ellet mentions only one Revolution case: "The wife of Col. Barnard Elliott presented to the second regiment, . . . a pair of richly embroidered colors, wrought by herself. They were planted, three years afterwards, on the British lines at Savannah, by Sergeant Jasper, who in planting them received his death wound." Elizabeth F. Ellet, *Domestic History of the American Revolution* (New York, 1850), 45. A few other instances are discussed in Edward W. Richardson, *Standards and Colors of the American Revolution* (Philadelphia: University of Pennsylvania Press, 1982). What stands out in the 1790s presentations is the publicity accorded the events, and especially the quite extensive transcriptions of the women's speeches on these occasions.

Laurel Thatcher Ulrich describes Maine women presenters between 1799 and 1805 in "'From the Fair to the Brave': Spheres of Womanhood in Federal Maine," in Laura Fecych Sprague, ed., *Agreeable Situations: Society, Commerce, and Art in Southern Maine, 1780-1830* (Kennebunk, Maine: Brick Store Museum), 215–225. My thanks to Albrecht Koschnik for bringing this source to my attention.

113. Elizabeth Powel to Captain Dunlap, March 16, 1797. Powel Collec-

tion, Elizabeth Powel Papers, Outgoing Correspondence, Box 1, folder 2, 1788–1799. See Richardson, 177, 240, 321–22.

114. *Philadelphia Gazette,* July 9, 1798: an "offering to Patriotism." Emily Mifflin Hopkinson (1773–1856) married Federalist Congressman Joseph Hopkinson (1770–1842) in 1794. For other examples of these presentations, see *Country Porcupine,* October 23 and 24, 1798. The Federalists' appropriation of Fourth of July festivals in 1798 is discussed in Newman, *Parades and the Politics of the Street,* chapter 4 and Len Travers, *Celebrating the Fourth: Independence Day and the Rites of Nationalism in the Early Republic* (Amherst: University of Massachusetts Press, 1997), chapter 5.

115. *Gazette of the United States,* May 14, 1798.

116. "Offering of Patriotism," *Gazette of the United States,* July 11, 1798.

117. *Country Porcupine,* October 23 and 24, 1798. Linda Kerber has remarked that the Democratic Republican newspapers of the decade were receptive to women in politics, while the Federalist press was not. This was clearly not the case in 1798. See *Women of the Republic,* 279.

118. *Country Porcupine,* October 23 and 24, 1798.

119. Eleanor Parke Custis to Elizabeth Bordley, May 14, 1798. In *George Washington's Beautiful Nelly,* 52.

120. For a discussion of the redefinition of political space, see Ozouf, *Festivals and the French Revolution,* chapter 6.

121. Newman, *Parades and the Politics of the Street,* chapter 5, and Travers, *Celebrating the Fourth,* chapter 4.

122. *Gazette of the United States,* July 11, 1798.

123. *Gazette of the United States,* July 26, 1798.

124. "Female Toasting," *Porcupine's Gazette,* July 14, 1798. Travers discusses women's participation in July Fourth celebrations in *Celebrating the Fourth,* 135–141.

125. Young, "The Women of Boston: 'Persons of Consequence' in the Making of the American Revolution, 1765–76," 192; *Porcupine's Gazette,* July 14, 1798.

126. Susan G. Davis, *Parades and Power: Street Theater in Nineteenth Century Philadelphia* (Philadelphia: Temple University Press, 1986), 6; Dominique Godineau, "Masculine and Feminine Political Practice during the French Revolution, 1793—Year III," 73–75; Joan Wallach Scott, "French Feminists and the Rights of 'Man': Olympe de Gouges's Declarations," *History Workshop Journal* (fall-winter 1989), 1–21; Lenora Cohen Rosenfield, "The Rights of Women in the French Revolution," *Studies in Eighteenth Century Culture* 7 (1976), 117–137; Jane Abray, "Feminism in the French Revolution," *American Historical Review* 80, no. 1 (February 1975), 43–62.

127. Koschnik, "Political Conflict and Public Context," 231.

128. David I. Kertzer, *Ritual, Politics, and Power* (New Haven: Yale University Press, 1988), 12. As David Waldstreicher as noted, they helped estab-

lish an "American national family." "Federalism, the Styles of Politics, and the Politics of Style," in Doron Ben-Atar and Barbara Oberg, eds., *Federalists Reconsidered* (Charlottesville: University Press of Virginia, 1998), 116.

129. Judith Sargent Murray to Sally Wood, November 25, 1800. Judith Sargent Murray Papers, Mississippi Department of Archives. Reprinted in *From Gloucester to Philadelphia in 1790,* 51.

130. Deborah Logan to Mary Norris, August 16, [1799], Deborah Logan Outgoing Correspondence 1798–1801, Robert R. Logan Collection. All the Logan material used in this chapter is in the Historical Society of Pennsylvania.

131. "He [George Logan] was fully aware of the misrepresentations to which his conduct would be liable, and, from the violence with which federalism at that period assailed its opponents, could hope for no quarter in case of a deviation from the most perfect prudence. He thought it best, therefore, by a solemn legal act to empower me to dispose of his estate in such a manner as to secure it from confiscation." Deborah Logan, *Memoir of Dr. George Logan of Stenton* (Philadelphia, 1899), 55; 54.

132. Of the latter Deborah Logan commented that he was "a character who has seemed to be possessed of a political life-boat with which he has in safety ridden on the tremendous surges of the Revolution." Ibid., 57–58.

133. Ibid., 58–59; 59; 57.

134. Ibid., 75–76.

135. Ibid., 75–76.

136. Cobbett was not being paid by the British. However, the British Minister in Philadelphia, Robert Liston, did offer Cobbett money, which he refused to accept, as reward for his stand against the French influence in America. Green, *Great Cobbett,* 141; *Porcupine's Gazette,* Wednesday, January 3, 1798, no. 269; "New Verses to an Old Tune," Reprinted from Fenno's paper, *Gazette of the United States,* in *Porcupine's Gazette,* no. 410, June 29, 1798.

137. *Porcupine's Gazette,* no. 400, June 18, 1798.

138. *Porcupine's Gazette,* July 21, 1798.

139. Deborah Logan, "Transactions on the Farm and Memoranda of Various Matters Commencing June 12th, 1798, the day on which my most tenderly beloved husband embarked for Europe," June 22, 1798.

140. Deborah Logan, "Transactions," August 4, August 21, September 11, and September 19, 1798.

141. Tolles, *George Logan,* 167; quoted in Tolles, *George Logan,* 166, from *Chronique universelle,* August 27, 1798.

142. *Memoir,* 82. Logan recorded in her "Transactions," September 7, 1798: "Paid Hagner's bill for Plaister of Paris. People of his description always enquire with great respect after my dear doctor Logan."

143. Deborah Logan, "Transactions," November 4, 1798, and *Memoir,* 79.

144. *Philadelphia Gazette and Universal Daily Advertiser,* no. 3143, Novem-

ber 9, 1798. Subsequently she also sent it to Bache's *Aurora. Memoir,* 79.

145. *Memoir,* 59–60; *Porcupine's Gazette,* November 10, 1798; *Memoir,* 80.

146. Deborah Logan to Mary Norris, Stenton, December 31, 1798, folder 37, Family letters vol. 1, Norris of Fairhill Papers, no. 2; *Memoir,* 87. See also Deborah Logan to Mary Norris, Stenton, December 31, 1798, Family letters vol. 1, folder 37, Norris of Fairhill Papers, no. 2; Deborah Logan, "Transactions," October 15, 1798. Although Federalist popularity was on the wane, they still controlled Congress. They were determined that no one else would repeat George Logan's performance, and steal thunder out from under the nose of the Adams administration. On January 7, 1799, the "Logan Act," as it came to be known, was introduced to the House. During the debate on the "Logan Act" the doctor was accused of corresponding with Talleyrand, of writing a letter of treasonable conspiracy. This prompted George Logan to respond first with his "Address to the Citizens of the United States," which the *Aurora* published on January 12. In this address the Doctor gave a full account of his visit to France, his motives and the outcome. A few days later he published a statement in which he denied the accusation of treasonous correspondence with Talleyrand. Tolles, *George Logan,* 194, quoting from *Annals,* 5th Congress, 3rd session, 2583–2584; Tolles, *George Logan,* 196–197; *Aurora,* January 16, 1799.

147. *Memoir,* 87.

148. Coguing meant dram-drinking.

149. Tolles, 193. His footnote for this information is *Messages and Papers of the Presidents,* I, 276; the poem was printed in *The Political Greenhouse for the Year 1798* (Hartford, 1799), 8.

150. *Aurora,* January 9, 1799, no. 2447; *Aurora,* nos. 2449 and 2455, January 11, 18, 1799.

151. *Porcupine's Gazette,* no. 602, February 9, 1799.

152. This is mentioned in Alexander Graydon, *Memoirs of a Life Chiefly Passed in Pennsylvania within the last sixty years* (Edinburgh, 1822), 405. Jean-Baptiste Louvet de Couvrai (c. 1760) was a revolutionary who ran a newspaper and wrote novels. His political opinions brought opponents to his store where they taunted him with digs at his wife, whom they called "Lodoiska" after a character in one of his books. See *Biographie Universelle Ancienne et Moderne,* 25:353–354. Philadelphia Democratic Republicans knew about Louvet de Couvrai's novel *Une Année de la Vie du Chevalier de Faublas* (1787) because it was translated and published in the city under the name *Love and Patriotism* (Mathew Carey, 1797). See Kathryn Norberg, "Love and Patriotism: Gender and Politics in the Life and Work of Louvet de Couvrai," in Sara E. Melzer and Leslie W. Rabine, eds., *Rebel Daughters: Women and the French Revolution* (New York: Oxford University Press, 1992), 38–53.

153. Waldstreicher, "Federalism, the Styles of Politics, and the Politics of Style," 167.

154. Rosemarie Zagarri, "Gender and the First Party System." Doron

Ben-Atar and Barbara Oberg, eds., *Federalists Reconsidered*, 5. *Porcupine's Gazette*, November 3, 1798.

CHAPTER 3. WOMEN AS AUTHORS, AUDIENCES, AND SUBJECTS IN THE AMERICAN THEATER

1. Heather Shawn Nathans discusses the Quaker opposition to theater in the colonial era in "'A Democracy of Glee': The Post-Revolutionary Theater of Boston and Philadelphia" (Ph.D. diss., Tufts University, 1999), 10–14.

2. Nathans, "'A Democracy of Glee,'" 42–43.

3. This brief history of Philadelphia's theater in the eighteenth century is gleaned from the following sources: Richard D. Stine, "The Philadelphia Theater, 1682–1829" (Ph.D. diss., University of Pennsylvania, 1951); Arthur Hornblow, *A History of the Theater in America From Its Beginnings to the Present Time* (New York, 1919); and Charles Durang, *History of the Philadelphia Stage from 1749 to 1821* (Philadelphia, 1854).

4. In 1794, for example, the *Gazette of the United States* announced that dancer Madame Gardie was to perform a pantomime "as performed at the Theatre de mes plaisirs at Paris with unbounded applause, called harlequin Pastry Cook. In the course of the Pantomime, madame Gardie will sing a French song, called Le Mot Vaut Mieux que la Chose, et la Chose Vaut Mieux que le Mot." *Gazette of the United States*, November 18, 1794.

5. Gerald Bordman, *The Oxford Companion to American Theater* (New York: Oxford University Press, 1984). *The Contrast*, by Royall Tyler, performed in New York in 1787, was the first play written in the United States. America did have one female playwright before the 1790s. Mercy Otis Warren wrote two plays about the Revolution, *The Adulator* (1773), a satire on Gov. Thomas Hutchinson, and *The Group* (1775), about the king's abrogation of Massachusetts's charter. They were printed but never performed. See Rosemarie Zagarri, *A Woman's Dilemma: Mercy Otis Warren and the American Revolution* (Wheeling, Ill.: Harlan-Davidson, 1995).

6. Thomas Clark Pollock, *The Philadelphia Theater in the Eighteenth Century* (Philadelphia: University of Pennsylvania Press, 1933), 54; *Dunlap's American Daily Advertiser*, February 4, 1793. Quoted in Nathans, "Forging a Powerful Engine," 129.

7. *Porcupine's Gazette* (Philadelphia), March 7, 1797.

8. The New Theater on March 24, 1794. Paul Leicester Ford, *Washington and the Theatre* (1899; reprint, New York: Benjamin Blom, 1967), 55–58.

9. Review by "Columbus," *Aurora*, January 2, 1798.

10. Judith Sargent Murray, July 10, June 14, 1790, Murray Letterbook 4. My thanks to Sheila Skemp for providing these letters from the Mississippi State Archives. They are also included in *From Gloucester to Philadelphia in*

1790: Observations, Anecdotes, and Thoughts from the Eighteenth-Century Letters of Judith Sargent Murray, ed. Bonnie Hurd Smith (Cambridge, Mass.: Judith Sargent Murray Society, 1998).

11. Murray, *From Gloucester to Philadelphia*, June 14, July 3, 1790, pp. 112, 168. Women were among the most celebrated performers of the day. Many, like Susanna Rowson and Henry, began their careers on the English stage and continued them, well into late middle age, in America. Rowson proudly advertised her novels as written by an "author and actress." After her retirement from the stage, Boston parents entrusted their daughters' educations and reputations to the former thespian turned educator and magazine editor.

Theater offered one of the few ways for women to earn a living and to continue their work once married. American theater companies employed dozens of married couples. Many actresses managed their performing schedules around childrearing. Children were raised in the theater, often performing themselves, and creating theatrical dynasties. A few women became theater managers, taking over from their deceased husbands. Anne Bruton Merry, for example, began her American career in 1796. Following the death of her husband in 1803, she took over management of Philadelphia's Chestnut Street theater. Faye E. Dudden, *Women in the American Theater: Actresses and Audiences, 1790–1870* (New Haven: Yale University Press, 1994), 12.

12. *Philadelphia Monthly Magazine*, April 1798, 188.

13. Stine, "The Philadelphia Theater," 99; Hornblow, *A History of the Theater*, 204.

14. Moreau de Saint Méry, *Moreau de Saint Méry's American Journey: 1793–1798*, ed. and trans. Kenneth Roberts and Anna M. Roberts (Garden City, N.Y.: Doubleday, 1947), 347.

15. Méry, *American Journey*, 347.

16. Review of historical play *Columbus* at the New Theater. *Aurora*, January 2, 1798.

17. One of the combatants was Mary Wollstonecraft's brother Charles. Charles Wollstonecraft worked for Alexander Hamilton Rowan at his calico mill in Wilmington, Delaware, for a time. Rowan was an Irishman who had escaped from a Dublin prison after his conviction for sedition. He first traveled to Paris, where he formed a friendship with Mary Wollstonecraft, who was anxious to have her brother settled in business. By 1796, Charles Wollstonecraft resided near the Philadelphia waterfront, in the High Street ward, close by the Imlay brothers' store on Front Street. Emily W. Sunstein, *A Different Face: The Life of Mary Wollstonecraft* (New York, 1975), 264, 296.

Wollstonecraft and merchant Robert Andrews argued over which of them was Mary Meredith's rightful suitor. The young gentlemen may have confronted each other in the foyer outside the boxes, an area where, as Charles Haswell remembered, "it was customary for the male portion of the audience during the acts to promenade." He is describing the Park Theater in New

York City (built in 1798), but the Philadelphia theater had a similar interior. Charles Haswell, *Reminiscences of New York by an Octogenarian (1816-1860)* (New York: Harper, 1896), chapter 3.

Mary's mother described the confrontation: "One evening Robert accompany'd us to the theater & leaving the box to walk in the lobby W[ollstonecraft] accosted him in very plain language & an altercation ensu'd.—I suppose being call'd a D—d R—l is an afront in publick that few gentlemen wou'd forgive without resentment. Mr. Meredith steps in. W[ollstonecraft] apologizes, saying he had drank too much, didn't like being called names. The next day W[ollstonecraft] stayed home expecting Andrews to challenge him to a duel, but A[ndrews] doesn't." Elizabeth Meredith to David Meredith, September 24, 1796, Meredith Family Papers, Historical Society of Pennsylvania.

18. *Dunlap's American Daily Advertiser,* June 5, 1792.

19. Ford, *Washington and the Theater,* 47. The President was feted even in absentia. The Federal Street theater in Boston celebrated George Washington's birthday in 1797 with the performance of *The Man of Ten Thousand, Solomon's Temple* (a Masonic presentation), and *The Birthday; or a Rural Fete.* Also on the bill of entertainment that evening was the display of a statue of Washington, "The Hero, Friend, and Patriot." Dorothy M. Bonowitz, "The History of the Boston Stage from the Beginning to 1810" (Ph.D. diss., Pennsylvania State University, 1936), 118–119.

20. See Tryna Zeedyk, "Political Issues on the Philadelphia Stage: Susanna Rowson's *Slaves in Algiers* and Its Critics" (unpublished essay, Northern Illinois University, 1990), 3–4.

21. See, for example the announcement of a comedy called *A Cure for the Heartache* at the New Theater, *Aurora,* January 1, 1798.

22. Coad, 213; Dunlap, *A History of the American Theater* (1832, reprint, New York: Burt Franklin, 1963) 140–141. The content of plays could also draw a political response from the audience. In Boston, "It was customary for the actors, who were all immigrants from the English stage, to interpolate jests and witticisms at the expense of the French and these often gave offence and sometimes created serious disturbances in the house." Hornblow, *History of the Theater,* 237.

23. Alfred F. Young, *The Democratic-Republicans of New York* (Chapel Hill: University of North Carolina Press, 1967), 364 [quoting *New York Journal, or General Advertiser* (New York) February 23, 1793].

24. Known as the "French Theater," the Church Street theater was started in 1794 by a group of refugees from Saint Domingue and Continental France. The theater quickly drew American patrons as well as patrons from the refugee community. Its politics, judging from this particular occasion, seem to have favored the Revolution. Eola Willis, *The Charleston Stage in the Eighteenth Century* (Columbia, S.C.: State Company, 1924), 243.

25. *Aurora General Advertiser*, February 28, 1794, and February 17, 1794. See Laura Mason, "'Ca Ira' and the Birth of the Revolutionary Song," *History Workshop Journal* 28 (autumn 1989), 22–38.

26. Bonowitz, "History of the Boston Stage," 121. The Federal Street theater was a Federalist theater. Its rival, the Haymarket, was Democratic Republican.

27. *Gazette of the United States*, April 17, 1798.

28. *Porcupine's Gazette*, April 28, 1798.

29. Henrietta Liston to James Jackson, May 3, 1798. "A Diplomat's Wife in Philadelphia: Letters of Henrietta Liston, 1779–1800," ed. Bradford Perkins, *William and Mary Quarterly* 11, no. 4 (October 1954), 616. The incident was also reported in *Porcupine's Gazette*, May 2, 1798.

30. Charleston's "French" Theater, 1794. Willis, *The Charleston Stage*, 251.

31. Willis, *The Charleston Stage*, 245–246; Bonowitz, "History of the Boston Stage," 93–94. Mrs. Marriott composed at least one other piece for the theater, a farce called *The Chimera; or The Effusions of Fancy*, performed by the Old American Company at Southwark Theater for her benefit night in 1794. *Gazette of the United States*, November 10, 1794.

32. *Gazette of the United States*, April 26, 1798.

33. *New York Journal*, March 12, 1794, quoted in George C. Odell, *Annals of the New York Stage* (New York: 1927; reprint 1970), 347. Charlotte Melmoth (1749–1823), "a tragic actress of great power, though no longer young nor slender," made her debut in Philadelphia with the Old American Company for its final season, September-December 1794. Pollock, *The Philadelphia Theater*, 57. After a long acting career, Melmoth, like Susanna Rowson, established a female seminary. Bordman, *The Oxford Companion to American Theater*; Virginia Blain et al., *The Feminist Companion to Literature in English* (New Haven: Yale University Press, 1990).

34. Hatton earned the title of "poetess" to the society after she penned an ode celebrating the French victory at Toulon. Odell, *Annals of the New York Stage*, 348; George O. Seilhamer, *History of the American Theater: New Foundations* (Philadelphia, 1891; reprint Grosse Pointe, Mich.: Scholarly Press, 1968), 85–86; Young, *The Democratic Republicans*, 202–203. The play was performed October 18 and November 10 at the Southwark (South, or Cedar Street) Theater by the Old American Company. See the *Gazette of the United States*, October 18 and November 19, 1794. The songs of the play have survived, but not the text.

35. Gary E. Wilson, "American Hostages in Moslem Nations, 1784–1796: The Public Response," *Journal of the Early Republic* 2 (summer 1982), 123–141.

36. Amelia Howe Kritzer, "Feminism and Nationalism in the Plays of Late Eighteenth-Century American Women," paper presented to the American Society for Eighteenth-Century Studies, March 1994, 6.

37. The following sources offer useful Rowson information: Eve Kornfield, "Women in Post-Revolutionary American Culture: Susanna Haswell Rowson's American Career 1793–1824," *Journal of American Culture* 6 (winter 1983), 56–62; Dorothy Weil, *In Defense of Women* (University Park: Pennsylvania State University Press, 1976); Ellen B. Brandt, *Susanna Haswell Rowson, America's First Best-Selling Novelist* (Chicago: 1975); Patricia L. Parker, *Susanna Rowson* (Boston: 1986); Tryna Zeedyk, "Political Issues on the Philadelphia Stage"; Doreen Alvarez Saar, "Susanna Rowson: Feminist and Democrat," in *Curtain Calls: British and American Women and the Theater, 1660-1820,* ed. Mary Anne Schofield and Cecilia Macheski (Athens: Ohio University Press, 1991), 231–246.

38. Pollock, *The Philadelphia Theater in the Eighteenth Century,* contains the performances for all the Philadelphia theaters in the 1790s. *Slaves in Algiers* appeared at least once a season.

39. Cobbett, *A Kick for a Bite,* 16. Englishwoman Helen Maria Williams was another favorite target for Cobbett. She moved to France in 1788 and from there wrote an eyewitness account of the Revolution. She entertained many "liberal English and American literary and political figures." Frederick B. Tolles, "Unofficial Ambassador: George Logan's Mission to France, 1798," *William and Mary Quarterly* 7, no. 1 (January 1950), 3–25.

40. *Porcupine's Gazette,* July 11, 1797.

41. Roland M. Baumann, "John Swanwick: Spokesman for 'Merchant-Republicanism' in Philadelphia, 1790–1798," *Pennsylvania Magazine of History and Biography* 97, no. 2 (April 1973); John Swanwick, *A Rub from Snub; or a Cursory Analytical Epistle: Addressed to Peter Porcupine, Author of the Bone to Gnaw, Kick for a Bite, &c. &c., Containing Glad Tidings for the DEMOCRATS and a Word of Comfort to Mrs. S. Rowson* (Philadelphia, 1795), 76.

Rowson wrote another play for which no printed copies can be located *The Female Patriot; or Nature's Rights,* also performed in 1794. Judging by its title, this second play also linked nationalism with women's roles. The following year her third play, *The Volunteers,* appeared. Like *Slaves in Algiers, The Volunteers* addressed a current political issue, the Whiskey Rebellion. Though no copy of the play exists, its songs demonstrate that Rowson supported the Federalist interpretation of the events of the rebellion. President and Mrs. Washington attended the second performance in January 1795, thus giving the play a Federalist seal of approval. Kritzer, *Plays By Early American Women: 1794-1844,* 11. See Thomas P. Slaughter, *The Whiskey Rebellion: Frontier Epilogue to the American Revolution* (New York: Oxford University Press, 1986).

42. Inchbald's first novel, *Nature and Art* (published in London and Philadelphia in 1796), which she herself described as "a socio-political fable," was heavily influenced by her friendship with William Godwin. Inchbald was a rival, rather than a friend, of Mary Wollstonecraft. Before his relationship with Wollstonecraft, Godwin proposed marriage to Inchbald, but she turned

him down. Yet all three writers were part of the same intellectual circle, which caused critics to label Inchbald's work a "Jacobin novel." Her novel is not overtly feminist, but expresses sympathy for the female characters, who are limited in their choices and activities and are often allowed to become victims of seduction. Roger Manvell, *Elizabeth Inchbald: England's Principal Woman Dramatist and Independent Woman of Letters in Eighteenth Century London: A Biography* (Lanham, Md.: University Press of America, 1987), 109.

43. George C. Odell, *Annals of the New York Stage*, 1, 354; Seilhamer, *History of the American Theater* 3, 243; David Ritchey, *A Guide to the Baltimore Stage in the Eighteenth Century* (Westport, Conn: Greenwood Press, 1982), 28. In the play, comic effect is presented by a constantly bickering couple, Mr. and Mrs. Placid (played by Susanna Rowson and Mr. Moreton in Philadelphia). President Washington and his family attended this play twice in March 1794. Ford, *Washington and the Theater*, 53–55.

44. Elizabeth Inchbald, *Everyone Has His Fault (As Performed at the New Theater, Philadelphia. Marked with Alterations {By Permission of the Managers} by William Rowson, Prompter)* (Philadelphia: H. and P. Rice, and Mathew Carey, 1794). The prologue is included in this Philadelphia edition of the play, but is not in the reprinted collection, Inchbald, *Selected Comedies* (Lanham, Md.: University Press of America, 1987). A New Jersey author "borrowed" Inchbald's words six years later in a poem on the subject of women's rights submitted to the *Centinel of Freedom* (Newark), September 22, 1801.

45. David A. Wilson, *United Irishmen, United States, Immigrant Radicals in the Early Republic* (Ithaca: Cornell University Press, 1998), 103–106; Len Travers, *Celebrating the Fourth: Independence Day and the Rites of Nationalism in the Early Republic* (Amherst: University of Massachusetts Press, 1997), 126.

46. John Murdock, *The Politicians*, act 1, scene 1.

47. Murdock signed himself anonymously as "An American and a Citizen of Philadelphia." A previous play, *The Triumphs of Love; Or Happy Reconciliation* (1795), had one performance at the Chestnut Street theater with many changes to the script unauthorized by the author. Murdock's problems with Wignell and Reinagle, based in part on his Democratic Republican politics and nonelite origins, are detailed in Nathans, "A Democracy of Glee," 141–142.

48. Mercy Otis Warren's *Ladies of Castille* (1790), published but never performed, also asserts the strength and self-reliance of American women.

49. Murray's *Virtue Triumphant* was the first American play originally produced in Boston, performed under the title *The Medium* at the Federal Street theater in March 1795. Both Murray's plays were printed as part of the collection *The Gleaner* in 1798. Judith Sargent Murray, *The Gleaner*, introduction by Nina Baym (Schenectady, N.Y.: Union College Press, 1992), 560–561, 572, 560, 590.

50. *Virtue Triumphant*, despite the fact that it was proudly advertised as

"Written by a Citizen of the United States," was not well received by its audience. According to Murray, "the players were generally deficient in their parts they came on the stage with scarce a recollection of the sentiment which they were to express," *The Gleaner*, 605, 544.

51. Ibid., 650.
52. Judith Sargent Murray, *The Traveler Returned*, act 4.
53. Kritzer, "Feminism and Nationalism," 3.
54. Seilhamer, *History of the American Theater*, 304–305.

CHAPTER 4. THE CREATION OF THE AMERICAN POLITICAL SALON

1. Awareness of the existence of salon culture in post-Revolutionary American society is not new. Over 140 years ago historian Rufus Griswold explored at great length the elite political and social networks in the new nation. At the beginning of the twentieth century, historian Anne Hollingsworth Wharton detailed the prominent role of Philadelphia women in these eighteenth-century networks. Griswold and Wharton copiously quoted from contemporaries who remarked on the charms, beauty, and grace of the nation's elite women. None of these historians considered the impact of these new circumstances on gender relations and women's access to public roles. Rufus Wilmot Griswold, *The Republican Court; or, American Society in the Days of Washington* (New York: D. Appleton, 1867); Anne Hollingsworth Wharton, *Salons, Colonial and Republican* (Philadelphia: J. B. Lippincott, 1900).

My information concerning French salon culture is taken from Dena Goodman's insightful work *The Republic of Letters: A Cultural History of the French Enlightenment* (Ithaca: Cornell University Press, 1994).

2. Goodman, *The Republic of Letters*, 4, 6 and 9.
3. Ibid., 75. This was equally true of Philadelphia's salons. See Susan Stabile's discussion of sororal intellectual networks in her dissertation, "Philadelphia Women's Literary Circle, 1760–1820" (University of Delaware, 1996).
4. Goodman, *The Republic of Letters*, 101.
5. Samuel Johnson was not known for his tact or gratitude. His definition of a patron in his *Dictionary* was "a wretch who supports with insolence and is paid with flattery." Quoted in Chauncey Brewster Tinker, *The Salon and English Letters* (New York: Macmillan, 1915), 32. Johnson was awarded a small pension (£300) by the crown in 1792 for his literary efforts. See W. Jackson Bate, *Samuel Johnson* (New York: Harcourt Brace Jovanovich, 1975), 355.
6. Tinker, *The Salon*, 30.
7. From its origins as the name of a heterosocial literary club, the word "bluestocking" evolved in the later eighteenth and nineteenth centuries into a

term referring exclusively to intellectual women. For a full treatment of the club and its influence on English women writers, see Sylvia Harcstark Myers, *The Bluestocking Circle: Women, Friendship, and the Life of the Mind in Eighteenth-Century England* (Oxford: Clarendon Press, 1990).

8. David S. Shields identifies the rise of this practice in the 1730s when the tea table became a social location which attracted "men of sense into the company by extending the promise that conversation with women would be to their advantage." *Civil Tongues and Polite Letters in British America* (Chapel Hill: University of North Carolina Press, 1997), 119.

9. Wharton, *Salons*, 13–21. Wharton mentions Mrs. Simon Bradstreet, Mrs. James Warren, Mrs. John Adams, and Mrs. Richard Stockton as other colonial American salonnières. David S. Shields discusses Graeme Ferguson extensively in *Civil Tongues and Polite Letters*, 120–140. Also see *Only for the Eye of a Friend: The Poems of Annis Boudinot Stockton*, ed. Carla Mulford (Charlottesville: University Press of Virginia, 1995) for Annis Boudinot Stockton as a pre- and post-Revolution salonnière.

10. Wharton, *Salons*, 11.

11. Mulford, introduction to *Only for the Eye of a Friend: The Poems of Annis Boudinot Stockton*, and Karin Wulf's introduction to *Milcah Martha Moore's Book: A Commonplace Book from Revolutionary America*, ed. Catherine La Courreye Blecki and Karin A. Wulf (University Park: Pennsylvania State University, 1997).

12. Part of the absence of politics from French salons of the ancien régime can be explained by censorship—something which did not exist (until the Sedition Act of 1798) in the United States.

Not all post-Revolutionary salons were directly connected to the political society. David Shields mentions New England and New York salons which retained a primarily literary character. Shields, *Civil Tongues and Polite Letters*, 311 n. 4.

13. Ethel E. Rasmusson, "Capital on the Delaware: The Philadelphia Upper Class in Transition, 1789–1801" (Ph.D. diss., Brown University, 1962), 87.

14. E. F. Ellet, *Court Circles of the Republic* (Philadelphia: Philadelphia Publishing Company, 1872), 16–17. Ellet may have been writing with a touch of elitist nostalgia generated in the late nineteenth century.

15. Judith Sargent Murray to her parents, August 14, 1790. *From Gloucester to Philadelphia in 1790: Observations, Anecdotes, and Thoughts from the Eighteenth-Century Letters of Judith Sargent Murray*, ed. Bonnie Hurd Smith (Cambridge, Mass.: Judith Sargent Murray Society, 1998), 254.

16. Ibid.

17. Douglas Southall Freeman, *George Washington, A Biography*, 7 vols. (New York: Scribners, 1948–1957), 213–14, 295.

18. Murray, *From Gloucester to Philadelphia in 1790*, 254.

19. Marital alliances between the sons and daughters of congressmen also furthered political interests. Freeman, *George Washington*, 211; Shields, *Civil Tongues*, 320; Daphne Hamm O'Brien, "The First Congress, Polite Society, and Courtship in New York City: The Case of Margaret Lowther," paper presented at the Sixteenth Annual Meeting of the Society for Historians of the Early Republic, Boston, July 15, 1994.

20. Kenneth R. Dowling and Helen E. Veit, eds., *The Diary of William Maclay, and Other Notes on Senate Debates* (Baltimore: Johns Hopkins University Press, 1988), 70, 349.

21. After the first federal election, senators were given a two, four, or six-year term. Maclay received a two-year term of office. See Dowling and Veit's introduction to *The Diary of William Maclay*, xvi.

22. Quoted in Margaret C. S. Christman, *The First Federal Congress, 1789–1791* (Washington, D.C.: Smithsonian, 1989), 197.

23. Wharton, *Salons*, 53; Maclay, *Diary*, 74.

24. Maclay, *Diary*, 60, 71.

25. Henrietta Liston, wife of the British ambassador, recalled being seated so near to the president at one of these official ceremonies in Philadelphia that she could see the "extreme agitation He felt when He mentioned the *French*." Henrietta Liston, letter, December 9, 1796, "A Diplomat's Wife in Philadelphia: Letters of Henrietta Liston, 1779–1800," ed. Bradford Perkins, *William and Mary Quarterly* 11, no. 4 (October 1954), 606.

26. Murray, *From Gloucester to Philadelphia in 1790*, 96.

27. Legislators themselves apparently escorted women to Congress. William Maclay recorded that he had "promised Mrs. Bell to go with her to the Hall." Maclay, *Diary*, 84.

28. Maclay, *Diary*, 298. Bell's sister had married Maclay's brother.

29. Carl and Jessica Bridenbaugh, *Rebels and Gentlemen: Philadelphia in the Age of Franklin* (New York: Oxford University Press, 1962); Ethel E. Rasmusson, "Capital on the Delaware"; Russell F. Weigley, *Philadelphia: A Three Hundred Year History* (New York: Norton, 1982).

30. See Washington's diaries from May to September 1787 in Philadelphia for descriptions of his numerous visits to the Morris, Powel and Bingham families. *The Diaries of George Washington*, ed. Donald Jackson and Dorothy Twohig (July 1786 to December 1789) (Charlottesville: University Press of Virginia, 1979), vol. 5.

Diplomats in the capital also regularly hosted dinners and "at homes." Henrietta Liston, wife of the British minister from 1796 to the end of the century, scheduled Monday evenings to receive visitors and offer "tea, coffee, and cards." She made a deliberate effort to make her gatherings attractive to Philadelphia's women, noting that "publick tea parties seem to be an amusement of which the Ladies in this Country are particularly fond, and mine will have the advantage of *Cards* over Mrs. Washington." And though by 1796 there were sharp fractures between Federalists and Republicans, Liston boasted that partisanship was no barrier to sociability; even "the greatest Democrats in Town," including Dr. Joseph Priestley, attended her parties. "A Diplomat's Wife in Philadelphia: Letters of Henrietta Liston, 1779–1800," 607, 608.

31. Charles Brockden Brown, "The Essayist," in *Ladys Magazine* (Philadelphia) November 1792, 255; see also "Address to the Ladies," June 1792. Cited in Steven Watts, *The Romance of Real Life: Charles Brockden Brown and the Origins of American Culture* (Baltimore: Johns Hopkins University Press, 1994), 60.

32. Wharton, *Salons*, 134.

33. Anne-Catherine de Ligniville Helvétius; Claude-Anne Lopez, *Mon Cher Papa: Franklin and the Ladies of Paris* (New Haven: Yale University Press, 1966), chapter 9.

34. Robert C. Alberts, *The Golden Voyage: The Life and Times of William Bingham, 1752–1804* (Boston: Houghton Mifflin, 1969), 142–147.

35. Abigail (Nabby) Adams diary entry, October 1784, Caroline Amelia Smith DeWindt, ed., *Journal and Correspondence of Miss Adams,* 2 vols. (Boston: Wiley and Putnam, 1841), quoted in Alberts, *Golden Voyage*, 143.

36. Bingham to Thomas Jefferson, June 1787. *The Papers of Thomas Jefferson* ed. Julian P. Boyd, et al. (Princeton: Princeton University Press, 1950–96), 11: 392. Reproduced in Alberts, *Golden Voyage*, 464–466. David Shields suggests that Bingham's salon was probably the first American one to be wholly modeled on the French. *Civil Tongues*, 199 n. 32.

37. Powel herself acknowledged her part in shaping Anne's character. Writing about her niece during the Binghams' stay in Europe, Powel commented, "It will be happy for her if she has retained some of the ancient impressions that I was so solicitous to make on her mind when I was her oracle." Elizabeth Powel (1743–1830) to Margaret Hare (Powel's sister), October 2, 1783, Elizabeth Powel Personal Correspondence, 1783–1786, Historical Society of Pennsylvania. Quoted in Wendy Anne Nicholson, "Making the Private Public: Anne Willing Bingham's Role as a Leader of Philadelphia's Social Elite in the Late Eighteenth Century" (master's thesis, University of Delaware, 1988), 21.

Nicholson contrasts contemporary advice books for men and women with Anne Bingham's behavior. She suggests that Bingham diverged from the precepts for young women in social gatherings and more readily fits the behavior suggested for young men in Lord Chesterfield's *Letters to His Son*. Elizabeth Powel's influence may have had something to do with Bingham's more outgoing, less passive personality. Powel highly disapproved of Chesterfield's opinions, especially concerning women: "On most points his sentiments are dangerous, with submission to his Lordship's judgement, they are generally weak and too often wicked when he speaks of our sex." Powel to Mary (Willing) Byrd, 1783, Elizabeth Powel Personal Correspondence, 1783–1786, Elizabeth Powel Papers, Historical Society of Pennsylvania.

Chesterfield considered women "only children for a larger growth; they have an entertaining tattle and sometimes wit; but for solid reasoning, good sense, I never knew one in my life that had it." Lord Chesterfield, *Letters to His Son*, ed. Oliver H. Lehigh, 2 vols. (New York: Tudor Publishing Company, 1937), 1:107. Quoted in Nicholson, "Making the Private Public," 15.

38. James Thomas Flexner, *George Washington and the New Nation (1783-1793)* (Boston: Little, Brown, 1970), 321.

39. Bingham was speaker of the Pennsylvania House of Representatives and was elected a senator for Pennsylvania in 1795.

40. This is Wendy Nicholson's reconstruction of the floor plan. Nicholson, "Making the Private Public," 34–35.

41. Items mentioned are in the 1805 house inventory, cited in Nicholson, "Making the Private Public," 60–66.

42. Richard L. Bushman, *The Refinement of America: Persons, Houses, Cities* (New York: Knopf, 1992), 126.

43. Arthur Lee to James Warren, December 12, 1782, *The Warren Adams Letters, Being Chiefly a Correspondence among John Adams, Samuel Adams, and James Warren*, 2 vols. (Boston: Massachusetts Historical Society, 1925), 184. Quoted in Nicholson, "Making the Private Public," 51.

44. *The Diaries of George Washington*, 5:159; 6:326.

45. Maclay, *Diary*, 357.

46. Abigail Adams, December 26, 1790, Charles Francis Adams, *Letters of Mrs. Adams*, enlarged 4th ed. (Boston: Little and Brown, 1848), 351; Quoted in Alberts, *Golden Voyage*, 212.

47. Alberts, *Golden Voyage*, 213.

48. Charlotte Chambers to her mother, Philadelphia, February 25, 1795, *Memoir of Charlotte Chambers* (Philadelphia, 1856), 16. Quoted in Rasmusson, "Capital on the Delaware," 53; Abigail Adams Smith, *Journal and Correspondence of Miss Adams, Daughter of John Adams*, ed. Caroline Amelia Smith de Windt 1:29. Quoted in Rasmusson, 51.

49. Charles Page Smith, *John Adams*, 2 vols. (New York: Doubleday, 1962), 864, 911. Quoted in Alberts, *Golden Voyage*, 214.

50. Jefferson to James Madison, Philadelphia, March 1793, *The Writings of Thomas Jefferson*, ed. Paul Leicester Ford, 10 vols. (New York: G. P. Putnam's Sons, 1892–1899), 6 (1895): 192–193.

51. Coffin diary entry for August 15, 1796, "Missionary Tour in Maine," Maine Historical Society, 326–327. Quoted in Alberts, *Golden Voyage*, 288.

52. Jefferson to Anne Bingham, Paris, May 11, 1788, *The Papers of Thomas Jefferson* 13:151–152. Jefferson did not reserve his opinions on gender roles for Anne Bingham alone. To Angelica Church he expressed similar ideas the following year during the ratification debates in New York. He assured her that

she need not feel agitated by the question of an American Constitution, because "The tender breasts of ladies were not formed for political convulsion." Jefferson must have been greatly disturbed by what he saw in France, for he repeated to her his condemnation of French women who "miscalculate much their own happiness when they wander from the true field of their influence into that of politics." Two months later he complained to George Washington on the same topic. He described the "desperate state to which things are reduced in this country [France] from the omnipotence of an influence which, fortunately for the happiness of the sex itself, does not endeavor to extend itself in our country beyond the domestic line." September 21, 1788, *Papers* 13:623; November 4, 1788, *Papers* 14:330. Jefferson's need to voice his disapproval of female political behavior to several different audiences, male and female, suggests his deep discomfort with the transgression of traditional gender roles.

53. This letter is the only piece of Bingham's correspondence known to exist. Quoted in Alberts, *The Golden Voyage*, 464–465.

54. *Aurora*, January 20, 1791. In a letter to the editor, the anonymous Mr. "C" recalled the topic under discussion at what was presumably such a social occasion. My thanks to Keith Arbour for bringing this source to my attention and discussing the implications of this source for my arguments on the public arenas within which gender roles and gender relations were being reformulated.

Other print versions of salon culture of the day include *Effusions of Female Fancy* (New York, 1784) and Richard Johnson's *Tea-Table Dialogues* (Philadelphia, 1789).

55. *Weekly Magazine of Original Essays* (Philadelphia), 1798. Brown himself participated in the Friendly Club, begun by a group of young men in 1793 or 1794 for the purpose of pursuing "intellectual growth and human progress through readings, critical discussions, writing and conversation." But these young men intentionally sought the intellectual company of young women of their acquaintance as a complement to their homosocial society. See Fredrika J. Teute, "Reading Men and Women in Late Eighteenth-Century New York," paper presented at the American Society for Eighteenth-Century Studies, Charleston, S.C., 1994, 7, 9–13.

CONCLUSION

1. *Centinel of Freedom* (Newark), July 29, 1800; *Genius of Liberty* (Morristown), July 31, 1800. Quoted in Judith Apter Klinghoffer and Lois Elkis, "'The Petticoat Electors': Women's Suffrage in New Jersey, 1776–1807," *Journal of the Early Republic* 12 (summer 1992), 180. Ironically, New Jersey did curtail their female citizens' rights when the state disenfranchised women in 1807.

2. See Nina Baym, *Woman's Fiction: A Guide to Novels by and About Women in America, 1820–1870* (Ithaca: Cornell University Press, 1978), and *American Women Writers and the Work of History, 1790–1860* (New Brunswick, N.J.: Rutgers University Press, 1995).

3. *The Port Folio* was begun by Joseph Dennie in 1801. For Dennie's "Federalist feminism," see William C. Dowling, *Literary Federalism in the Age of Jefferson* (Columbia: University of South Carolina Press, 1999), 80–81. Carr's *Tea Tray* lasted only a year, from 1814–1815. Louis Godey's magazine began in 1830 and lasted almost sixty years. *Philadelphia Repository and Weekly Register*, edited by David Hogan, was published from 1800 until 1806.

4. David Kaser, *A Book for a Sixpence: The Circulating Library in America* (Pittsburgh: Beta Phi Mu, 1980), 117, 77.

5. Ronald J. Zboray and Mary Saracino Zboray, "Whig Women, Politics, and Culture in the Campaign of 1840: Three Perspectives from Massachusetts," *Journal of the Early Republic* 17, no. 2 (summer 1997), 278–315; Elizabeth R. Varon, "Tippecanoe and the Ladies, Too: White Women and Party Politics in Antebellum Virginia," *Journal of American History* 82 (September 1995), 494–521.

6. This is Varon's term. "Tippecanoe and the Ladies, Too," 495.

7. Ibid., 499; 501.

8. Announcement in *United States Gazette*, November 11, 1808, quoted in Reese D. James, *Old Drury of Philadelphia: A History of the Philadelphia Stage, 1800-1835* (Philadelphia: University of Pennsylvania Press, 1932), 13.

9. These examples are cited in Faye E. Dudden, *Women in the American Theater: Actresses and Audiences, 1790–1870* (New Haven: Yale University Press, 1994), 24–25.

10. Margaret Bayard Smith to Jane B. Kirkpatrick, March 13, 1814, *First Forty Years of Washington Society*, ed. Gaillard Hunt (New York: Charles Scribner's Sons), 94–97. Quoted in Fredrika J. Teute, "Roman Matron on the Banks of Tiber Creek: Margaret Bayard Smith and the Politicization of Spheres in the Nation's Capital," in *"A Republic for the Ages": The United States Capitol and the Political Culture of the Early Republic*, ed. Donald R. Kennon and Barbara Wolanin (Charlottesville: University of Virginia Press, 1999). Teute is currently writing a biography of Smith, *Writing a Woman's Life in the Early Republic: The Liberation of Margaret Bayard Smith, 1778–1844*.

11. Madison was not the only Washington woman who exercised political influence. See Catherine Allgor, "Political Parties: Society and Politics in Washington City, 1800–1832" (Ph.D. diss., Yale University, 1998), chapter 2. Jan Lewis also discusses the political culture of early Washington in "Politics and the Ambivalence of the Private Sphere: Women in Early Washington, D.C.," in *"A Republic for the Ages": The United States Capitol and the Political Culture of the Early Republic*, ed. Donald Kennon and Barbara Wolanin (Charlottesville: University Press of Virginia, 1999). Women's identity as

political beings in the 1820s is addressed by Norma Basch in "Equity vs. Equality: The Concept of Women's Political Status in the Age of Jackson," *Journal of the Early Republic* 3 (fall 1983), 297–318; and in Kirsten E. Wood, "'One Woman So Dangerous to Public Morals': Gender and Power in the Eaton Affair," *Journal of the Early Republic* 17, no. 2 (summer 1997), 237–275.

12. Len Travers, *Celebrating the Fourth: Independence Day and the Rites of Nationalism in the Early Republic* (Amherst: University of Massachusetts Press, 1997), 221. The most comprehensive discussion of women's emergence into the public sphere through benevolent organizations is Lori D. Ginzberg, *Women and the Work of Benevolence: Morality, Politics, and Class in the Nineteenth-Century United States* (New Haven: Yale University Press, 1990).

Bibliography

MANUSCRIPT SOURCES
American Antiquarian Society
  Carey Papers
American Philosophical Society
  Bache Collection
  Bache Papers—Castle Collection
  Benjamin Franklin Bache Papers
  Bradford Collection
  Hewson Family Papers
  Miscellaneous Manuscript Collection
Historical Society of Pennsylvania
  Drinker Papers
  Gibbons Collection Manuscripts, 1760-1837
  Robert R. Logan Collection
  Logan Family Papers
  Maria Dickinson Logan Family Papers
  Loudoun Papers
  Meredith Family Papers
  Norris of Fairhill Papers
  Pennsylvania Land Records, Book E, F 10,
  Pennsylvania Abolition Society, Manumission Book C
  Elizabeth Powel Papers, Powel Collection
Library Company of Philadelphia
  William Bingham Papers
  Dillwyn Family Papers
Library of Congress
  Rebecca Gratz Collection
Rosenbach Museum and Library
  Rush-Biddle-Williams Collection

NEWSPAPERS

American Star (Philadelphia)
Aurora General Advertiser (Philadelphia)
Boston Gazette (Boston)
Columbian Centinel (Boston)
Courrier de la France et des Colonies (Philadelphia)
Dunlap's American Daily Advertiser (Philadelphia)
Federal Gazette and Philadelphia Daily Advertiser (Philadelphia)
Gazette of the United States (New York, Philadelphia)
Independent Chronicle and the Universal Advertiser (Boston)
Independent Gazetteer and Agricultural Repository (Philadelphia)
Massachusetts Mercury (Boston)
National Gazette (Philadelphia)
New York Journal and Weekly Register (New York)
Philadelphia Gazette and Universal Daily Advertiser (Philadelphia)
Porcupine's Gazette (Philadelphia)

MAGAZINES

American Magazine (New York)
American Museum or Universal Magazine (Philadelphia)
American Museum or Repository of Ancient and Modern Fugitive Pieces (Philadelphia)
Columbian Magazine (Philadelphia)
Gentleman and Lady's Town and Country Magazine (Boston)
Gentleman and Lady's Town and Country Magazine: or, Repository of Instruction and Entertainment (Boston)
Intellectual Regale, or Ladies' Tea-Tray (Philadelphia)
Lady's Magazine and Repository of Entertaining Knowledge (Philadelphia)
Lady's Magazine, or Entertaining Companion for the Fair Sex (London)
Literary Magazine and American Register (Philadelphia)
National Magazine (Richmond, Virginia)
New York Journal and Weekly Register (New York)
Philadelphia Minerva (Philadelphia)
Philadelphia Monthly Magazine (Philadelphia)
South Carolina Weekly Museum (Charleston)
Theatrical Censor and Critical Miscellany (Philadelphia)

Weekly Magazine of Original Essays, (Philadelphia)
Weekly Museum (Baltimore)

PUBLISHED PRIMARY SOURCES

Adams, Abigail. *New Letters of Abigail Adams, 1788-1801*. Edited by Stewart Mitchell. Boston, 1947.

————. *The Book of Abigail and John: Selected Letters of the Adams Family, 1762-1784*. Edited by Lyman H. Butterfield et al. Cambridge, Mass.: Harvard University Press, 1975.

Alexander, William. *History of Women from the Earliest Antiquity to the Present Time*. London, 1782.

The American Ladies Pocketbook. Philadelphia: John Morgan, 1802.

Biddle, Clement. *The Philadelphia Directory*. Philadelphia, 1791.

Bingham, Caleb. *American Preceptor*. Boston, 1813.

Boston City Directory. Boston: Manning & Loring, 1796.

Burr, Aaron. *Memoirs of Aaron Burr*. Edited by Matthew L. Davis. 1836. Reprint, Freeport, N.Y.: Books for Libraries Press, 1970.

Catalogue of the Annapolis Circulating Library. 1783.

Catalogue of Books to be sold at Hearn's Book Store. Savannah, Ga., 1790.

Cobbett, William (Peter Porcupine). *A Kick for a Bite: or Review Upon Review: with a Critical Essay on the Works of Mrs. Rowson: in A Letter to the Editor, or Editors of the American Monthly Review* (1795).

————. *The Bloody Buoy, Thrown out as a warning to the political pilots of America. Or a faithful Relation of Multitude of Acts of Horrid Barbarity. such as the eye never witnessed, the tongue never expressed, or the imagination conceived, until the commencement of the French Revolution*. Philadelphia: Benjamin Davies, 1796.

————. *Porcupine's Works: Containing Various Writings and Selections, Exhibiting a Faithful Picture of the United States of America from the End of the War, in 1783, to the Election of the President, in March, 1801*. 12 vols. London: Cobbett and Morgan, 1801.

Drinker, Elizabeth. *Extracts from the Journal of Elizabeth Drinker, From 1759 to 1807, A.D.* Edited by Henry D. Biddle. Philadelphia: J. P. Lippincott, 1889.

————. *The Diary of Elizabeth Drinker*. Edited by Elaine F. Crane. 3 vols. Boston: Northeastern University Press, 1991.

Emerson, Mary Moody. *Selected Letters of Mary Moody Emerson*. Ed.

Nancy Craig Simmons. Athens: University of Georgia Press, 1993.

Godwin, William. *Memoirs of Mary Wollstonecraft Godwin, Author of "A Vindication of the Rights of Woman."* Philadelphia, 1799.

Graydon, Alexander. *Memoirs of a Life Chiefly Passed in Pennsylvania Within the Last Sixty Years.* Edinburgh, 1822.

Gregory, John. *A Father's Legacy to His Daughters.* 1774. Reprint, New York: Garland, 1974.

Haswell, Charles. *Reminiscences of New York by an Octogenarian (1816-1860).* New York: Harper, 1896.

Hogan, Edmund. *The Prospect of Philadelphia.* Philadelphia, 1795.

Hopkinson, Francis. *An Account of the Grand Federal Procession, Performed at Philadelphia on Friday, the 4th of July 1788.* Philadelphia: Mathew Carey, 1788.

Inchbald, Elizabeth. *Everyone Has His Fault (As Performed at the New Theater, Philadelphia. Marked with Alterations (By Permission of the Managers) by William Rowson, Prompter.* Philadelphia: H. & P. Rice, and Mathew Carey, 1794.

Jefferson, Thomas. *The Writings of Thomas Jefferson.* Edited by Paul Leicester Ford. 10 vols. New York: G. P. Putnam's Sons, 1892-1899.

———. *The Papers of Thomas Jefferson.* Edited by Julian P. Boyd et al. 28 vols. to date. Princeton: Princeton University Press, 1950-1996.

Lewis, Eleanor Parke Custis. *George Washington's Beautiful Nelly: The Letters of Eleanor Parke Custis Lewis to Elizabeth Bordley Gibson, 1794-1851.* Edited by Patricia Brady. Columbia: University of South Carolina Press, 1991.

Liston, Henrietta. "A Diplomat's Wife in Philadelphia: Letters of Henrietta Liston, 1779-1800." Edited by Bradford Perkins. *William and Mary Quarterly* 11, no. 4 (October 1954), 592-632.

Logan, Deborah Norris. *Memoir of Dr. George Logan of Stenton.* Edited by Frances A. Logan. Philadelphia, 1899.

Maclay, William. *The Diary of William Maclay, and Other Notes on Senate Debates.* Edited by Kenneth R. Bowling and Helen E. Veit. Baltimore: Johns Hopkins University Press, 1988.

Méry, Moreau de Saint. *Moreau de Saint Méry's American Journey: 1793-1798.* Edited and translated by Kenneth and Anna M.

Roberts. Garden City, N.Y.: Doubleday, 1947.

Miller, Rev. Samuel. "The Appropriate Duty and Ornament of the Female Sex." In *The Columbian Preacher, Or, A Collection of Original Sermons, from Preachers of Eminence in the United States. Embracing the Distinguishing Doctrines of Grace.* Catskill, N.Y., 1808.

Moore, Milcah Martha. *Milcah Martha Moore's Book: A Commonplace Book from Revolutionary America.* Edited by Catherine La Courreye Blecki and Karin A. Wulf. University Park: Pennsylvania State University Press, 1997.

Murray, Judith Sargent. *Judith Sargent Murray: A Brief Biography with Documents.* Edited by Sheila L. Skemp. Boston: Bedford Books, 1998.

————. *The Gleaner.* Introduction by Nina Baym. Schenectady, N.Y.: Union College Press, 1992.

————. *Selected Writings of Judith Sargent Murray.* Edited by Sharon M. Harris. Oxford: Oxford University Press, 1995.

————. *From Gloucester to Philadelphia in 1790: Observations, Anecdotes, and Thoughts from the Eighteenth-Century Letters of Judith Sargent Murray.* Edited by Bonnie Hurd Smith. Cambridge, Mass.: Judith Sargent Murray Society, 1998.

Murdock, John. *The Politicians.* Philadelphia, 1798.

Nelson, John Dixon. *Nelson's Charleston Directory and Strangers' Guide for 1801.* Charleston, S.C.: John Dixon Nelson, 1801.

Playfair, William. *The History of Jacobinism, Its Crimes, Cruelties and Perfidies: Comprising an Inquiry Into the Manner of Discriminating, Under the Appearance of Philosophy and Virtue, Principles Which Are Equally Subversive of Order, Virtue, Religion, Liberty and Happiness. By William Playfair. With an Appendix by Peter Porcupine, Containing a History of the American Jacobins, Commonly Denominated Democrats.* 2 vols. Philadelphia: for William Cobbett, 1796.

Reflections on Courtship and Marriage. Philadelphia, 1746.

Ridgelys of Delaware and Their Circle: What Them Befell in Colonial and Federal Times: Letters, 1751-1890. Edited by Mabel L. Ridgely. Portland, Me., 1949.

Ross and Douglas. *Catalogue of Books.* Petersburg, Va., 1800.

Rousseau, Jean Jacques. *Emile.* Translated by Barbara Foxley. London:

Everyman, 1993.

Rowson, Susanna. *Slaves in Algiers*. Philadelphia, 1795.

Rudiments of Taste in a Series of Letters from a Mother to Her Daughters. Philadelphia: William Spotswood, 1790.

Rules of the Carlisle Library Company with a Catalogue of Books. Carlisle, Pa., 1797.

Rush, Benjamin. *Thoughts upon Female Education, Accommodated to the Present State of Society, Manners and Government in the United States of America.* Philadelphia, 1787.

———. *The Rise and Progress of the Young Ladies' Academy of Philadelphia.* Philadelphia, 1794.

"Sacramental Registers at St. Joseph's Church, Philadelphia, Pennsylvania." *American Catholic Historical Society Records*, 16 (1905).

Stockton, Annis Boudinot. *Only for the Eye of a Friend: The Poems of Annis Boudinot Stockton.* Edited by Carla Mulford. Charlottesville, Va.: University of Virginia Press, 1995.

Swanwick, John. *Some Observations on the State of the Commerce of the United States in General in 1796.* Philadelphia, 1796.

———. *Thoughts on Education Addressed to the Visitors of the Young Ladies' Academy of Philadelphia.* Philadelphia, 1787.

———. *A Rub from Snub; or a Cursory Analytical Epistle: Addressed to Peter Porcupine, Author of the Bone to Gnaw, Kick for a Bite, &c. &c., Containing Glad Tidings for the Democrats and a Word of Comfort to Mrs. S. Rowson.* Philadelphia, 1795.

———. *Poems on Several Occasions.* Philadelphia, 1797.

Wansey, Henry. *An Excursion to the United States of North America in the Summer of 1794.* Salisbury, England, 1798.

"Washington's Household Account Books, 1793-1797." *Pennsylvania Magazine of History and Biography* 29 (1905) and 30 (1906).

Washington, George. *The Diaries of George Washington.* Edited by Donald Jackson and Dorothy Twohig. 6 vols. Charlottesville: University Press of Virginia, 1976–1979.

Watson, John F. *The Annals of Philadelphia and Pennsylvania.* 3 vols. Philadelphia: Edwin S. Stuart, 1905.

White, Francis. *The Philadelphia Directory.* Philadelphia: Young, Stewart and McCulloch, 1785.

Wollstonecraft, Mary. *A Vindication of the Rights of Woman*. In *The Vindications: The Rights of Men, The Rights of Woman*. Edited by D. L. Macdonald and Kathleen Scherf. Ontario: Broadview Literary Texts, 1997.

SECONDARY SOURCES

Abray, Jane. "Feminism in the French Revolution." *American Historical Review* 80, no. 1 (February 1975), 43-62.

Akers, Charles W. *Abigail Adams, An American Woman*. Boston: Little, Brown, 1980.

Alberts, Robert C. *The Golden Voyage: The Life and Times of William Bingham, 1752-1804*. Boston: Houghton Mifflin, 1969.

Alderson, Robert. "'This Bright Era of Happy Revolutions': M.-A.-B. de Mangourit in Charleston, S.C., 1792-1794." Ph.D. diss., University of Georgia.

Aronson, Amy Beth. "Understanding Equals: Audience and Articulation in the Early American Women's Magazine." Ph.D. diss., Columbia University, 1996.

Barker-Benfield, G. J. *The Culture of Sensibility: Sex and Society in Eighteenth-Century Britain*. Chicago: University of Chicago Press, 1992.

Basch, Norma. "Equity vs. Equality: The Concept of Women's Political Status in the Age of Jackson." *Journal of the Early Republic* 3 (fall 1983), 297-318.

Bate, W. Jackson. *Samuel Johnson*. New York: Harcourt Brace Jovanovich, 1975.

Baumann, Roland M. "Merchant-Republicanism: Philadelphia, 1789-1794." Master's thesis, Northern Illinois University, 1966.

———. "The Democratic-Republicans of Philadelphia: The Origins, 1776-1797." Ph.D. diss., Pennsylvania State University, 1970.

———. "John Swanwick: Spokesman for 'Merchant-Republicanism' in Philadelphia, 1790-1798." *Pennsylvania Magazine of History and Biography* 97, no. 2 (April 1973).

Bell, Whitfield Jenks, Jr. "The Federal Processions of 1788." *New York Historical Society Quarterly* 66 (1962).

Berkin, Carol. *First Generations: Women in Colonial America*. New

York: Hill and Wang, 1998.

Bodle, Wayne. "Jane Bartram's 'Application': Her Struggle for Survival, Stability, and Self-Determination in Revolutionary Pennsylvania." *Pennsylvania Magazine of History and Biography* 115, no. 2 (1991), 185-220.

Bonowitz, Dorothy M. "The History of the Boston Stage from the Beginning to 1810." Ph.D. diss., Pennsylvania State University, 1936.

Bordman, Gerald. *The Oxford Companion to American Theater.* New York: Oxford University Press, 1984.

Boudreau, George W. "The Surest Foundation of Happiness: Education and Society in Franklin's Philadelphia." Ph.D. diss., Indiana University, 1998.

Boydston, Jeanne. "The Woman Who Wasn't There: Women's Market Labor and the Transition to Capitalism in the United States." *Journal of the Early Republic* 16, no. 2 (summer 1996), 183-206.

Brandt, Ellen B. *Susanna Haswell Rowson, America's First Best-Selling Novelist.* Chicago, 1975.

Braudel, Fernand. *The Structures of Everyday Life.* Translated by Siân Reynolds. New York: Harper and Row, 1979.

Brookes, George S. *Friend Anthony Benezet.* Philadelphia, 1837.

Brown, Chandos Michael. "Mary Wollstonecraft, or The Female Illuminati: The Campaign Against Women and 'Modern Philosophy' in the Early Republic." *Journal of the Early Republic* 15 (fall 1995), 389-424.

Bushman, Richard L. *The Refinement of America: Persons, Houses, Cities.* New York: Knopf, 1992.

Childs, Frances S. *French Refugee Life in the United States, 1790-1800: An American Chapter of the French Revolution.* Baltimore: Johns Hopkins University Press, 1940.

Christman, Margaret C. S. *The First Federal Congress, 1789-1791.* Washington, D.C.: Smithsonian, 1989.

Coad, Oral Sumner. "Stage and Players in Eighteenth Century America." *Journal of English and Germanic Philology* 19 (April 1920).

Colwill, Elizabeth. "Just Another Citöyenne? Marie Antoinette on Trial 1790-93." *History Workshop Journal* 28 (September 1989).

Combs, Jerald A. *The Jay Treaty, Political Battleground of the Founding Fathers.* Berkeley: University of California Press, 1970.

Conway, Jill K. "Perspectives on the History of Women's Education in the United States." *History of Education Quarterly* 14, no. 1 (spring 1974), 1-12.

Cott, Nancy F. "Divorce and the Changing Status of Women in Eighteenth-Century Massachusetts." *William and Mary Quarterly* 33 (October 1976).

———. *The Bonds of Womanhood: "Woman's Sphere" in New England, 1780-1835.* New Haven: Yale University Press, 1977.

Crane, Elaine F. "Dependence in the Era of Independence: The Role of Women in a Republican Society." In *The American Revolution, Its Character and Limits.* Edited by Jack P. Greene. New York: New York University Press, 1987.

Davidson, Cathy N. "The Matter and Manner of Charles Brockden Brown's *Alcuin.*" In *Critical Essays on Charles Brockden Brown.* Edited by Bernard Rosenthal. Boston: G.K. Hall, 1981.

———. *Revolution and the Word: The Rise of the Novel in America.* New York: Oxford University Press, 1986.

———. "The Novel as Subversive Activity." in *Beyond the American Revolution: Explorations in the History of American Radicalism.* Edited by Alfred F. Young. Dekalb: Northern Illinois University Press, 1993.

Davis, Susan G. *Parades and Power: Street Theater in Nineteenth Century Philadelphia.* Philadelphia: Temple University Press, 1986.

De Conde, Alexander. *The Quasi-War: The Politics and Diplomacy of the Undeclared War with France, 1797-1801.* New York, 1966.

———. *Entangling Alliance: Politics and Diplomacy Under George Washington.* Durham, N.C.: Duke University Press, 1958.

Dowling, William C. *Literary Federalism in the Age of Jefferson: Joseph Dennie and The Port Folio, 1801-1812.* Columbia: University of South Carolina Press, 1999.

Dudden, Faye E. *Women in the American Theater: Actresses and Audiences, 1790-1870.* New Haven: Yale University Press, 1994.

Elkins, Stanley, and Eric McKitrick. *The Age of Federalism: The Early American Republic, 1788-1800.* New York: Oxford University Press,

1993.

Ellet, Elizabeth F. *Court Circles of the Republic.* Philadelphia: Philadelphia Publishing Company, 1872.

———. *The Women of the American Revolution.* 2 vols. 1848-50. Reprint, Philadelphia, 1900.

———. *Domestic History of the American Revolution.* New York, 1850.

Evans, Elizabeth. *Weathering the Storm: Women of the American Revolution.* New York: Charles Scribner's Sons, 1975.

Ford, Paul Leicester. *Washington and the Theatre.* 1899. Reprint, New York: Benjamin Blom, 1967.

Fraser, Nancy. "Rethinking the Public Sphere: A Contribution to the Critique of Actually Existing Democracy." In *Habermas and the Public Sphere.* Edited by Craig Calhoun. Cambridge, Mass.: MIT Press, 1992.

Freeman, Douglas Southall. *George Washington, A Biography.* 7 vols. New York: Scribners, 1948-57.

Garcia, Hazel. "Of Punctilios Among the Fair Sex: Colonial American Magazines, 1741-1776." *Journalism History* 3, no. 2 (summer 1976).

Ginzberg, Lori D. *Women and the Work of Benevolence: Morality, Politics, and Class in the Nineteenth-Century United States.* New Haven: Yale University Press, 1990.

Godineau, Dominique. "Masculine and Feminine Political Practice during the French Revolution, 1793—Year III." In *Women and Politics in the Age of the Democratic Revolution.* Edited by Harriet Branson Applewhite and Darline G. Levy. Ann Arbor: University of Michigan Press, 1990.

Goodman, Dena. *The Republic of Letters: A Cultural History of the French Enlightenment.* Ithaca: Cornell University Press, 1994.

Gordon, Ann D. "The Young Ladies Academy of Philadelphia." In *Women of America: A History.* Edited by Carol Ruth Berkin and Mary Beth Norton. Boston: Houghton Mifflin, 1979.

Green, Daniel. *Great Cobbett, The Noblest Agitator.* London, 1983.

Griswold, Rufus Wilmot. *The Republican Court; or American Society in the Days of Washington.* New York: D. Appleton, 1867.

Gundersen, Joan R. "Independence, Citizenship, and the American

Revolution." *Signs* 13 (autumn 1987), 59-77.

Gutwirth, Madelyn. *The Twilight of the Goddesses: Women and Representation in the French Revolutionary Era.* New Brunswick, N.J.: Rutgers University Press, 1992.

Habermas and the Public Sphere. Edited by Craig Calhoun. Cambridge, Mass.: MIT Press, 1992.

Harris, Jennifer. "The Red Cap of Liberty: A Study of Dress Worn by French Revolutionary Partisans, 1789-94." *Eighteenth-Century Studies* 14, no. 3 (spring 1981), 283-312.

Hazen, Charles Downer. *Contemporary American Opinion of the French Revolution.* Baltimore, 1897. Reprint, Gloucester, Mass., 1964.

Hebert, Catherine Anne Bieri. "The Pennsylvania French in the 1790s: The Story of Their Survival." Ph.D. diss., University of Texas at Austin, 1981.

Hoff, Joan. *Law, Gender, and Injustice: A Legal History of U.S. Women.* New York: New York University Press, 1991.

Hornblow, Arthur. *A History of the Theater in America from Its Beginnings to the Present Time.* New York, 1919.

Hufton, Olwen H. *Women and the Limits of Citizenship in the French Revolution.* Toronto: University of Toronto Press, 1992.

Hunt, Lynn. "The Many Bodies of Marie Antoinette: Political Pornography and the Problem of the Feminine in the French Revolution." In *Eroticism and the Body Politic.* Edited by Lynn Hunt. Baltimore: Johns Hopkins University Press, 1991.

————. *Politics, Culture and Class in the French Revolution.* Berkeley: University of California Press, 1982.

Janes, R. M. "On the Reception of Mary Wollstonecraft's A Vindication of the Rights of Woman." *Journal of the History of Ideas* 39 (April-June 1978), 293-302.

Kaminski, John P. and Gaspare J. Saladino, eds. *The Documentary History of the Ratification of the Constitution.* Madison: State Historical Society of Wisconsin.

Kaser, David. *A Book for a Sixpence: The Circulating Library in America.* Pittsburgh: Beta Phi Mu, 1980.

Kates. Gary. "'The Powers of Husband and Wife Must Be Equal and Separate': The Cercle Social and the Rights of Women, 1790-91."

In *Women and Politics in the Age of the Democratic Revolution*. Edited by Harriet Branson Applewhite and Darline G. Levy. Ann Arbor: University of Michigan Press, 1990.

Kerber, Linda K. *Women of the Republic: Intellect and Ideology in Revolutionary America*. Chapel Hill, North Carolina, 1980.

―――. " 'History Can Do It No Justice': Women and the Reinterpretation of the American Revolution." In *Women in the Age of the American Revolution*. Edited by Ronald Hoffman and Peter J. Albert. Charlottesville: University Press of Virginia, 1989.

―――. " 'I Have Don ... much to Carrey on the Warr': Women and the Shaping of Republican Ideology After the American Revolution." In *Women and Politics in the Age of the Democratic Revolution*. Edited by Harriet Branson Applewhite and Darline G. Levy. Ann Arbor: University of Michigan Press, 1990.

―――. "The Republican Mother: Women and the Enlightenment— An American Perspective." In *Toward an Intellectual History of Women*. Chapel Hill: University of North Carolina Press, 1997, 41-62.

―――. "The Republican Ideology of the Revolutionary Generation." In *Toward an Intellectual History of Women*. Chapel Hill: University of North Carolina Press, 1997, 131-156.

Kerber, Linda K., et al. "Beyond Roles, Beyond Spheres: Thinking About Gender in the Early Republic." *William and Mary Quarterly* 46, no. 3 (July 1989), 565-585.

Kertzer, David I. *Ritual, Politics, and Power*. New Haven: Yale University Press, 1988.

Kierner, Cynthia A. *Beyond the Household: Women's Place in the Early South, 1700-1835*. Ithaca: Cornell University Press, 1998.

Klinghoffer, Judith Apter, and Lois Elkis. "'The Petticoat Electors': Women's Suffrage in New Jersey, 1776-1807." *Journal of the Early Republic* 12 (summer 1992), 159-193.

Kornfield, Eve. "Women in Post-Revolutionary American Culture: Susanna Haswell Rowson's American Career 1793-1824." *Journal of American Culture* 6 (winter 1983), 56-62.

Koschnik, Albrecht. "Political Conflict and Public Contest: Rituals of National Celebration in Philadelphia, 1788-1815." *Journal of the*

Early Republic 68, no. 3 (July 1994), 209-248.

Kritzer, Amelia Howe. *Plays By Early American Women: 1794-1844.* Ann Arbor: University of Michigan Press, 1995.

Levy, Darline G., and Harriet B. Applewhite. "Women, Radicalization, and the Fall of the French Monarchy." In *Women and Politics in the Age of the Democratic Revolution.* Edited by Harriet Branson Applewhite and Darline G. Levy. Ann Arbor: University of Michigan Press, 1990.

Lewis, Jan. "The Republican Wife: Virtue and Seduction in the Early Republic." *William and Mary Quarterly* 44 (1987), 689-721.

———. "'Of every age sex and condition': The Representation of Women in the Constitution." *Journal of the Early Republic* 15, no. 3 (fall 1995), 359-388.

List, Karen K. "The Post-Revolutionary Woman Idealized: Philadelphia Media's 'Republican Mother'." *Journalism Quarterly* 66 (spring 1989), 65-75.

Manvell, Roger. *Elizabeth Inchbald, England's Principal Woman Dramatist and Independent Woman of Letters in Eighteenth Century London: A Biography.* Lanham, Md.: University Press of America, 1987.

Mason, Laura. "'Ça Ira' and the Birth of the Revolutionary Song." *History Workshop Journal* 28 (autumn 1989), 22-38.

McMaster, John Bach. *A History of the People of the United States from the Revolution to the Civil War.* 6 vols. New York, 1896.

Mott, Frank Luther. *A History of American Magazines, 1741-1850.* Cambridge, Mass.: Harvard University Press, 1939.

Nathans, Heather Shawn. "'A Democracy of Glee': The Post-Revolutionary Theater of Boston and Philadelphia." Ph.D. diss., Tufts University, 1999.

Newman, Simon P. "American Popular Political Culture in the Age of the French Revolution." Ph.D. diss., Princeton University, 1991.

———. *Parades and the Politics of the Street: Festive Culture in the Early American Republic.* Philadelphia: University of Pennsylvania Press, 1997.

Nicholson, Wendy Anne. "Making the Private Public: Anne Willing Bingham's Role as a Leader of Philadelphia's Social Elite in the

Late Eighteenth Century." Master's thesis, University of Delaware, 1988.

Nord, David Paul Nord. "A Republican Literature: Magazine Reading and Readers in Late-Eighteenth-Century New York." In *Reading in America: Literature and Social History*. Edited by Cathy N. Davidson. Baltimore: Johns Hopkins University Press, 1989, 114-139.

Norton, Mary Beth. *Liberty's Daughters: The Revolutionary Experience of American Women, 1750-1800*. Boston: Little, Brown, 1980.

O'Brien, Daphne Hamm. "The First Congress, Polite Society, and Courtship in New York City: The Case of Margaret Lowther." Paper presented at the Sixteenth Annual Meeting of the Society for Historians of the Early Republic, Boston, July 15, 1994.

Odell, George C. *Annals of the New York Stage*. New York, 1927. Reprint, 1970.

Ozouf, Mona. *Festivals and the French Revolution*. Translated by Alan Sheridan. Cambridge, Mass.: Harvard University Press, 1988.

Parker, Patricia L. *Susanna Rowson*. Boston: Twayne, 1986.

Pollock, Thomas Clark. *The Philadelphia Theater in the Eighteenth Century*. Philadelphia: University of Pennsylvania Press, 1933.

Rasmusson, Ethel E. "Capital on the Delaware: The Philadelphia Upper Class in Transition, 1789-1801." Ph.D. diss., Brown University, 1962.

———. "Democratic Environment-Aristocratic Aspiration." *Pennsylvania Magazine of History and Biography* 90, no. 2 (April 1966), 155-182.

Remer, Rosalind. *Printers and Men of Capital: Philadelphia Book Publishers in the New Republic*. Philadelphia: University of Pennsylvania Press, 1996.

Ribeiro, Aileen. *Fashion in the French Revolution*. New York: Holmes and Meier, 1988.

Richardson, Edward W. *Standards and Colors of the American Revolution*. Philadelphia: University of Pennsylvania Press, 1982.

Ritchey, David. *A Guide to the Baltimore Stage in the Eighteenth Century*. Westport, Conn.: Greenwood Press, 1982.

Rosenberg, Nancy F. "An Uncommon Language: Education and Social Perceptions in Eighteenth and Early Nineteenth Century

Philadelphia." Paper presented to the Annual Meeting of the American Historical Association, Washington, D.C., 1987.

———. "The Word Within, the World Without: Quaker Education in Philadelphia, 1682-1837." Ph.D. diss., University of Michigan, 1991.

Rosenfield, Lenora Cohen. "The Rights of Women in the French Revolution." *Studies in Eighteenth-Century Culture* 7 (1976), 117-137.

Saar, Doreen Alvarez. "Susanna Rowson: Feminist and Democrat." In *Curtain Calls: British and American Women and the Theater, 1660-1820.* Edited by Mary Anne Schofield and Cecilia Macheski. Athens: Ohio University Press, 1991.

Scharf, J. Thomas, and Thompson Westcott. *The History of Philadelphia, 1609-1884.* 3 vols. Philadelphia: L. H. Everts, 1884.

Scott, Joan Wallach. "French Feminists and the Rights of 'Man': Olympe de Gouges's Declarations." *History Workshop Journal* (fall-winter 1989), 1-21.

Seilhamer, George O. *History of the American Theater: New Foundations.* Philadelphia, 1891. Reprint, Grosse Pointe, Mich.: Scholarly Press, 1968.

Sharp, James R. *American Politics in the Early Republic: The New Nation in Crisis.* New Haven: Yale University Press, 1993.

Shelton, Cynthia J. *The Mills of Manayunk: Industrialization and Social Conflict in the Philadelphia Region, 1787-1837.* Baltimore: Johns Hopkins University Press, 1986.

Shera, Jesse H. "The Beginnings of Systematic Bibliography in America, 1642-1799." In *Essays Honoring Lawrence C. Wrath.* Edited by Frederick Richmond Goff et al. Portland, Me.: Anthoesen Press, 1951.

Shevelow, Kathryn. *Women and Print Culture: The Construction of Femininity in the Early Periodical.* London: Routledge, 1989.

Shields, David S. *Civil Tongues and Polite Letters in British America.* Chapel Hill: University of North Carolina Press, 1997.

Slaughter, Thomas P. *The Whiskey Rebellion: Frontier Epilogue to the American Revolution.* New York: Oxford University Press, 1986.

Slotten, Martha C. "Elizabeth Graeme Ferguson: A Poet in 'The

Athens of North America.'" *Pennsylvania Magazine of History and Biography* (1984), 259-288.

Smith, Billy G. *The "Lower Sort": Philadelphia's Laboring People, 1750-1800.* Ithaca: Cornell University Press, 1990.

Smith, Bonnie G. *Changing Lives: Women in European History Since 1700.* Lexington, Mass.: D. C. Heath, 1989.

Stearns, Bertha M. "Early New England Magazines for Ladies." *New England Quarterly* 2 (1929), 421.

———."Before Godey's." *American Literature* 2 (1930).

———. "A Speculation Concerning Charles Brockden Brown." *Pennsylvania Magazine of History and Biography* 59 (1935), 99-105.

———. "Early Philadelphia Magazines for Ladies." *Pennsylvania Magazine of History and Biography* 64, (1940), 479-491.

Stine, Richard D. "The Philadelphia Theater, 1682-1829." Ph.D. diss., University of Pennsylvania, 1951.

Sunstein, Emily W. *A Different Face: The Life of Mary Wollstonecraft.* New York: Harper & Row, 1975.

Teute, Fredrika J. "Roman Matron on the Banks of Tiber Creek: Margaret Bayard Smith and the Politicization of Spheres in the Nation's Capital." In *"A Republic for the Ages": The United States Capitol and the Political Culture of the Early Republic.* Edited by Donald R. Kennon and Barbara Wolanin. Charlottesville: University Press of Virginia, 1999.

Thiebaux, Marelle. "Mary Wollstonecraft in Federalist America: 1791-1802." In *The Evidence of the Imagination: Studies of Interactions Between Life and Art in English Romantic Literature.* Edited by Donald H. Reiman et al. New York: New York University Press, 1978.

Tinker, Chauncey Brewster. *The Salon and English Letters.* New York: Macmillan, 1915.

Tolles, Frederick B. *George Logan of Philadelphia.* New York, 1953.

Travers, Len. *Celebrating the Fourth: Independence Day and the Rites of Nationalism in the Early Republic.* Amherst: University of Massachusetts Press, 1997.

Trouille, Mary Seidman. *Sexual Politics in the Enlightenment: Women Writers Read Rousseau.* Albany: State University of New York Press, 1997.

Ulrich, Laurel Thatcher. "'From the Fair to the Brave': Spheres of Womanhood in Federal Maine." In *Agreeable Situations: Society, Commerce, and Art in Southern Maine, 1780-1830*. Edited by Laura Fecych Sprague. Kennebunk, Me.: Brick Store Museum, 1987.

Varon, Elizabeth R. "Tippecanoe and the Ladies, Too: White Women and Party Politics in Antebellum Virginia." *Journal of American History* 82 (September 1995), 494-521.

Waldstreicher, David. *The Making of American Nationalism: Celebrations and Political Culture, 1776-1820*. Chapel Hill: University of North Carolina Press, 1997.

———. "Federalism, the Styles of Politics, and the Politics of Style." In *Federalists Reconsidered*. Edited by Doron Ben-Atar and Barbara Oberg. Charlottesville: University Press of Virginia, 1998.

Watts, Steven. *The Romance of Real Life: Charles Brockden Brown and the Origins of American Culture*. Baltimore: Johns Hopkins University Press, 1994.

Weigley, Russell F. *Philadelphia: A Three Hundred Year History*. New York: Norton, 1982.

Weil, Dorothy. *In Defense of Women: Susanna Rowson (1752-1824)*. University Park: Pennsylvania State University, 1976.

Welter, Barbara. "The Cult of True Womanhood: 1820-1860." *American Quarterly* 18 (1966), 151-174.

Wharton, Anne Hollingsworth. *Salons, Colonial and Republican*. Philadelphia: J. B. Lippincott, 1900.

Willis, Eola. *The Charleston Stage in the Eighteenth Century*. Columbia, S.C.: The State Company, 1924.

Wilson, David A. *United Irishmen, United States, Immigrant Radicals in the Early Republic*. Ithaca: Cornell University Press, 1998.

Wilson, Gary E. "American Hostages in Moslem Nations, 1784-1796: The Public Response." *Journal of the Early Republic* 2 (summer 1982), 123-141.

Winans, Robert B. "The Growth of a Novel-reading Public in Late Eighteenth-Century America." *Early American Literature* 9 (1975).

———. *A Descriptive Checklist of Book Catalogues Separately Printed in America 1693-1800*. Worcester, Mass.: American Antiquarian Society, 1981.

Women's Periodicals and Newspapers from the Eighteenth Century to

1981. Edited by James P. Danky. Boston, 1982.

Wood, Kirsten E. "'One Woman So Dangerous to Public Morals': Gender and Power in the Eaton Affair." *Journal of the Early Republic* 17, no. 2 (summer 1997), 237-275.

Woody, Thomas. *A History of Women's Education in the United States*. 2 vols. New York, 1929.

Wulf, Karin A. "'My Dear Liberty': Quaker Spinsterhood and Female Autonomy in Eighteenth-Century Pennsylvania." In *Women and Freedom in Early America*. Edited by Larry D. Eldridge. New York: New York University Press, 1997.

———. *Not All Wives: Women of Colonial Philadelphia*. Ithaca: Cornell University Press, 1999.

Young, Alfred F. *The Democratic Republicans of New York*. Chapel Hill: University of North Carolina Press, 1967.

———. "The Women of Boston: 'Persons of Consequence' in the Making of the American Revolution, 1765-76." In *Women and Politics in the Age of the Democratic Revolution*. Edited by Harriet Branson Applewhite and Darline G. Levy. Ann Arbor: University of Michigan Press, 1990.

Zagarri, Rosemarie. "Morals, Manners, and the Republican Mother." *American Quarterly* 44, no. 2 (June 1992).

———. *A Woman's Dilemma: Mercy Otis Warren and the American Revolution*. Wheeling, Ill.: Harlan-Davidson, 1995.

———. "Gender and the First Party System." In *Federalists Reconsidered*. Edited by Doron Ben-Atar and Barbara Oberg. Charlottesville: University Press of Virginia, 1998.

———. "The Rights of Man and Woman in Post-Revolutionary America." *William and Mary Quarterly* 55, no. 2 (April 1998).

Zboray, Ronald J., and Mary Saracino Zboray. "Whig Women, Politics, and Culture in the Campaign of 1840: Three Perspectives from Massachusetts." *Journal of the Early Republic* 17, no. 2 (summer 1997), 278-315.

Zeedyk, Tryna. "Political Issues on the Philadelphia Stage: Susanna Rowson's *Slaves in Algiers* and Its Critics." Unpublished essay, Northern Illinois University, 1990.

Index

Inchbald, Elizabeth: performances of *Everyone Has His Fault*, 117; prologue to *Everyone Has His Fault*, 117–118

Jacobins: closing women's political clubs, 62
Jay Treaty, 81, 112
Jefferson, Thomas: comments on women talking politics, 138; letter to Anne Bingham, 58, 139; sends Bingham French fashion journals, 68; confirms George Logan's citizenship, 88; offers Deborah Logan advice, 89
Journal de la Mode et de Goût: bonnet "à l'americaine," 69
Journal des Dames et des Modes: "fichu à la Marat," 69
July Fourth celebrations, 56, 83, 85–86

Kemble, Fanny, 147
Kenney, Lucy, 147
Knox, Lucy Fluckner: desire for "equal command," 11

Ladies Association of Philadelphia, 11
Ladies Magazine. See Lady's Magazine
Lady and Gentlemen's Pocket Magazine of Literary and Polite Amusement (New York), 25; importance of the fair sex, 26
Lady's Magazine and Musical Repository, 52
Lady's Magazine and Repository of Entertaining Knowledge (Philadelphia): 25, 27, 29; offers readers an education, 15; selections from *A Vindication of the Rights of Woman*, 39; topics of interest to women, 21; the word "obey," 28
Lady's Magazine, or Entertaining Companion for the Fair Sex (London), 25
Lancaster, Pa.: July Fourth celebration, 56
Lee, Arthur: criticizes Binghams' ostentation, 136
Léon, Pauline, 61
Liston, Henrietta: wife of British ambas-

sador, 81; reports on Federalist theater audience, 110
Literacy, 22
Lockean liberalism, 4
Logan Act, 94
Logan, Deborah, 87–98
Logan, George: peace mission to France, 87
Logan, James, 91
Louvet de Couvrai, Jean-Baptiste, 96

Maclay, William, Senator: calls on politicians' wives, 131; complains about President's levees, 130
MacPherson's Blues, 84
Madison, Dolly: as salonnière, 149
Magazines: anonymity of contributors, 26; antifeminist material, 30; characteristics of, 23–24; contents of, 26–32; discussion of women's roles, 27; female readership, 15; fiction in, 26; first ones directed at women, 24–25; nonfiction in, 26–27; theater announcements, 102
Mangourit, Monsieur M.A.B., 79
Marat, Jean-Paul: funeral procession of, 60
Marie Antoinette, Queen: capture of, 58; trial and execution of, 63–64
Martin v. Massachusetts, 12
Mason, Priscilla: commencement address to Young Ladies Academy of Philadelphia, 45–46; urges women to adopt American style of dress, 69–71
Massachusetts Magazine (Boston), 25; appeals to female readership, 26; and Judith Sargent Murray, 26, 32
McClenahan, Blair: leads protest against British Minister, 76
McKean, Pennsylvania Chief Justice, 88
Melmoth, Mrs.: refuses to perform in anti-British play, 111
Menotomy, Mass.: celebration of Valmy victory, 78–79
Meredith, Elizabeth, 39
Merry, Anne Bruton: member of

Acknowledgments

This book has been through many incarnations over the years. I must begin by thanking those people who helped and encouraged me during my graduate study at Northern Illinois University, especially Allan Kulikoff and Elizabeth Schulman. As a dissertation fellow at the Philadelphia (now McNeil) Center for Early American Studies I was lucky enough to enjoy the scholarly companionship and encouragement of Aaron Fogleman, Brendan McConville, and Leslie Patrick. Susan Klepp has graciously shared her knowledge, sources, and time with me from start to finish. I thank her for her friendship and generosity.

My research for this book was carried out at several Philadelphia institutions, including the Historical Society of Pennsylvania, where former Curator of Manuscripts Linda Stanley's comprehensive knowledge of the collections was an invaluable aid to my work. At the American Philosophical Society, Librarian Roy Goodman was always resourceful and encouraging and Elizabeth Carroll-Horrocks spent many patient hours helping me in the manuscript room. A good part of my work was done at the Library Company of Philadelphia, where James Green and Philip Lapsansky are the dream team of the researcher's world.

Three individuals have been involved with my project since its inception. To them I owe a great deal of thanks. My advisor, Alfred Young, has seen more drafts of this book than any other human being. As many American historians have reason to know, he is not only generous with his time, but he is also one of the best and fairest of critics. Richard Dunn, as former Director of the Philadelphia Center and series editor for the University of Pennsylvania Press, has encouraged my work for a number of years. Last, but not least, Simon Newman has been a good colleague, critic, and friend. I have relied on his clear-headed way of cutting to the heart of many a problem as this project evolved.

My thanks are also due to several people who have helped me develop as a scholar: Kenneth Margerison at Southwest Texas State University, Stephanie Cole and Christopher Morris of the Dallas Area Social History group, and my friends and colleagues at the University of Texas at Dallas: Michael Wilson, Erin Smith, and Patricia Michaelson. I also owe a thank you to the School of Arts and Humanities at the University of Texas at Dallas for providing financial assistance for this project.

In the final stages of the process, I have been fortunate to have found three more generous and encouraging readers, Sheila Skemp, Dallett Hemphill, and Robert Lockhart. As Penn's history and American studies editor, Bob has shown a great deal of patience, consideration, and confidence. He is not only a terrific editor, but also a good historian.

Family members tend to receive their thanks last in acknowledgments. This seems unfair in many ways since they are the people who have put up with the process the longest and many times have seen the less pleasant side of the author's nature. But I have saved the best for last. Jaki Gottfried has always been my cheerleader. My parents and my sisters, Kathryn Schwartz and Lisa Forrest, have unfailingly shown their confidence in my abilities, even when I wasn't so sure myself. And finally, to the two people without whom nothing would be worth doing, Mark and Kaitlin—thank you for your love.